Fourth Edition

W9-CZZ-214

Correct Writing

Eugenia Butler
University of Georgia

Mary Ann Hickman
Gainesville Junior College

Lalla Overby
Brenau College

D.C. Heath and Company
Lexington, Massachusetts ■ Toronto

To the Instructor

Correct Writing, Fourth Edition, is a revision of past editions, enlarging and improving the material contained in those earlier editions. It has been updated in the light of universal needs in colleges which now find it necessary to return to the teaching of basic grammar, punctuation, and mechanics before moving on to instruction in composition and rhetoric. The authors have amplified the body of grammatical information to a considerable degree through the addition of definitions of terms and careful explanations of the principles involved in sentence structure. These definitions and explanations come at the earliest mention of a term, so that students will not have to continue their study of a grammatical principle without a clear understanding of what they have already been told. Discussions which may be enlarged upon in other chapters carry convenient cross-references that point the reader to further information available on a given topic. Moreover, for handy reference, a new feature of the Fourth Edition is a comprehensive Glossary of Grammatical Terms, with easily grasped examples accompanying the definitions.

As it has done since its first edition, *Correct Writing* combines the best features of a textbook of grammar and composition, a workbook of exercises, and a reference handbook. Wherever possible, the exercises have been simplified to make them more than usually illustrative of the grammatical principles involved. The exposition of the various aspects of grammar and sentence structure is presented to the student in as simple terms as possible and is more extensive than that in most other workbooks. Although the discussion of many aspects of grammar is not intended to be exhaustive, information in this book is thorough enough for a student to grasp and to learn without having constantly to rely on the instructor's further discussion. The Glossary of Faulty Diction, which has been updated and enlarged for this edition, is an especially useful feature, and it is accompanied by exercises so that the information it contains may be applied in a practical way as well as used for reference.

The treatment of punctuation is a strong feature of *Correct Writing*, because rules of punctuation are given in individual chapters in relation to the basic principles of sentence structure under discussion. When students reach Chapter 19, which is devoted exclusively to punctuation, they will already have learned most of the rules in the chapter. This chapter can then serve as a review of the subject instead of a listing of arbitrary rules to be memorized. There are, however, some occasions when it seems appropriate simply to cite a rule without attempting theoretical explanations that would defeat the purpose of the text as an elementary handbook for grammar and composition. A rule governing punctuation, grammar, or sentence structure may be susceptible to modification or exception, but it is nevertheless useful for being arbitrarily stated. If students do not know that their sentences contain faulty parallelism, for example, they are hardly able at an early stage to explore the subtleties of such constructions.

A section of paragraph tests has been added to this edition as a new feature with strong, practical application for both instructor and student. These tests are whole, integrated paragraphs like those students encounter in their everyday reading of newspapers, magazines, or any other form of printed material. Within these paragraphs are various errors of all the kinds studied in this book; they provide a realistic method of determining whether students have learned to be alert to unexpected errors in their everyday reading and writing.

One central point which should emerge through a student's careful use of this text is that the study of grammar and sentence elements is valuable primarily as a practical means of improving communication and understanding.

The following individuals generously helped us with their suggestions for this edition: Burton Dwyre, New Mexico Highlands University; Dennis Thompson, Macomb County College; Harvey Summers, San Antonio College; and Fran Johnson, Louisiana Technical University.

To the Student

This book is a combination textbook, workbook, and reference handbook. It contains a great deal of information in the various chapters that precede the exercises. It is a workbook in which you will be able to write your answers concerning grammatical principles that you have just studied. When you have worked all the exercises as well as the Review and Achievement Tests, you will still have a convenient reference handbook in which you can check points of grammar, usage, punctuation, and mechanics whenever you need to. The enlarged Glossary of Faulty Diction and the new Glossary of Grammatical Terms will be of special help to you in questions of usage and in providing familiarity with grammatical terminology that you are likely to encounter.

Working conscientiously through the chapters and exercises of *Correct Writing* will put you well on your way to a mastery of grammar and usage, which in turn will help you to write and speak accurately and effectively.

Contents

xi

Diagnostic Test

A. In the following sentences identify the part of speech of each *italicized* word by writing one of the following numbers in the space at the right:

1 if it is a *noun*,	**5** if it is an *adverb*,
2 if it is a *pronoun*,	**6** if it is a *preposition*,
3 if it is a *verb*,	**7** if it is a *conjunction*,
4 if it is an *adjective*,	**8** if it is an *interjection*.

1. She greeted *both* men with a smile. _____
2. The door *burst* open, and Tommy ran in. _____
3. Ralph felt *confident* that he had passed the exam. _____
4. There is no reason for your *anger*. _____
5. What Jeff reported is *absolutely* true. _____
6. *Every* generation learns to preserve its natural resources. _____
7. *After* you have read the chapter, write a summary. _____
8. The tour *guide* will take care of our luggage. _____
9. Jennifer and her family are moving *to* New York this summer. _____
10. The tornado *barely* missed the governor's house. _____
11. *Are* you *attending* the opera this season? _____
12. Each evening *I* walk down to the square. _____
13. Before she answered, she hesitated *briefly*. _____
14. *Fast-food* chains feed millions of Americans each day. _____
15. Dr. Pepperdine is a woman of *vision* and integrity. _____
16. *Underneath* the basket you will find the Easter egg. _____
17. I lost the pendant *that* was my great-grandmother's. _____
18. The missing kittens tumbled out of the *laundry* basket. _____
19. *Oh*, what are you doing here so early? _____
20. Can *you* believe she wants to be a ventriloquist? _____
21. *Behind* the television set is an electrical outlet. _____
22. Success depends on understanding *oneself*. _____
23. Religion *in* America is in transition. _____
24. A student planning to attend college *needs* English, science, and mathematics. _____
25. The children wanted ice cream *and* cake before going to bed. _____

B. Each of the following sentences either contains an error in grammar or is correct. Indicate the error or the correctness by writing one of the following numbers in the space at the right:

1 if the *case of the pronoun* is incorrect,
2 if the *subject and verb do not agree*,
3 if a *pronoun and its antecedent do not agree*,
4 if an *adjective or an adverb is used incorrectly*,
5 if the *sentence is correct*.

26. Our committee works together quite good.   _____

27. Carrie invited me to the tennis tournament.   _____

28. Each tourist said that they must have a private bath.   _____

29. Have either of these letters been answered?   _____

30. I am sure that Betsy and him will be here soon.   _____

31. It was Alice who I think took the car.   _____

32. The media sometimes makes the news rather than reports it.   _____

33. I did not like him wearing my shirts.   _____

34. Yes, it is I who am responsible for arranging the dance.   _____

35. The theme of *A Clockwork Orange* was not real clear.   _____

36. Please give these top hats to whoever is in the costume room.   _____

37. Aunt Ethel often tells Dana and I that we ought to eat vegetables instead of hamburgers and french fries.   _____

38. The mayor as well as the other members of the city council are advocating an increase in the millage.   _____

39. Do you think that my new lipstick is some brighter than yours?   _____

40. Neither of those toys are suitable for your two-year-old nephew.   _____

41. Me and my friend Al are planning to drive down to Santa Fe tomorrow.   _____

42. When we play softball on Saturday, everybody will have to bring their own glove.   _____

43. The bell on that telephone sounds very loudly to me.   _____

44. Whom do you think wrote the lead editorial in Sunday's paper?   _____

45. Phyllis is one of those women who thoroughly enjoys shopping for bargains.   _____

46. The Carnegie Foundation always sends our library their annual report.   _____

47. The three of us — Sarah, Lori, and me — have volunteered to solicit donations for the Community Chest.   _____

48. Janie is the quietest of the two Portman sisters.   _____

49. Mick, along with a girl from Springfield, are coming to the party tonight. _____

50. As soon as the ship docks at Newport, the crew are looking forward to going home.   _____.

C. Each of the following sentences either contains an error in sentence structure or is correct. Indicate the error or correctness by writing one of the following numbers in the space at the right:

> **1** if the sentence contains a *dangling modifier,*
> **2** if the sentence contains a *misplaced modifier,*
> **3** if the sentence contains a *faulty reference of a pronoun,*
> **4** if the sentence contains *faulty parallelism,*
> **5** if the sentence is *correct.*

51. One must have the correct change if you want to use the photocopier.   _____

52. The magazine salesman appeared enthusiastic, energetic, and was all smiles.   _____

53. We have only seen one of the films that Dan rented for the weekend.   _____

54. I stumbled as I was running up the stairs, which caused me to drop my books and papers.   _____

55. While skating with my brothers, my ankle turned, and I sprawled across the ice.   _____

56. This house needs not only to be painted, but it also needs a new roof.   _____

57. Calvin hopes to in the immediate future show his paintings at the local gallery.   _____

58. Eloise nearly spent all her allowance for a pair of red satin sandals.   _____

59. To be objective, both sides of an issue must be considered.   _____

60. Dr. West is a respected physician and who serves on the staff of the Oakbridge Hospital.   _____

61. Having been gathered by several research assistants, the data were fed into the computer last week.   _____

62. Tracy has a bearskin rug, but I don't think that he shot it.   _____

63. The train runs on a high wooden trestle headed for Denver.   _____

64. Susie wrote that she is delighted but a little surprised at your decision to go camping with us.   _____

65. Hiking along the bank of the stream, our shoes soon became wet.   _____

66. If Wendy opens a bookshop, she will spend all her time reading them.   _____

67. If anyone thinks that they can come up with a solution to the problem, they should talk to me immediately.   _____

68. Bart is not only cheerful and friendly but also he is ambitious.   _____

69. The man that was fishing for tarpon in the boat looked strong and capable.   _____

70. While talking with Louise, she told me that Sara is in the hospital.   _____

71. Swinging about in its cage, we saw the monkey run suddenly to its food dish. _____

72. His handwriting is interesting; the downward loops are long, wide, and they slant to the right. _____

73. In order to practice law, Angela, the bar exam must be passed. _____

74. By washing the dishes last night, they are all nice and clean for breakfast. _____

75. Graham remarked to Alex that he was losing weight. _____

D. Each of the following sentences contains an error of punctuation or mechanics, or is correct. Indicate the error or correctness by writing one of the following numbers in the space at the right:

   1 if a *comma* has been omitted,
   2 if a *semicolon* has been omitted,
   3 if an *apostrophe* has been omitted,
   4 if *quotation marks* have been omitted,
   5 if the sentence is *correct.*

76. When you have finished your supper please give me some help with this letter I'm trying to write. _____

77. Melinda shouted, Ken wants us to go with him to the lake tomorrow. _____

78. I suppose its too late now to make the matinee performance of *Guys and Dolls.* _____

79. Fran made a cake for the picnic, and Don made lemonade Lucy made just peanut butter sandwiches. _____

80. When I was heading for the library I saw Melvin riding his bicycle toward my house. _____

81. It was an ugly drizzly day, but the warmth of the fire made things cozy inside. _____

82. Jane Carey my childhood friend is coming for a visit in July. _____

83. My dog, said Isabel, is tracking the rug with his muddy feet. _____

84. Dont try to get away from here without cleaning your room, Thomas. _____

85. I wonder whether grade-school children still recite Joyce Kilmer's poem Trees. _____

86. Hank was furious with us for eating all the chocolate cake he soon recovered, however, when we took him out for a pizza. _____

87. After we had finished eating the dishes had to be washed. _____

88. As we arrived a pretty slender girl took our coats. _____

89. Rudy has always written his 7s in the European way. _____

90. One of the loveliest sonnets I know is Gerard Manley Hopkins's God's Grandeur. _____

91. I was rushing to finish my letter Ned, nevertheless, kept calling to me to hurry. _____

92. In his letter John reminded us that we had promised to spend Christmas with him and his family. _____

93. I don't think that we should go out on this rainy night without an umbrella do you? _____

94. Ginny went to the closet she put on her coat and she stalked out of the house. _____

95. I warned Steve several times about his grades but could not make him listen. _____

96. Beth asked Ward, "Dont you like these turnip greens?" _____

97. You are no longer a child, Susan you must learn not to pity yourself. _____

98. While I was studying the textbook fell out of my hands, and I went to sleep. _____

99. Martin's old car, which he calls Old Bessie, finally broke down yesterday. _____

100. To get to Jacksonville in five hours you would have to drive much too fast, Harry. _____

Fourth Edition

Correct Writing

The Parts of Speech

Our own language is one of the most fascinating subjects that we can investigate, and those of us who speak and write English can find pleasure in seeking to understand its various aspects. The concern of this book is Standard English and its use in contemporary writing. The study and description of Standard English, based on the thoughtful use of language by educated people, provide standards for correct writing. Although the English language is flexible and continually changing, it is possible to follow certain principles and to observe certain characteristics of usage which can make grammar a relatively exact study and one which can widen the scope of the individual in a satisfying way.

An understanding of the accurate and effective use of English is important not only as a means of communication but also as a vital element of creative thought. Because words are used to formulate conscious thought, precise grammatical usage promotes clear thinking and encourages logical and systematic transmission of ideas.

Knowledge of Standard English and its acceptable forms is basic to the education of all college students. Learning grammatical terms is an essential first step toward understanding what is correct and what is incorrect in the writing of English prose. The best place to begin this learning of terms is with the various elements that make up a sentence, elements called **parts of speech.** Many words may function as more than one part of speech, and any word's designation as a particular part of speech depends entirely upon its use within its sentence. (See Section 1i as well as the "Glossary of Grammatical Terms" at the end of this book.) The names of the eight parts of speech are as follows:

noun	verb	conjunction
pronoun	adverb	interjection
adjective	preposition	

■ 1a Noun

A **noun** (from Latin *nomen*, name) is the name of a person, place, thing, or idea. All nouns are either proper nouns or common nouns. A **proper noun** is the name of a particular person, place, or thing and is spelled with a capital letter:

John F. Kennedy	London, England
California	The Washington Monument
The Vatican	O'Keefe Junior High School

A **common noun** is the name of a class of persons, places, things, or ideas and is not capitalized:

girl	park	honesty
teacher	street	disgust
student	dog	friendship
home	automobile	poverty

Nouns may also be classified as **individual** or **collective**. **Collective** nouns name groups of persons, places, or things that sometimes function as units:

flock	team	the rich
jury	dozen	club

Finally, nouns may be classified as **concrete** or **abstract**. The **concrete** noun names a person, place, or thing that can be perceived by one of the five senses. It can be seen, felt, smelled, heard, or tasted. Here are some examples of concrete nouns:

door	woman	scream
dress	city	snow
tree	odor	museum

An **abstract** noun is the name of a quality, condition, action, or idea. The following are examples of abstract nouns:

beauty	truth	kindness
fear	loneliness	campaign
dismissal	hatred	courtesy

A noun is said to belong to the **nominative,** the **objective,** or the **possessive case,** depending upon its function within a sentence. Subjects are in the nominative case (The *truck* stopped), objects are in the objective case (He saw the *parade*), and nouns showing possession are in the possessive case (That car is *John's*). As you can see, there is no difference in form between nouns in the nominative and the objective cases. The possessive case, however, changes a noun's form. (See Chapter 11 for a thorough discussion of case.)

A noun may be **singular** or **plural,** forming its plural generally by the addition of -*s* or -*es* to the end of the singular form (*girl, girls; potato, potatoes*).

Nouns, together with pronouns and other words or expressions that function as nouns, are sometimes called **substantives.**

■ 1b Pronoun

A **pronoun** (from Latin *pro*, for, and *nomen*, name) is a word used in place of a noun. A pronoun usually refers to a noun or other substantive already mentioned, which is called its **antecedent** (from Latin *ante*, before, and *cedere*, to go). Most pronouns have antecedents, but some do not.

Pronouns are divided into seven categories:

PERSONAL PRONOUNS: I, you, he, it, they, etc.

DEMONSTRATIVE PRONOUNS: this, that, these, those

INDEFINITE PRONOUNS: each, anyone, everyone, either, several, some, etc.

INTERROGATIVE PRONOUNS: who, which, what

RELATIVE PRONOUNS: who, which, that

REFLEXIVE PRONOUNS: myself, yourself, herself, themselves, etc.

INTENSIVE PRONOUNS: I *myself*, you *yourself*, she *herself*, they *themselves*, etc.

The personal pronouns have differing forms depending upon whether they are subjects (*I* will help Mr. Curtis) or objects (Gene told *him* the plan) or show possession (The red coat is *hers*). These differences in form, which are seen only in the possessive case of nouns, occur in all three cases (*nominative, objective,* and *possessive*) of these pronouns.

Personal pronouns, like nouns, are singular and plural, but their plurals are irregularly formed: I, *we;* she, *they;* it, *they;* etc. The following table shows the various forms of the personal pronouns:

Singular			
	Nominative	Objective	Possessive
1st person	I	me	my, mine
2nd person	you	you	your, yours
3rd person	he, she, it	him, her, it	his, her, hers, its
Plural			
	Nominative	Objective	Possessive
1st person	we	us	our, ours
2nd person	you	you	your, yours
3rd person	they	them	their, theirs

■ 1c Adjective

An **adjective** (from Latin *adjectivum*, something that is added) modifies, describes, limits, or adds to the meaning of a noun or pronoun (*strange, lovely, three, French, those*). In other words, adjectives modify substantives. The articles *the, a,* and *an* are adjectives. Nouns in the possessive case (*Martha's* book, the *cat's* whiskers) and some possessive forms of the personal pronouns are used as adjectives:

my	our
your	your
his, her, its	their

Many demonstrative, indefinite, and interrogative forms may be used as either pronouns or adjectives:

DEMONSTRATIVE: this, that, these, those

INDEFINITE: each, any, either, neither, some, all, both, every, many, most

INTERROGATIVE: which, what, whose

When one of these words appears before a noun or other substantive, describing it or adding to its meaning (*this* cake, *those* gloves, *any* person, *some* food, *which* dress), it is an adjective. When the word stands in the place of a noun (*Those* are pretty roses), it is, of course, a pronoun.

Adjectives formed from proper nouns are called **proper adjectives** and are spelled with a capital letter **(German, Christian, Shakespearean).**

■ 1d Verb

A **verb** (from Latin *verbum*, word) is a word used to state or ask something and usually expresses an action (*spoke, tells, ran, argued, fights*) or a state of being (*is, seemed, existed, appears*). As its Latin origin indicates, the verb is *the* word in the sentence, for every sentence must have a verb, either expressed or understood.

Transitive and Intransitive Verbs

A verb is called **transitive** if its action is directed toward some receiver, which may be the object of the verb or even its subject. (*David flew the plane*, or *The plane was flown by David*. Whether *plane* is the subject or object of the verb, the fact remains that David flew the plane, making *plane* in both sentences the receiver of the verb's action.)

Note: The term *action* should not be misinterpreted as always involving physical activity. The so-called "action" of a verb may not refer to a physical action at all: Mr. Lee *considered* the plan, Amanda *believed* Frank's story, Louise *wants* a new car. The verbs *considered, believed,* and *wants* are transitive verbs; and their objects *plan, story,* and *car* are receivers of their "action," even though there is no physical action involved.

A verb is called **intransitive** if its action is not directed toward some receiver. (*Lightning strikes. Mother is ill.*) Most verbs may be either transitive or intransitive, simply depending on whether or not a receiver of the verb's action is present in the sentence: *Lightning strikes tall trees* (*strikes* is transitive because *trees* is its object). *Lightning strikes suddenly* (*strikes* is intransitive because no receiver of its action is present). The action is complete without an object.

Linking Verbs

There is a special group of intransitive verbs that make a statement not by expressing action but by indicating a state of being or a condition. These verbs are called **linking verbs** because their function is to link the subject of a sentence with a noun, pronoun, or other substantive that identifies it or with an adjective that describes it. A subject and a linking verb cannot function together as a complete sentence without the help of the substantive or adjective needed to complete the thought; for example, in the sentence *Dorothy is my sister* the word *sister* is necessary to complete the sentence, and it identifies *Dorothy*, the subject. In the sentence *Dorothy is vigorous* the word *vigorous* is necessary, and it describes the subject.

The most common linking verb is the verb *to be* in all its forms (see table on pages 8–9), but any verb that expresses a state of being and is followed by a noun or an adjective identifying or describing the subject is a linking verb. Following is a list of some of the most commonly used linking verbs:

appear	look	smell
become	remain	sound
feel	seem	taste*
grow		

You will notice that those verbs referring to states of being perceived through the five senses are included in the list: *look, feel, smell, sound,* and *taste.* (Sally *looks* happy, I *feel* chilly, The coffee *smells* good, The ticking of the clock *sounded* loud, The plum pudding *tastes* spicy.)

Active and Passive Voice

Transitive verbs are said to be in the **active voice** or the **passive voice. Voice** is the form of a verb that indicates whether the subject of the sentence performs the action or is the receiver of the action of the verb. If the subject performs the action, the verb is in the *active voice* (*Andy ate soup for lunch today*). If the subject receives the action, the verb is in the *passive voice* (*Soup was eaten by Andy for lunch today*).

Tense

Tense is the form a verb takes in order to express the time of an action or a state of being, as in these examples: *Helen walks* **(present tense)**; *Helen walked* **(past tense).** These two tenses, present and past, change the verb's simple form to

---

*These verbs are not exclusively linking verbs; they may also be used in an active sense, possibly having objects, as in the following:

The dog cautiously *smelled* the food in its bowl.
We *looked* everywhere for the lost key.
Sharon *felt* the warmth of the log fire across the room.
Nick *tasted* the chowder and then added salt.

show the time of the verb's action. The other four of the six principal tenses found in English verbs are formed through the use of **auxiliary** (helping) verb forms like the following:

am	was	have
are	were	has
is	will	had

The use of these auxiliary verbs creates **verb phrases** (groups of related words that function as single parts of speech). These verb phrases enable the writer to express time and time relationships far beyond those found in the simple present and past forms: She *has gone* to the office; Maggie *will ride* with me; He *had expected* to win the prize; I *am planning* a trip. Verb phrases are also created by the combination of verbs and words like *must, can,* and *do,* often called modal auxiliaries: I *can walk* to class in five minutes; You *must finish* your dinner; *Do* you *have* the time?

Conjugation of Verbs

Showing all forms of a verb in all its tenses is called **conjugation.** Any verb may be conjugated if its **principal parts** are known. These are (1) the first person singular, present tense, (2) the first person singular, past tense, (3) the past participle. (The **participle** is a verbal form that must always be accompanied by an auxiliary verb when it is used to create one of the verb tenses.)

The principal parts of the verb *to call* are (1) *call,* (2) *called,* (3) *called.* The first two of these provide the basic forms of the simple tenses; the third is used with the auxiliary verbs to form verb phrases for the other tenses. The conjugation in the **indicative mood** (that form used for declarative sentences, which make a statement, or interrogative sentences, which ask a question) of the verb *to call* is given below:

ACTIVE VOICE	
Present tense	
Singular	Plural
1. I call	We call
2. You call	You call
3. He, she, it calls	They call
Past tense	
1. I called	We called
2. You called	You called
3. He, she, it called	They called
Future tense	
1. I will (shall) call	We will (shall) call
2. You will call	You will call
3. He, she, it will call	They will call

Present perfect tense	
1. I have called	We have called
2. You have called	You have called
3. He, she, it has called	They have called

Past perfect tense	
1. I had called	We had called
2. You had called	You had called
3. He, she, it had called	They had called

Future perfect tense	
1. I will (shall) have called	We will (shall) have called
2. You will have called	You will have called
3. He, she, it will have called	They will have called

PASSIVE VOICE

Present tense	
1. I am called	We are called
2. You are called	You are called
3. He, she, it is called	They are called

Past tense	
1. I was called	We were called
2. You were called	You were called
3. He, she, it was called	They were called

Future tense	
1. I will (shall) be called	We will (shall) be called
2. You will be called	You will be called
3. He, she, it will be called	They will be called

Present perfect tense	
1. I have been called	We have been called
2. You have been called	You have been called
3. He, she, it has been called	They have been called

Past perfect tense	
1. I had been called	We had been called
2. You had been called	You had been called
3. He, she, it had been called	They had been called

Future perfect tense	
1. I will (shall) have been called	We will (shall) have been called
2. You will have been called	You will have been called
3. He, she, it will have been called	They will have been called

Note: You have probably noticed that in the future and future perfect tenses the auxiliary verb *shall* is used as an alternate to *will* in the first persons singular and plural. Traditionally, written English has required *shall,* but contemporary grammarians now suggest that the distinction need be made only rarely and that *will* may be used throughout a conjugation. For emphasis, however, *shall* may occasionally be needed, especially to express strong determination or invitation:

We *shall* overcome!

Shall we dance?

Progressive Tenses

To express an action or state in progress either at the time of speaking or at the time spoken of, forms of the auxiliary verb *to be* are combined with the present participle (see Chapter 4, Section C) as follows:

Progressive present tense	
1. I am calling	We are calling
2. You are calling	You are calling
3. He, she, it is calling	They are calling
Progressive past tense	
1. I was calling	We were calling
2. You were calling	You were calling
3. He, she, it was calling	They were calling

This process may be continued through the various tenses of the active voice, as indicated below:

PROGRESSIVE FUTURE TENSE: I will (shall) be calling, etc.

PROGRESSIVE PRESENT PERFECT TENSE: I have been calling, etc.

PROGRESSIVE PAST PERFECT TENSE: I had been calling, etc.

PROGRESSIVE FUTURE PERFECT TENSE: I will (shall) have been calling, etc.

In the passive voice, the progressive is generally used only in the simple present and past tenses:

PROGRESSIVE PRESENT TENSE: I am being called, etc.

PROGRESSIVE PAST TENSE: I was being called, etc.

In the remaining tenses of the passive voice, the progressive forms — though feasible — become awkward (I will be being called, I have been being called, etc.).

Auxiliary Verbs *To Be* and *To Have*

As you have seen, the verbs *to be* and *to have* are used to form certain tenses of all verbs. Following are the conjugations of these two auxiliary verbs in the indicative mood, active voice:

The principal parts of *to be* are (1) *am*, (2) *was*, and (3) *been*.

Present tense	
Singular	Plural
1. I am	We are
2. You are	You are
3. He, she, it is	They are
Past tense	
1. I was	We were
2. You were	You were
3. He, she, it was	They were
Future tense	
1. I will (shall) be	We will (shall) be
2. You will be	You will be
3. He, she, it will be	They will be
Present perfect tense	
1. I have been	We have been
2. You have been	You have been
3. He, she, it has been	They have been
Past perfect tense	
1. I had been	We had been
2. You had been	You had been
3. He, she, it had been	They had been
Future perfect tense	
1. I will (shall) have been	We will (shall) have been
2. You will have been	You will have been
3. He, she, it will have been	They will have been

The principal parts of the verb *to have* are (1) *have,* (2) *had,* and (3) *had.*

Present tense	
Singular	Plural
1. I have	We have
2. You have	You have
3. He, she, it has	They have
Past tense	
1. I had	We had
2. You had	You had
3. He, she, it had	They had
Future tense	
1. I will (shall) have	We will (shall) have
2. You will have	You will have
3. He, she, it will have	They will have

Present perfect tense	
1. I have had	We have had
2. You have had	You have had
3. He, she, it has had	They have had

Past perfect tense	
1. I had had	We had had
2. You had had	You had had
3. He, she, it had had	They had had

Future perfect tense	
1. I will (shall) have had	We will (shall) have had
2. You will have had	You will have had
3. He, she, it will have had	They will have had

Mood

Mood is the form a verb may take to indicate whether it is intended to make a statement, to give a command, or to express a condition contrary to fact. Besides the **indicative** mood shown in the conjugations above, there are the **imperative** and the **subjunctive** moods.

The **imperative** mood is used in giving commands or making requests, as in *TAKE me out to the ball game.* Here *TAKE* is in the imperative mood. The subject of an imperative sentence is *you*, usually understood, but sometimes expressed for the sake of emphasis, as in *You get out of here!*

The **subjunctive** mood is most often used today to express a wish or a condition contrary to fact. In the sentences *I wish I WERE going* and *If I WERE you, I would not go*, the verbs in capitals are in the subjunctive mood.

■ 1e Adverb

An *adverb* (from Latin *ad*, to or toward, and *verbum*, word) usually modifies or adds to the meaning of a verb, an adjective, or another adverb. Sometimes, however, it may be used to modify or qualify a whole phrase or clause, adding to the meaning of an idea that the sentence expresses. The following sentences illustrate the variety of uses of the adverb:

He ran *fast*. [*Fast* modifies the verb *ran*.]

The judges considered the contestants *unusually* brilliant. [*Unusually* modifies the adjective *brilliant*.]

She sang *very* loudly. [*Very* modifies the adverb *loudly*.]

The doves were flying *just* outside gun range. [*Just* modifies either the preposition *outside* or the whole prepositional phrase *outside gun range*.]

He had driven carefully *ever* since he was injured. [*Ever* modifies either the conjunction *since* or the whole clause *since he was injured*.]

Unfortunately, she has encountered rejection everywhere. [*Unfortunately* modifies the whole idea expressed in the sentence and cannot logically be attached to a single word.]

■ 1f Preposition

A **preposition** (from Latin *prae*, before, and *positum*, placed) is a word placed usually before a substantive, called the *object of the preposition*, to show relationship between that object and some other word in the sentence. The combination of a preposition, its object, and any modifiers of the object is called a **prepositional phrase** (*in the mood, on the porch, of human events, toward the beautiful green lake*). You will see how necessary prepositions are to our language when you realize how often you use most of the ones in the group below, which includes some of the most commonly used prepositions:

about	below	except	through
above	beneath	for	throughout
across	beside	from	to
after	besides	in	toward
against	between	into	under
along	beyond	like	underneath
amid	but (meaning	of	until
among	*except*)	off	up
around	by	on	upon
at	concerning	over	with
before	down	past	within
behind	during	since	without

Ordinarily a preposition precedes its object, as its name indicates. Although a sentence ending with a preposition is frequently unemphatic or clumsy, it is in no way contrary to English usage. *She asked what they were cooked in* is better English than *She asked in what they were cooked*.

■ 1g Conjunction

A **conjunction** (from Latin *conjungere*, to join) is a word used to join words or groups of words. There are two kinds of conjunctions: **coordinating conjunctions** and **subordinating conjunctions.**

Coordinating Conjunctions

Coordinating conjunctions join sentence elements of equal rank. In the sentence *She was poor but honest* the conjunction *but* joins the two adjectives *poor* and *honest*. In *She was poor, but she was honest* the conjunction *but* joins the two independent statements *She was poor* and *she was honest*. The common coordinating conjunctions are the following:

and	or	for
but	nor	

Yet in the sense of *but*, and *so* in the sense of *therefore* are also coordinating conjunctions. **Correlative conjunctions,** which are used in pairs (*either . . . or . . . , neither . . . nor . . .*), are coordinating conjunctions also.

Subordinating Conjunctions

Subordinating conjunctions introduce certain subordinate or dependent elements and join them to the main or independent part of the sentence. In *Jack has gone home because he was tired* the subordinating conjunction *because* subordinates the clause that it is part of and joins it to the main part of the sentence, *Jack has gone home.* There are many subordinating conjunctions. Some common ones are the following:

after	as	if
unless	when	while
although	before	since
until	whether	

Note: Words like *however, therefore, nevertheless, moreover, in fact, consequently, hence,* and *accordingly* are essentially adverbs, not conjunctions; they are sometimes called **conjunctive adverbs.**

■ 1h Interjection

An **interjection** (from Latin *inter*, among or between, and *jectum*, thrown) is an exclamatory word like *oh, ouch, please, why, hey* thrown into a sentence or sometimes used alone. An interjection is always grammatically independent of the rest of the sentence. Adjectives, adverbs, and occasionally other parts of speech become interjections when used as independent exclamations (*good! horrible! fine! what! wait!*).

■ 1i Varying Sentence Functions of Words

The introductory paragraphs in this chapter pointed out that there are many words in the English language that may function as more than one part of speech and that the designation of a word as a particular part of speech is dependent upon its function within its own sentence. It will be helpful for you to see a few examples of this assertion. The word *cause*, for instance, may be a noun, as in the sentence *What was the cause of her distress?* or a transitive verb, as in the sentence *Will the rain cause a delay in the baseball game?* The word *fire* may be a noun, a verb, or an adjective, as shown in the following sentences: *The fire at the warehouse was set by an arsonist; John fired the pistol;* and *We had a fire drill at school yesterday.* The word *near* may be an adverb, an adjective, or a preposition, as in the following sentences: *The end of the year is drawing near; I will make my decision in the near future; Our house is near the campus.*

Exercise 1 Nouns and Pronouns

Write in the first column at the right any *italicized* word that is a *noun* and in the second any that is a *pronoun*.

	Noun	**Pronoun**
Example: *He* is an articulate *person*.	*person*	*He*
1. *Children* ask many questions, don't *they*?		
2. Jess will wait for *you* at the *hotel*.		
3. The main problem for *him* is *procrastination*.		
4. *I* recently bought a portable electronic *typewriter*.		
5. Bring *me* a *loaf* of bread.		
6. *These* are our *arrangements* for the party.		
7. In high school John excelled in *math* and *science*.		
8. *One* of the department *heads* will visit us today.		
9. *She* is an ambitious professional *woman*.		
10. Do you project a positive *image* of *yourself*?		
11. A liberal arts background is a great *asset* for *anyone*.		
12. Gloria has brought *everyone* a *present*.		
13. She has read *everything* connected with *computers*.		
14. Her transition from teacher to bank *president* wasn't easy.		
15. Can *you* go to the *beach* with us?		
16. *What* did you see at the *movie*?		

13

	Noun	Pronoun
17. I have not read that *book myself*.	_____	_____
18. No, that *hat* is not *mine*.	_____	_____
19. *Who* bought Nelson's *house*?	_____	_____
20. *What* are your *priorities*?	_____	_____
21. Sometime between lunch and supper Kyle will mow the *lawn* for *you*.	_____	_____
22. *We* will leave early in the morning for the *mountains*.	_____	_____
23. It was *I* who made the *pizza*.	_____	_____
24. After a while his constant *chatter* causes *me* to lose my temper.	_____	_____

Exercise 2 — Pronouns

In the sentences below identify the *italicized* pronouns by writing one of the following abbreviations in the space at the right:

P for personal,   **Inter** for interrogative,
D for demonstrative,   **Inten** for intensive,
I for indefinite,   **Ref** for reflexive.
Rel for relative,

Example: Are you going with *us*?   _P_

1. Did you notify *everyone* of the time change?   _____

2. *I* can't imagine Laura's being at a loss for words.   _____

3. Tell *me* about your style of management.   _____

4. John said he would paint the house *himself.*   _____

5. *She* attempted all summer to learn to water ski.   _____

6. *That* is where I parked the car.   _____

7. Has *anyone* responded to the invitation?   _____

8. *Who* is bringing the hamburgers?   _____

9. Michael, *who* is shortstop for our team, was chosen most valuable
    player.   _____

10. I studied the outline *that* you suggested.   _____

11. Have *you* seen Russell today?   _____

12. Dr. Gibson is a professor who is respected by *all* of her students.   _____

13. Our children are grown and can take care of *themselves.*   _____

14. The orders *that* you placed last week have arrived.   _____

15. Can you open this can for *me*?   _____

16. Ralph *himself* said the movie was boring.   _____

17. *This* cannot be the only way out.   _____

18. *Who* wrote the novels about the Snopes family?   _____

19. *Several* of us are going to London after Christmas.   _____

20. *One* of the players won a scholarship to West Point.   _____

21. Had you called *me* earlier?   _____

22. *We* are looking forward to my cousin's visit.   _____

15

Exercise 3   Adjectives and Adverbs

In the following sentences underline once all the adjectives and words used as adjectives except the articles **a, an,** and **the.** Underline all the adverbs twice.

Example: Aunt Ellie was an <u>extremely</u> <u>proud</u> woman.

1. Dr. Webb normally gives a test on Friday.
2. Anna is a very lovely woman.
3. Heroic figures sometimes appear almost too perfect.
4. There are currently five houses for sale on Bay Street.
5. Some states are experiencing a shortage of cheap, clean water.
6. The United States is rapidly moving from an industrial society to an informational society.
7. We were not the only strangers there.
8. Uncle Ned walks several miles daily.
9. The decrepit old man quietly entered the room.
10. Brenda is a hard worker, and she also works fast.
11. We seldom attend professional football games.
12. Laura is somewhat anxious.
13. He turned around and recognized us immediately.
14. At practice the soccer team was surprised by the college president.
15. Neither sirloin steak nor hamburger is very cheap now.
16. It is almost impossible to study and watch television simultaneously.
17. She prepares for her interviews very carefully.
18. Each meeting lasted nearly two hours.
19. Joel's manners are abominable.
20. Jan will always remember the challenge of her first race.

Exercise 4 Verbs

In the following sentences underline all verbs, and then write them in the first column at the right. In the second column write **A** if the verb is in the active voice, **P** if it is in the passive voice. In the last column write **T** if the verb is transitive, **I** if it is intransitive.

	Verb	A/P	T/I
Example: The women in her stories thrive on romance.	*thrive*	*A*	*I*
1. We are a nation of moviegoers.			
2. Almost everyone fled from the main hall after the speech.			
3. Suddenly the silence was broken.			
4. Chuck's job is a very important one.			
5. Margaret wears beautifully tailored clothes.			
6. Remember me to your family.			
7. Her discussions of the novel were quite informative.			
8. Draft a statement for the press.			
9. Miriam was chosen captain of the team.			
10. Have you read Nell P. Eurich's *Corporate Classrooms*?			
11. I always considered my father's advice useful.			
12. Did she appear somewhat distant last night?			
13. No, Reid is not my brother.			
14. Karla instructed us carefully.			
15. The area that is Arkansas was visited by Hernando de Soto in 1541.			

	Verb	A/P	T/I
16. Among other things, Dr. Ellison did not like my thesis statement.	_____	___	___
17. I really don't feel good today.	_____	___	___
18. Will you have lunch with Grand-mother and me?	_____	___	___
19. Paul has been out of town for several weeks.	_____	___	___
20. The woman by the window is our new club president.	_____	___	___
21. Anna will finish law school this year.	_____	___	___
22. The issue of student aid has become important to every college.	_____	___	___
23. Most of the adult students are professional and technical workers.	_____	___	___

Exercise 5 Prepositions

Write the prepositions in the following sentences in the spaces of the first column to the right. Write the objects of the prepositions in the second column. If a sentence contains no preposition, leave the spaces blank.

	Prep.	**Object**
Example: Among my favorite possessions is an old writing desk.	*Among*	*possessions*
1. How did you fall down the stairs?		
2. I can come anytime except Sunday.		
3. The umbrella is behind the door.		
4. You cannot both go at the same time.		
5. During lunch we will plan the conference.		
6. Shirley is coming within the hour.		
7. Did you notice the Queen Anne's lace along the roadside?		
8. Jennifer would not walk across the swinging bridge.		
9. Ed seldom plans beyond the present moment.		
10. Kennebunkport is not far from my hometown.		
11. Beth is not interested in her courses.		
12. Marie has a romantic view of the past.		
13. Uncle Wayne is taking us to the opera this Friday.		
14. I believe that his family lives in Scotland.		
15. You aren't surprised by my news?		
16. Los Angeles is between San Diego and San Francisco.		
17. There is something very adventurous about mountain climbing.		
18. Join us for a midnight party.		

	Prep.	**Object**
19. Have you heard any news about our reservations?	_____	_____
20. The prize is hidden under the couch.	_____	_____
21. Comets are the building blocks of solar systems.	_____	_____
22. Without my glasses I can't see anything.	_____	_____
23. You will find his office down this hall.	_____	_____
24. The snake moved quickly across the road.	_____	_____

Exercise 6   Conjunctions

In the following sentences there are both coordinating and subordinating conjunctions. Underline all conjunctions, and then write them in the first column at the right. In the second column write **C** if the conjunction joins sentence elements of equal rank, **S** if it joins unequal elements.

	Conj.	C/S
Example: <u>While</u> I was in London, I met an old school friend.	*While*	*S*
1. After you finish your homework, we'll go to get some pizza.		
2. Benjamin Franklin was a philosopher and a scientist.		
3. I am sorry, but I didn't order an avocado pear filled with crabmeat.		
4. When Kate finally arrived, she was rather badly dressed.		
5. He is taking physics even though his advisor counseled against the idea.		
6. Neither Clyde nor Kenneth went to England this summer.		
7. I will meet you at the airport if I can.		
8. Sea turtles are toothless, but they can eat crisp vegetation.		
9. Bart was unable to play in Friday night's game because he was injured last week.		
10. Either you or Robyn must attend Gary's graduation.		
11. Both my sister and her husband play in the Chicago Symphony.		
12. As you turn the corner, you will see our house on the right.		
13. She has wanted to be a doctor since she was six years old.		

23

	Conj.	C/S
14. Neither time nor place has been announced for the meeting.	_____	_____
15. Although he is my supervisor, we do not always agree.	_____	_____
16. Unless I hear from you tomorrow, I'll expect you for Sunday supper.	_____	_____
17. The blind man hesitated before he crossed the street.	_____	_____
18. Marlene and Gloria have been accepted by Smith College.	_____	_____
19. I was not only puzzled but also distressed by his attitude.	_____	_____
20. Our cat sat in the window and watched the snow fall.	_____	_____

Exercise 7   Review of Parts of Speech

In the following sentences identify the part of speech of each *italicized* word by writing one of the following abbreviations in the space at the right:

N for noun,   **Adv** for adverb,
V for verb,   **Prep** for preposition,
P for pronoun,   **C** for conjunction,
Adj for adjective,   **I** for interjection.

Example: You were *unusually* quiet at the party tonight.   *Adv*

1. Can you help *me* bring in the groceries?   _____

2. *No!* I told you I don't want to go.   _____

3. Robert Hutchins became president of the University of Chicago *at* the age of thirty.   _____

4. This report *responds* to your questions about the writing program.   _____

5. The *average* person's perception of crime is colored by the crimes reported on television.   _____

6. Mrs. Holcomb's yard *or* house is always full of children.   _____

7. How many classes are you taking this *semester*?   _____

8. The profession of medicine is *rapidly* changing.   _____

9. *Do* you *support* Roger's opinion?   _____

10. The *initial* phase of the project will begin next month.   _____

11. *What!* Are you sure the caterer has dropped the wedding cake?   _____

12. The state's population has increased *over* the last ten years.   _____

13. Except for Al, *everyone* plans to attend the play.   _____

14. The conference sponsored by the University of Wisconsin emphasized the need for *communication* skills.   _____

15. The contributions of the *poet* to society are equal to those of the engineer.   _____

16. The library is the *largest* building on the campus.   _____

17. Early *this* morning Ben left for Australia.   _____

18. The faculty *and* staff enjoyed the director's report.   _____

19. Pamela left *herself* open for criticism.   _____

20. Julian is a research engineer *at* the California Institute of Technology.   _____

21. As the president's secretary, he spends *many* hours on the telephone.   _____

Exercise 8   Review of Parts of Speech

In the following sentences identify the part of speech of each *italicized* word by writing one of the following abbreviations in the space at the right:

N for noun,   **Adv** for adverb,
V for verb,   **Prep** for preposition,
P for pronoun,   **C** for conjunction,
Adj for adjective,   **I** for interjection.

Example: Tommy is not a *typical* college student.   *Adj*

1. Downtown Atlanta appears deserted *at* night. _____

2. The Panama Canal connects the Gulf of Mexico *with* the Pacific Ocean. _____

3. *Despite* Rick's explanation, I still did not understand the question. _____

4. *Preventive* medicine involves more than protection against disease. _____

5. Bonnie is a polite, energetic woman with a pleasing *personality.* _____

6. Dr. Bishop became Tom's *mentor.* _____

7. Baylor University rewards *both* faculty *and* students for achievement. _____

8. I do not see *enough* emphasis on oral reports. _____

9. Our old hound spends most of *his* time under the porch. _____

10. *At last!* You finally got somewhere on time. _____

11. Fluffy's kittens are *too* cute for words. _____

12. Did you see Russ *before* he moved to Seattle? _____

13. The committee will establish *emergency* procedures. _____

14. During the next few months we *will study* German literature. _____

15. A great deal has been written *about* computer literacy. _____

16. Most professors are articulate *and* can talk for hours. _____

17. There will be a few *modifications* in your design. _____

18. The Australian government *plans* to restrict future enrollment of foreign students. _____

19. *These* are the extra tickets to the Saturday afternoon performance. _____

20. The Portland School of Art *was founded* in 1882. _____

2

Recognizing Subjects, Verbs, and Complements

■ 2a The Sentence

A **sentence** is made up of single parts of speech combined into a pattern that expresses a complete thought. In other words, a sentence is a group of words that expresses a complete thought. When written, it begins with a capital letter and ends with a period, a question mark, or an exclamation mark. In its simplest form this complete statement is an independent clause or a **simple sentence.**

■ 2b Subject and Predicate

Every simple sentence must have two basic elements: (1) the thing we are talking about, and (2) what we say about it. The thing we are talking about is called the **subject,** and what we say about it is called the **predicate.** The subject is a noun, a pronoun, or some other word or group of words used as a noun. The essential part of the predicate is a verb — a word that tells something about the subject. It tells that the subject *does* something or that something *is true* of the subject. A subject and a verb are, therefore, the fundamental parts of every sentence. In fact, it is possible to express meaning with just these two elements:

Pilots fly.

Flowers bloom.

She sings.

Note that in each example the verb says that the subject does something.

■ 2c Finding the Verb

Finding verbs and subjects of verbs in a sentence is the first step in determining whether or not a group of words expresses a complete thought. Look first for the verb, the most important word in the sentence, and then for its subject.

The verb may sometimes be difficult to find. It may come anywhere in the sentence; for instance, it may precede the subject, as in some interrogative sentences (*Where is my pencil?*). It may consist of a single word or a group of two or more words; it may have other words inserted within the verb phrase; it may be combined with the negative *not* or with a contraction of *not*. To find the verb, look for the word or group of words that expresses an action or a state of being. In the following sentences the verbs are in italics:

> His friend *stood* at his side. [The verb *stood* follows the subject *friend.*]
>
> At his side *stood* his friend. [The verb *stood* precedes the subject *friend.*]
>
> His friend *was standing* at his side. [The verb *was standing* consists of two words.]
>
> His friend *can*not *stand* at his side. [The verb *can* is combined with the negative adverb *not,* which is not part of the verb.]
>
> *Did* his friend *stand* at his side? [The two parts of the verb *did stand* are separated by the subject.]

■ 2d Finding the Subject

Sometimes finding the subject may also be difficult, for, as we have just seen, the subject does not always come immediately before the verb. Often it comes after the verb; often it is separated from the verb by a modifying element. Always look for the noun or pronoun about which the verb asserts something and disregard intervening elements:

> *Many* of the children *come* to the clinic. [A prepositional phrase comes between the subject and the verb. The object of a preposition is never a subject.]
>
> There *are flowers* on the table. [The subject comes after the verb. The word *there* is never a subject; in this sentence it is an **expletive,** an idiomatic introductory word.]
>
> In the room *were* a *cot* and a *chair.* [The subjects come after the verb.]

In an imperative sentence, a sentence expressing a command or a request, the subject *you* is usually implied rather than expressed. Occasionally, however, the subject *you* is expressed:

> Come in out of the rain.
>
> Shut the door!
>
> *You* play goalie.

Either the verb or the subject or both may be **compound;** that is, there may be more than one subject and more than one verb:

The *boy* and the *girl* played. [Two subjects.]

The boy *worked* and *played*. [Two verbs.]

The *boy* and the *girl worked* and *played*. [Two subjects and two verbs.]

In the first sentence the compound subject is *boy* and *girl*. In the second sentence there is a compound verb, *worked* and *played*. In the third sentence both the subject and the verb are compound.

■ 2e Complements

Thus far we have discussed two functions of words: that of nouns and pronouns as subjects and that of verbs as predicates.

A third function of words that we must consider is that of completing the verb. Nouns, pronouns, and adjectives are used to complete verbs and are called **complements.** A complement may be a **direct object,** an **indirect object,** a **predicate noun** or **pronoun,** a **predicate adjective,** an **objective complement,** or a **retained object.**

A **direct object** is a noun or noun equivalent that completes the verb and receives the action expressed in the verb:

The pilot flew the plane. [*Plane* is the direct object of *flew*. Just as the subject answers the question *"who?"* or *"what?"* before the verb (Who flew?), so the direct object answers the question *"whom?"* or *"what?"* after the verb (Flew what?).]

An **indirect object** is a word (or words) denoting the person or thing indirectly affected by the action of a transitive verb. It is the person or thing to which something is given or for which something is done. A sentence cannot contain an indirect object without also containing a direct object. Such words as *give, offer, grant, lend, teach,* and the like represent the idea of something done for the indirect object:

We gave *her* the book. [*Her* is the indirect object of *gave*. The indirect object answers the question *"to (for) whom or what?"* after the verb *gave* (Gave to whom?).]

Certain verbs that represent the idea of taking away or withholding something can also have indirect objects:

The judge *denied him* the opportunity to speak in his own defense.

Father *refused Frances* the use of the car.

A **predicate noun** (also called **predicate nominative**) is a noun or its equivalent that renames or identifies the subject and completes such verbs as *be, seem, become,* and *appear* (called linking verbs):

The woman is a *doctor*. [The predicate noun *doctor* completes the intransitive verb *is* and renames the subject *woman*.]

My best friends are *she* and her *sister*. [The predicate pronoun *she* and the predicate noun *sister* complete the intransitive verb *are* and rename the subject *friends*.]

Mary has become a *pilot*. [The predicate noun *pilot* completes the intransitive verb *has become* and renames the subject *Mary*.]

A **predicate adjective** is an adjective that completes a linking verb and describes the subject:

The man seems *angry*. [The predicate adjective *angry* completes the intransitive verb *seems* and describes the subject *man*.]

An **objective complement** is a noun or an adjective that completes the action expressed in the verb and refers to the direct object. If it is a noun, the objective complement is in a sense identical with the direct object; if it is an adjective, it describes or limits the direct object. It occurs commonly after such verbs as *think, call, find, make, consider, choose,* and *believe:*

Jealousy made Othello a *murderer*. [The objective complement *murderer* completes the transitive verb *made* and renames the direct object *Othello*.]

She thought the day *disagreeable*. [The objective complement *disagreeable* is an adjective that describes the direct object *day*.]

A **retained object** is a noun or noun equivalent that remains as the object when a verb having both a direct and an indirect object is put into the passive voice. The other object becomes the subject of such a verb. Although either object may become the subject, the indirect object more commonly takes that position, and the direct object is retained:

The board granted him a year's leave of absence.
He was granted a year's leave of absence.

[In the second sentence the verb has been put into the passive voice, the indirect object of the first sentence has become the subject of the second, and the direct object has been retained.]

The teacher asked the student a difficult question.
A difficult question was asked the student.

[In the second sentence the verb has been put into the passive voice, the direct object of the first sentence has become the subject of the second, and the indirect object has been retained.]

Exercise 9   Subjects and Verbs

In each of the following sentences underline the subject once and the verb twice. Then write the subject in the first column and the verb in the second column at the right.

	Subject	Verb
Example: The students at St. Pius High School excelled in the debate.	*students*	*excelled*
1. Today's sea turtles have a history of at least 120 million years.		
2. Many academic programs have survived despite their mediocrity.		
3. Betsy and Roy will be here for lunch.		
4. The University of Cincinnati is recognized for its music program.		
5. Our company purchased a million-dollar computer last year.		
6. There are two vacant apartments in our building.		
7. Over the years she has gained the respect of the legal community.		
8. Don't let the cat in.		
9. Last week Mr. Everett announced his retirement date.		
10. Behind the barn you will find the tractor.		
11. Recently Chris was nominated chairman of the faculty senate.		
12. Both Ned and Judy are taking piano lessons this year.		
13. There are too many courses on this term's schedule.		
14. Have you been to the races lately?		
15. I eat too fast.		

	Subject	Verb
16. Each group of students has a different advisor.	_____	_____
17. Guatemala was visited by the delegation.	_____	_____
18. Many well-preserved dinosaur skeletons have been found in the South and Southwest.	_____	_____
19. Traffic at five o'clock in the afternoon is chaotic.	_____	_____
20. The admissions committee did not meet today.	_____	_____

Exercise 10   Subjects and Verbs

In each of the following sentences underline the subject(s) once and its verb(s) twice. Then copy the subject(s) in the first column and the verb(s) in the second column at the right.

	Subject	Verb
Example: Beverly Sills is a great performer.	*Beverly Sills*	*is*
1. My father wrote and spoke flawless English and German.		
2. The tall, handsome foreigner stood, then left the room.		
3. The Smithsonian delights everyone.		
4. Each Agatha Christie mystery provides excitement.		
5. Keys are traditional symbols of authority.		
6. In the summer of 1984 I accompanied my parents to Ontario.		
7. One of the secrets of Helen's success is time management.		
8. On winter evenings Marshall entertains us with hilarious stories.		
9. Lee's parents were immigrants.		
10. On Mother's Day everyone left for home.		
11. His charm and adaptability open many doors to him.		
12. The dog across the street belongs to the neighborhood.		
13. Trinity College advertised for a biophysicist.		
14. Before rapid transit they almost always drove to work.		

	Subject	Verb

15. We will probably see Gene next week.

16. At the bottom of the stairs sat Rob and his new puppy.

17. Most of the offices will be closed on Monday.

18. Shortly after the game the remnants of the crowd had gone.

19. With some hesitation I entered the long, dark hallway.

20. Willa Cather, a major American writer, attended the University of Nebraska.

21. Nobody has ever created a Utopia here on earth.

22. Of course, moral courage is the major qualification for a leader.

23. Few critics questioned the genius of Thomas Jefferson.

24. Funds for the dance will be raised by the sorority.

25. Sooner or later Ada will take chemistry.

Exercise 11   Direct Objects and Predicate Nouns

In each of the following sentences underline the complement. Then identify the complement by writing in the space at the right one of the following abbreviations:

DO if it is a direct object,
PN if it is a predicate noun.

Example: Our main goal is quality <u>performance</u>.   *PN*

1. We had an excellent dinner at the new restaurant.   _____

2. The recent storm destroyed our fishing cabin.   _____

3. Ralph's mother is an executive secretary.   _____

4. I really would like more time with my family.   _____

5. Jesse bought his wife a red Porsche.   _____

6. Dr. Hooper became department chairman last year.   _____

7. Microelectronics is a fairly new field of science.   _____

8. Rudy bought his father's company.   _____

9. The forest provides a great resource for the region.   _____

10. Dr. O'Rear studied medicine at the University of Arkansas. _____

11. Is she a corporate lawyer?   _____

12. The Research Center will consider Karen's proposal at its next
    meeting.   _____

13. This new legislation will benefit business and industry.   _____

14. Did you send a letter of recommendation for Paul?   _____

15. You are comparing apples and oranges.   _____

16. The cost of the building is an outrage.   _____

17. Do you have any other questions?   _____

18. Fire ants are a major problem to many farmers.   _____

19. Their fraternity bought six personal computers for the members' use. _____

20. Everyone has a wish list.   _____

Exercise 12   Indirect Objects and Objective Complements

In each of the following sentences identify the *italicized* complement by writing in the space at the right one of the following abbreviations:

    IO if it is an indirect object,
    OC if it is an objective complement.

Example: The shopping trip made my niece *happy*.   *OC*

1. The tennis pro gave *several* of us free lessons.   _____
2. The company quickly appointed Joe *director*.   _____
3. Why did they paint their house royal *blue*?   _____
4. The team voted Paul the best *player*.   _____
5. They offered *her* the position.   _____
6. At lunch I gave *them* my new address.   _____
7. The board of directors appointed Lloyd Anderson *president* of the association.   _____
8. We all considered her report *excellent*.   _____
9. Bring *me* your letter, and I will mail it.   _____
10. Aunt Jessie always sends *each* of us a present.   _____
11. I offered your *sister* a ride.   _____
12. Only Margaret thought Josh's experiences *interesting*.   _____
13. Judge Warren denied *him* bail.   _____
14. Really, I thought the entire story *incredible*.   _____
15. The hostess served *us* tea and cakes.   _____
16. All the professors believed Marty very *capable*.   _____
17. Dr. Walkins gave my *brother* a clean bill of health.   _____
18. Will you send *me* a Chinese garden stool from Hong Kong?   _____
19. The alumnae thought Dr. Winter's speech *inspiring*.   _____
20. Last night Dorothy dyed her hair jet *black*.   _____

Exercise 13 Complements

A. In each of the following sentences identify the *italicized* word by writing one of the following abbreviations in the space at the right:

PN if it is a predicate noun,	**IO** if it is an indirect object,
PA if it is a predicate adjective,	**OC** if it is an objective complement.
DO if it is a direct object,	

Example: Mozart was an accomplished *artist*.   _*PN*_

1. We have devoted too much *time* to this one problem. _____

2. Just remember that the people elected him *governor*. _____

3. In the first quarter Jim threw two touchdown *passes*. _____

4. Your nephew is quite *handsome*. _____

5. I hope that I did not appear too *bored*. _____

6. The prize is a new Buick *convertible*. _____

7. Before you leave, will you bring *me* the paper? _____

8. I consider Brian a *friend*. _____

9. I think Mother is cooking *us* spaghetti for supper. _____

10. Last week Susan began her first *semester* at Brown University. _____

11. Will the organization select *Nancy* or *Steve*? _____

12. Surely Mark will be a *politician* someday. _____

13. Is Denise still *petite*? _____

14. John Keats, the British poet, was a *contemporary* of Percy Shelley, another British poet. _____

15. Children love *Halloween*. _____

B. Write sixteen sentences, four of which contain direct objects; four, indirect objects; four, predicate nouns; four, predicate adjectives. In the space at the right, write **DO** (direct object), **IO** (indirect object), **PN** (predicate noun), or **PA** (predicate adjective) as the case may be.

1. _____ _____

2. _____ _____

3. _____ _____

4. _____   _____

5. _____   _____

6. _____   _____

7. _____   _____

8. _____   _____

9. _____   _____

10. _____   _____

11. _____   _____

12. _____   _____

13. _____   _____

14. _____   _____

15. _____   _____

16. _____   _____

3

The Sentence Fragment

▍ 3a Grammatical Fragments

If you are not careful to have both a subject and a predicate in your sentences and to express a complete thought, you will write sentence fragments instead of complete sentences. Observe, for example, the following:

> A tall, distinguished-looking gentleman standing on the corner in a pouring rain.
>
> Standing on the corner in a pouring rain and shielding himself from the deluge with a large umbrella.

The first of these groups of words is no more than the subject of a sentence or the object of a verb or preposition. It may be part of such a sentence, for example, as *We noticed a tall, distinguished-looking gentleman standing on the corner in a pouring rain.* The second group is probably a modifier of some kind, the modifier of a subject, for instance: *Standing on the corner in a pouring rain and shielding himself from the deluge with a large umbrella, a tall, distinguished-looking gentleman was waiting for a cab.*

Another type of fragment is seen in the following illustrations:

> Because I had heard all that I wanted to hear and did not intend to be bored any longer.
>
> Who was the outstanding athlete of her class and also the best scholar.
>
> Although he had been well recommended by his former employers.

Each of these groups of words actually has a subject and a predicate, but each is still a fragment because the first word of each is a subordinating element and clearly indicates that the thought is incomplete, that the thought expressed depends upon some other thought. Such fragments are subordinate parts of longer sentences like the following:

> I left the hall because I had heard all that I wanted to hear and did not intend to be bored any longer.

> The valedictorian was Alice Snodgrass, who was the outstanding athlete of her class and also the best scholar.

> He did not get the job although he had been well recommended by his former employers.

■ 3b Permissible Fragments

A sentence fragment is often the result of ignorance or carelessness and is the sign of an immature writer. On the other hand, much correctly spoken and written English contains perfectly proper fragments of sentences. The adverbs *yes* and *no* may stand alone, as may other words and phrases in dialogue (though our chief concern remains written prose). There is nothing wrong, for example, in such fragments as the following:

> The sooner, the better.

> Anything but that.

> Same as before.

Interjections and exclamatory phrases may also stand alone as independent elements. The following fragments are correct:

> Ouch!

> Tickets, please!

> Not so!

■ 3c Stylistic Fragments

There is another kind of fragment of rather common occurrence in the writing of some of the best authors. It is the phrase used for realistic or impressionistic effect, the piling up of words or phrases without any effort to organize them into sentences: "The blue haze of evening was upon the field. Lines of forest with long purple shadows. One cloud along the western sky partly smothering the red." This kind of writing, if it is to be good, is very difficult. Like free verse it may best be left to the experienced writer. You should learn to recognize a sentence fragment when you see one. You should use this form sparingly in your own writing. And you should remember two things: first, that the legitimacy of the sentence fragment depends upon whether it is used intentionally or not, and second, that *in an elementary course in composition most instructors assume that a sentence fragment is unintended.*

Study carefully the following sentence fragments and the accompanying comments:

A large woman of rather determined attitude who says that she wishes to see you to discuss a matter of great importance. [This is a typical fragment unintended by the writer, who seems to have felt that it is a complete sentence because there are a subject and a predicate in each subordinate clause.]

He finally decided to leave school. Because he was utterly bored with his work and was failing all his courses. [Here the second group of words is an unjustifiable fragment. It is a subordinate clause and should be attached to the main clause without a break of any kind.]

There were books everywhere. Books in the living room, books in the bedroom, books even in the kitchen. [The second group of words is a fragment, but it may be defended on grounds of emphasis. Many writers, however, would have used a colon after *everywhere* and made a single sentence.]

Exercise 14 The Sentence Fragment

Indicate in the space at the right by writing **C** or **F** whether the following groups of words are complete sentences or fragments of sentences. Rewrite any fragment, making it a complete sentence.

Example: That we have the flexibility to select our books.   _____F_____

That we have the flexibility to select our books is important.

1. Special programs planned for new employees.   _____

2. If you want to visit Portland.   _____

3. Karen, who is studying art at the Sorbonne this year.   _____

4. Only through the discovery of our potential as human beings can we develop wisdom.   _____

5. Dale, a graduate of Denison University in Ohio.   _____

6. Having spent four seasons at the Brunswick Music Theater in Maine. _____

7. My friend Ray, who always studies French with me.   _____

8. Students who feel that their professors really don't care.   ———

9. If you really want to learn the fundamentals of accounting.   ———

10. The boy who decided to run away from home.   ———

11. Because of its relevancy and its realism I suggest that you read *The Invisible Man* by Ralph Ellison.   ———

12. The snail's pace of progress which is often frustrating.   ———

13. It became clear that those who enjoy getting up early were in the minority.   ———

14. As I understand the directions, the room that is vacant down the hall.   ———

15. Her personality which is bubbly.   ———

16. While Mars, the god of war, seems always to be calling nations to war.   ———

17. What troubles me most in our video culture.   _____

18. The construction project which was delayed by the weather.   _____

19. At the head table, Janice Bostict, a woman of independent ideas.   _____

20. In Delaware fishing and waterfowl hunting in season.   _____

21. General Gates's house, located in York, Pennsylvania.   _____

22. Washington, D.C., designed by Major Pierre Charles L'Enfant, is the capital of the United States.   _____

23. The present wrapped in purple paper with an untied bow.   _____

24. After eating too much barbecue.   _____

25. Harold and Jean who both want to become engineers.   _____

Exercise 15   The Sentence Fragment

Some of the following groups are fragments. Some are fragments and sentences. Some are complete sentences. Rewrite in such a way as to leave no fragments. If the group of words is already a complete sentence, leave it as it is and mark it **C**.

Example: Stone Mountain is located in Georgia. Where each summer a laser show is presented.   ___F___

Stone Mountain, where each summer a laser show is presented, is located in Georgia.

1. Although he is not the banquet speaker. He is the president of the University of Utah.   _____

2. The youngest of six children. He grew up wanting to work with his hands.   _____

3. Having taken her parents' advice. She studied art and business.   _____

4. We thought Steve had forgotten to come. Because he was thirty minutes late.   _____

5. My old pick-up which I use nearly every day. The pick-up is over fourteen years old.   _____

6. The Oxford Used-Book Store which carries a variety of books by authors famous and out-of-print.   _____

7. Sandra Deer, author of *So Long on Lonely Street,* a play about choices. The gothic comedy set in the South.   _____

8. Two of humanity's most noble qualities, the capacity to endure and to grow in spirit.   _____

9. Having recently read Thomas Merton's *The Seven Storey Mountain.* Newman, who is an avid reader.   _____

10. Having flown first to Paris, we then flew to Rome.   _____

11. Ingram, who stayed at Biltmore House last year. He recommended staying there.   _____

12. Because he was early for his meeting, he walked across the street to the cafe for a cup of tea.   _____

13. Wilma glanced toward the door and slowly walked toward us. As we entered the room.   _____

14. Before returning to Australia. Louise planned a hiking trip through New Zealand.   _____

15. Throughout his successful drive for student government president. Rick maintained a 3.5 average.   _____

Exercise 16   The Sentence Fragment

Complete or revise the following sentence fragments in such a way as to make complete sentences.

Example: Deidre, having mailed her application to Hollins College.

Deidre, having mailed her application to Hollins College, now anxiously awaited an answer.

1. Those who are interested in learning how to cope with math anxiety.

2. Seniors and any other students wanting to attend Saturday's game.

3. Interviewing skills and tips on how to dress for interviews.

4. Free coffee and refreshments, which will be served in the West Terrace Room.

5. After the guests finally left.

6. Although we have no control over the final report.

7. If you or your company needs more information about the assistance program.

8. Even though Dan is blind.

9. The alarm clock having failed me.

10. Jeremy's tales of his experiences in the Navy.

4

Verbals

You may sometimes have trouble in recognizing sentence verbs because you may confuse them with certain verb forms that function partly as verbs and partly as other parts of speech. (The *sentence verb* is the verb that states something about the subject, one capable of completing a statement.) These other verb forms are made from verbs but also perform the function of nouns, adjectives, or adverbs. In other words, they constitute a sort of half-verb. They are called **verbals.** The three verbal forms are the **gerund,** the **participle,** and the **infinitive.**

■ 4a Verbals and Sentence Verbs

It is important that you distinguish between the use of a particular verb form as a verbal and its use as a main verb in a sentence. An illustration of the different uses of the verb form *running* will help you to make this distinction:

> *Running* every day is good exercise. [*Running* is a **gerund** and is the subject of the verb *is.*]

> *Running* swiftly, he caught the bandit. [*Running* is a **participle** and modifies the pronoun *he.*]

> The boy *is running* down the street. [*Is running* is the **sentence verb.** It is formed by using the present participle with the auxiliary verb *is.*]

It must be emphasized that *a verbal cannot take the place of a sentence verb* and that *any group of words containing a verbal but no sentence verb is a sentence fragment:*

> The boy *running* [A sentence fragment.]

> *To face* an audience [A sentence fragment.]

The boy *running* up the steps is Charles. [A complete sentence.]

To face an audience was a great effort for me. [A complete sentence.]

The following table shows the tenses and voices in which verbals appear:

Gerunds and participles		
Tense	Active voice	Passive voice
Present	doing	being done
Past		done (This form applies only to participles.)
Present perfect	having done	having been done
Progressive present perfect	having been doing	
Infinitives		
Tense	Active voice	Passive voice
Present	to do	to be done
Present perfect	to have done	to have been done
Progressive present	to be doing	
Progressive present perfect	to have been doing	

■ 4b The Gerund

A **gerund** is a verbal used as a noun and in its present tense always ends in *-ing*. Like a noun, a gerund is used as a subject, a complement, an object of a preposition, or an appositive. Do not confuse the gerund with the present participle, which has the same form but is used as an adjective:

Planning the work carefully required a great deal of time. [*Planning* is a gerund used as subject of the sentence.]

She was not to blame for *breaking* the vase. [*Breaking* is a gerund used as object of the preposition *for*.]

I appreciated your *taking* time to help me. [*Taking* is a gerund used as direct object of *appreciated*.]

His unselfish act, *giving* Marty his coat, plainly showed Ed's generosity. [*Giving* is a gerund used as the appositive of *act*.]

In the sentences above, you will note examples of gerunds functioning as nouns but also taking objects as verbs do. In the first sentence the gerund *planning* is used as the subject of the verb *required*. *Planning* itself, however, is completed by the object *work* and is modified by the adverb *carefully*. This dual functioning of the gerund is apparent in the other three sentences as well.

It is important to remember a rule concerning the modification of gerunds: Always use the possessive form of a noun or pronoun before a gerund. Because gerunds are nouns, their modifiers, other than the adverbial ones just mentioned, must be adjectival; therefore, the possessive form, which has adjectival function, is the correct modifier:

Mr. Bridges was surprised at *Doug's* offering him the motorboat.

NOT

Mr. Bridges was surprised at Doug offering the motorboat.

■ 4c The Participle

A **participle** is a verbal used as an adjective. The present participle is formed by adding *-ing* to the verb: *do — doing.* Again, remember not to confuse the gerund and the present participle, which have the same form but do not function similarly. The past participle is formed in various ways. It may end in *-ed, -d, -t,* or *-n: talk — talked, hear — heard, feel — felt, know — known.* It may also be formed by a change of vowel: *sing — sung.*

The baby, *wailing* pitifully, refused to be comforted. [*Wailing* is a present participle. It modifies *baby*.]

The *broken* doll can be mended. [*Broken* is a past participle, passive voice. It modifies *doll*.]

An old coat, *faded* and *torn*, was her only possession. [*Faded* and *torn* are past participles, passive voice, modifying *coat*.]

Having been warned, the man was sent on his way. [*Having been warned* is the present perfect participle, passive voice. It modifies *man*.]

Like the gerund, the participle may have a complement and adverbial modifiers. In the sentence *Wildly waving a red flag, he ran down the track,* the participle *waving* has the object *flag* and the adverbial modifier *wildly*.

■ 4d The Infinitive

An **infinitive** is a verbal consisting of the simple form of the verb preceded by *to* and used as a noun, an adjective, or an adverb:

To err is human. [*To err* is used as a noun, the subject of *is*.]

He wanted *to go* tomorrow. [*To go* is used as a noun, the object of the verb *wanted*.]

He had few books *to read*. [*To read* is used as an adjective to modify the noun *books*.]

Frank seemed eager *to go*. [*To go* is used as an adverb to modify the adjective *eager*.]

She rode fast *to escape* her pursuers. [*To escape* is used as an adverb to modify the verb *rode*.]

Sometimes the word *to* is omitted:

> Susan helped carry the packages. [*To* is understood before the verb *carry*. *(To) carry* is used as a noun and is the object of *helped*.]

Note: An adverbial infinitive can frequently be identified if the phrase "in order" can be placed before it, as in *Katy paid ten dollars* (in order) *to get good seats for the play*.

Like the gerund and the participle, the infinitive may have a complement and adverbial modifiers:

> He did not want *to cut the grass yesterday*. [The infinitive *to cut* has the object *grass* and the adverbial modifier *yesterday*.]

Exercise 17   Verbs and Verbals

In the following sentences identify each *italicized* expression by writing on the line at the right:

    V if it is a verb,   **Part** if it is a participle,
    Ger if it is a gerund,   **Inf** if it is an infinitive.

Example: Marvin's *reasoning* is circuitous.   *Ger*

1. *Reading* fills many lonely hours.   _____

2. For some *unknown* reason, I believed his story.   _____

3. The heron moved swiftly across the water *searching* for minnows.   _____

4. *Wide-ranging* citizen support exists for the highway bill.   _____

5. Have you decided *to go*?   _____

6. Cactus plants are not difficult *to grow.*   _____

7. Among those *attending* the conference were college presidents, state higher education executives, and governors.   _____

8. During times of disappointment we fall back on our *treasured* memories.   _____

9. Please do this chore for your *tired* old father.   _____

10. She channeled all her efforts toward one goal: *to run* in the Olympics.   _____

11. There were many issues *facing* the finance committee.   _____

12. The Board of Education *is studying* teachers' salaries.   _____

13. Her uncle is a *recognized* expert on telecommunications.   _____

14. We spent the evening *recalling* old stories.   _____

15. We tried not *to disappoint* our parents.   _____

16. The goal of the fashion world is *to capture* the fancy of the masses.   _____

17. The board of directors actually *is making* its decisions based on the facts.   _____

18. *Panning* for gold is fun.   _____

19. He got in trouble with my grandfather for *helping* himself to rhubarb from our garden.   _____

20. As she left, I saw Leola *looking* back over her shoulder.   _____

21. *Learning* my multiplication tables was very difficult.   _____

22. Louis's constant *bragging* really bores us.   _____

23. We remodeled the house *to sell* it quickly.   _____

24. I *am* not *planning* to lose the race.   _____

25. David finally decided *to clean* his apartment.   _____

Exercise 18 — Gerunds

In the following sentences underline each gerund. Copy the gerund in the first column at the right. In the second column write **S** if the gerund is the subject of the verb, **PN** if the gerund is the predicate nominative, **DO** if the gerund is the direct object, **OP** if the gerund is the object of the preposition.

	Gerund	Use
Example: Teaching offers many rewards.	*Teaching*	S

	Gerund	Use
1. Striking the proper balance between study and play can have a significant impact on a student's future.	_____	___
2. Walking is an excellent exercise.	_____	___
3. We had the responsibility of identifying the conference needs.	_____	___
4. Did you enjoy interviewing the candidates?	_____	___
5. Terry's favorite sport is swimming.	_____	___
6. Feeding the hungry is a major concern for Congress.	_____	___
7. Yes, we do learn best by doing.	_____	___
8. Clarence's method of reasoning is not often clear.	_____	___
9. Developing sensitivity to other cultures is a challenge to each of us.	_____	___
10. Reasons for joining the Peace Corps vary from person to person.	_____	___
11. Mollie's remembering our anniversary pleased us.	_____	___
12. Performing well contributes to job security.	_____	___
13. We enjoy white-water canoeing and mountain climbing.	_____	___
14. Ethel has no time for playing.	_____	___
15. His favorite pastime is listening to classical music.	_____	___
16. Bird-watching is particularly exciting in the fall.	_____	___

	Gerund	Use

17. Mr. Book had a lifelong interest in farming.

18. He did not explain his reasons for being late.

19. We did consider inviting the entire car pool to the party.

20. Walking on the edge of Saluth Ridge can be dangerous.

21. Cycling is only one of the sports at which Susan excels.

22. My job was sending the invitations.

23. His parents do not understand his wanting to major in art.

24. For Alma, learning aerobics was great fun.

25. Timing is often the most important part of any decision.

Exercise 19 Participles

Underline the participle in each of the following sentences, and then write in the space at the right the word that the participle modifies.

Example: Put the <u>stained</u> tablecloth in the washing
machine.   _*tablecloth*_

1. Medicine is an extremely demanding profession.   _____

2. Freddie is a fast-talking salesman.   _____

3. Her disgruntled response shocked all of us.   _____

4. The study concluded that most of the students surveyed objected to pop quizzes.   _____

5. Rembrandt is an internationally known artist.   _____

6. Fascinated, I stood and watched the gymnasts.   _____

7. He waited for some time on the deserted beach to see the sea turtles.   _____

8. He has looked everywhere for a furnished apartment.   _____

9. Leo devoured the hamburgers, spilling catsup all over his shirt.   _____

10. The staff quickly discovered Rose's inquiring mind.   _____

11. Walker Percy, a well-known author, will give three lectures today on Southern fiction.   _____

12. Did you clean up the broken glass?   _____

13. Our first meeting will be a planning meeting.   _____

14. Some summer camps feature accelerated programs in science.   _____

15. I remember the turning points of my life.   _____

16. Women's clothing is a reflection of changing lifestyles.   _____

17. A main concern in developing countries is energy.   _____

18. Increased interest and involvement of the citizen in the election process are necessary to maintain a democracy.   _____

19. I spent the entire afternoon mopping the kitchen floor.   _____

20. Dr. Russell's patronizing attitude infuriated me.   _____

63

21. The canned vegetables are located on Aisle 5.   _____

22. Mills College, small and stimulating, offers women a liberal arts education.   _____

23. I searched every bookstore for the required textbook in physics.   _____

24. Ms. Ward left work early, hoping to avoid the traffic.   _____

25. Joined by some of my colleagues, I spent an enjoyable evening at the theater.   _____

26. Relaxing on the beach, Shannon fell asleep.   _____

27. Mr. Ross owns ten restaurants, stretching from Santa Fe to Washington, D.C.   _____

28. Driving up the Maine coast, we spotted several whales.   _____

29. Are you going to repair my broken mower?   _____

30. The yard, trimmed and mowed, looked beautiful.   _____

Name _____   Score _____

Exercise 20 Infinitives

Underline the infinitive in each of the following sentences, and in the space at the right indicate its use in the sentence by writing **N** for noun, **Adj** for adjective, and **Adv** for adverb.

Example: I tried to call you yesterday.   _N_

1. Learning to deal with stress is an important part of education.   _____

2. Chris is preparing to teach history at the University of Virginia.   _____

3. Hamilton is attending that conference to make some professional
   contacts.   _____

4. The committee did not have time to read the report before the
   meeting.   _____

5. Our school group wanted very much to visit the museum.   _____

6. I hear that you want to be your own boss.   _____

7. Benton is having supper with us to tell us about his new job.   _____

8. I need to have the air conditioning on my car repaired.   _____

9. To reach our house, you go around the lake.   _____

10. Last night I decided to go to the play.   _____

11. My doctor's orders were to walk daily for my health.   _____

12. To take clearer pictures, keep the camera lens clean.   _____

13. To manage one's time well is one of the keys to success.   _____

14. Observe all posted signs to ensure your safety.   _____

15. I am the last person in the world to give advice on romance.   _____

16. Burke tried to be perfect.   _____

17. The desert can be an exciting place to visit.   _____

18. Professor Wright's question will be difficult to answer.   _____

19. Rodrigo managed to get a job at the American Embassy.   _____

20. It is probably not necessary to pay much attention to what she says.   _____

21. The director wants to work out a rehearsal schedule.   _____

22. In this course you will learn to drive defensively.   _____

65

23. The lighting has been lowered in the exhibition hall to preserve the textiles and costumes. _____

24. Our club plans to attend the annual azalea show. _____

25. A crowd had been gathered there for three or four hours to hear the election results. _____

26. The children continued to follow the parade down the street; nothing in the world could have stopped them. _____

27. Too many students are graduating without the ability to express themselves. _____

28. The campus was elated when Ann Beattie agreed to speak. _____

29. To complete the assignment on time, I spent all of yesterday in the library. _____

30. Her job is a difficult one to perform. _____

Exercise 21 Verbals

In the following sentences underline each verbal. In the first column at the right identify the *type* of verbal by writing

Ger for gerund,
Part for participle,
Inf for infinitive.

In the second column at the right indicate the *use* of the verbal by writing

Adj for adjective,	**PN** for predicate nominative,
Adv for adverb,	**DO** for direct object,
S for subject,	**OP** for object of a preposition.

	Type	Use
Example: I am planning <u>to go</u>.	*Inf*	*DO*
1. Writing poetry is difficult.		
2. We are not always able to fulfill all our dreams.		
3. Hugh is a very exciting pianist.		
4. The purpose of his committee is to promote industry in the state.		
5. The initial expense of building a house hardly compares with that of its upkeep.		
6. Two distinguished scientists will be here tomorrow.		
7. Understanding the theory of chaos is not as easy as it might first appear.		
8. Paris seems to suit Cameron quite well.		
9. We enjoy eating at the Peasant Restaurant.		
10. Laura couldn't go to see the exhibit.		
11. Did you know that whales sleep with one eye open and one eye closed?		
12. I thank you for coming.		
13. The rather broad parkway was bordered by moss-covered trees.		
14. Each of us hopes to visit the Tate Gallery in London.		

	Type	Use
15. I am afraid this tea is too hot to drink.	_____	_____
16. Sometimes staring at a blank wall is the only way to concentrate.	_____	_____
17. She seldom used her oven because she hated cleaning it.	_____	_____
18. There is no aroma quite like that of fresh-ground coffee.	_____	_____
19. I will need several more eggs to make an angel food cake.	_____	_____
20. Marty slipped on the ice, hurting his pride.	_____	_____
21. To prepare for the meeting took longer than I had planned.	_____	_____
22. After Quincy left, the cookie jar needed refilling.	_____	_____
23. One of her favorite sports is water-skiing.	_____	_____
24. Driving home, Sara passed Mike in his new truck.	_____	_____
25. But I don't mind your going with us.	_____	_____

5

Recognizing Phrases

A **phrase** is a group of related words, generally having neither subject nor predicate and used as though it were a single word. It cannot make a statement and is therefore not a clause.

A knowledge of the phrase and how it is used will suggest to you ways of diversifying and enlivening your sentences. Variety in using sentences will remedy the monotonous "subject first" habit. The use of the participial phrase, for instance, will add life and movement to your style because the participle is an action word, having the strength of its verbal nature in addition to its function as a modifier.

We classify phrases as **gerund, participial, infinitive, absolute, prepositional,** and **appositive.** The following sentences will show how the same idea may be expressed differently by the use of different kinds of phrases:

Sue swam daily. She hoped to improve her backstroke. ["Subject first" sentences.]

By *swimming daily,* Sue hoped to improve her backstroke. [Gerund phrase.]

Swimming daily, Sue hoped to improve her backstroke. [Participial phrase.]

Sue's only hope of improving her backstroke was *to swim daily.* [Infinitive phrase.]

With a daily swim Sue hoped to improve her backstroke. [Prepositional phrase.]

Sue knew of one way to improve her backstroke: *swimming daily.* [Appositive phrase.]

■ 5a The Gerund Phrase

A **gerund phrase** consists of a gerund and any complement or modifiers it may have. The function of the gerund phrase is always that of a noun:

69

Being late for breakfast is Joe's worst fault. [The gerund phrase is used as the subject of the verb *is.*]

She finally succeeded in *opening the camera.* [The gerund phrase is the object of the preposition *in.*]

Bill hated *driving his golf balls into the lake.* [The gerund phrase is the object of the verb *hated.*]

His hobby, *making furniture,* is enjoyable and useful. [The gerund phrase is an appositive.]

■ 5b The Participial Phrase

A **participial phrase** consists of a participle and any complement or modifiers it may have. It functions as an adjective:

Disappointed by his best friend, Roger refused to speak to him. [The participial phrase modifies the proper noun *Roger.*]

Having written the letter, Julie set out for the Post Office. [The participial phrase modifies the proper noun *Julie.*]

The boy *standing in the doorway* is the one who asked to borrow our rake. [The participial phrase modifies the noun *boy.*]

Punctuation: *Introductory participial phrases are set off by commas. Other participial phrases are also set off by commas unless they are essential to the meaning of the sentence. (See Chapter 19, Section b.)*

■ 5c The Infinitive Phrase

An **infinitive phrase** consists of an infinitive and any complement or modifiers it may have. Infinitives function as adjectives, adverbs, or nouns:

She had a plane *to catch at eight o'clock.* [The infinitive phrase modifies the noun *plane.*]

To be in Mr. Foster's class was *to learn the meaning of discipline.* [The first infinitive phrase is the subject of the verb *was.* The second infinitive phrase is the predicate nominative after the linking verb *was.*]

Millie left early *to avoid the heavy traffic.* [The infinitive phrase modifies the verb *left.*]

After the night outdoors we were happy *to be warm and dry again.* [The infinitive phrase modifies the adjective *happy.*]

Ted has no plans except *to watch television.* [The infinitive phrase is the object of the preposition *except.*]

We decided *to go for a long walk.* [The infinitive phrase is the direct object of the verb *decided.*]

Her fiancé seems *to be very pleasant.* [The infinitive phrase is the predicate adjective after the linking verb *seems.*]

Punctuation: *Introductory infinitive phrases used as modifiers are set off by commas. (See Chapter 19, Section b.)*

■ 5d The Absolute Phrase

A noun followed by a participle may form a construction grammatically independent of the rest of the sentence. This construction is called an **absolute phrase.** It is never a subject, nor does it modify any word in the sentence, but it is used *absolutely* or independently:

> *The bus having stopped,* the tourists filed out.
>
> *The theater being nearby,* I decided to walk.
>
> I shall do as I please, *all things considered.*

Punctuation: *An absolute phrase is always separated from the rest of the sentence by a comma. (See Chapter 19, Section b.)*

■ 5e The Prepositional Phrase

A **prepositional phrase** consists of a preposition followed by a noun or pronoun used as its object, together with any modifiers the noun or pronoun may have. The prepositional phrase functions usually as an adjective or an adverb:

> The plan *of the house* is very simple. [The prepositional phrase modifies the noun *plan.*]
>
> The river runs *through rich farmland.* [The prepositional phrase modifies the verb *runs.*]
>
> *Throughout the house* there was an aroma of corn beef and cabbage.

Punctuation: *An introductory prepositional phrase, unless unusually long, is not set off by a comma. (See Chapter 19, Section b.)*

■ 5f The Appositive Phrase

An **appositive** is a word or phrase that explains, identifies, or renames the word it follows. An appositive may be a noun phrase (that is, a noun and its modifiers), a gerund phrase, an infinitive phrase, or a prepositional phrase:

> This book, *a long novel about politics,* will never be a best seller. [Noun phrase used as an appositive.]
>
> Jean knew a way out of her difficulty: *telling the truth.* [Gerund phrase used as an appositive.]
>
> His greatest ambition, *to make a million dollars,* was doomed from the start. [Infinitive phrase used as an appositive.]

The rustler's hideout, *in the old cave by the river,* was discovered by the posse. [Prepositional phrase used as an appositive.]

An appositive may be **essential** (sometimes called **fused**) or **nonessential;** it is essential if it positively identifies that which it renames, frequently by use of a proper noun. Examples of both essential and nonessential appositives occur in the sentences below:

The Victorian poets *Tennyson and Browning* were outstanding literary spokesmen of their day. [The appositive, *Tennyson and Browning,* identifies *poets* and thus is essential.]

Tennyson and Browning, *two Victorian poets,* were outstanding literary spokesmen of their day. [The appositive, *two Victorian poets,* is nonessential because the poets are already identified by their names.]

Punctuation: *An appositive phrase is enclosed with commas unless it is essential.* (See Chapter 19, Section b.)

Exercise 22 Phrases

In each of the following sentences identify the *italicized* phrase by writing in the space at the right

Prep if it is a prepositional phrase,   **Inf** if it is an infinitive phrase,
Part if it is a participial phrase,   **App** if it is an appositive phrase,
Ger if it is a gerund phrase,   **Abs** if it is an absolute phrase.

Example: *Riding home,* I remembered that I had neglected to lock my office.   *Part*

1. *Reading C. S. Lewis* is an unforgettable experience.   _____

2. *A native of Massachusetts,* he worked one summer at the *Boston Globe.*   _____

3. *Writing a children's story* is not as easy as one might think.   _____

4. *Facing formidable opposition,* she decided against running for governor.   _____

5. Any one of the owners might be induced *to sell his condominium.*   _____

6. The purpose of this course is *to stimulate thinking.*   _____

7. A dish *of jalapeño jelly beans* was on the coffee table.   _____

8. My husband is very handy *around the house.*   _____

9. The politician launched an aggressive campaign *to get his bill passed.*   _____

10. *Funding education* is the best investment a country can make.   _____

11. When spring comes, I am ready *to take a vacation.*   _____

12. Science fiction often deals *with future possibilities,* not fantasy.   _____

13. John Muir, *a naturalist and philosopher,* spent several years making an inventory of California's giant sequoias.   _____

14. The company, *having spent thousands of advertising dollars,* finally admitted that the product was a failure.   _____

15. *Having read through the brochure,* the student became aware of the broad scope of the college's programs.   _____

16. At least once a month Bill spends an evening browsing *through the Oxford Bookstore.*   _____

17. Dr. Siegle, *an advisory council member,* delivered a speech that was thought-provoking, interesting, and timely.   _____

18. *The fog having thickened,* we decided to spend the night in Boston.   _____

19. I recently purchased the *Governor's Quail Family, a full-color lithograph,* by Rena Divine.   _____

20. *The conference having ended,* we all hurried to the airport to catch the first plane home.   _____

Exercise 23 Phrases

The sentences in the following exercise contain prepositional, verbal, and appositive phrases. Underline each phrase, and in the space at the right of each sentence show how each phrase is used by writing **Adj** for adjective, **Adv** for adverb, and **N** for noun.

Example: Are we ready <u>to present our report</u>?   _*Adv*_

1. Attending conference meetings all day is quite exhausting.   _____

2. This morning the professor began the class with a story.   _____

3. The most interesting point of the story is that it became a reality.   _____

4. Daphne, my cousin, told how she became a college professor.   _____

5. Richard Lamar, a graduate assistant, will lead our seminar today.   _____

6. The highest point in Maine is Mount Katahdin.   _____

7. Jane Duckett, an education specialist, explained her state's mathematics and science programs.   _____

8. Howard told Grace and me wild stories about his college days.   _____

9. I can't remember the title of James Baldwin's latest novel.   _____

10. Buying expensive clothes is Page's favorite pastime.   _____

11. Each new freshman has ten books to read this summer.   _____

12. Dora and Ed cleaned the garage for the rummage sale.   _____

13. The young, attractive woman looking this way is the new English professor.   _____

14. The jazz concert lasted until midnight.   _____

15. To read a Dickens novel takes several days.   _____

16. We enjoyed visiting the Jeffersonian Institute.   _____

17. What are your plans for this evening?   _____

18. The committee chairman said that the conflicting opinions would be resolved before the weekend.   _____

19. Inside the barn you will find the rake, the hoe, and the tractor.   _____

20. Grant refused to discuss his final grade.   _____

21. To improve her skills, Jessica is taking a computer course.   _____

22. Naturally, the window facing east gets the early morning sun.   _____

23. I hope that you will put Lynn on the steering committee.   _____

24. Engineers are discovering new ways to increase automobile safety.   _____

25. Brad cannot afford to miss another chemistry class.   _____

Exercise 24 Phrases

In each of the following sentences underline the phrase. In the first column at the right identify the *type* of phrase by writing

Prep for prepositional phrase,   **Inf** for infinitive phrase,
Part for participial phrase,   **App** for appositive phrase.
Ger for gerund phrase,

Then in the second column indicate its *use* by writing **Adj, Adv,** or **N.**

	Type	Use
Example: Tammy, <u>a former water-polo player</u>, was named swimming coach.	*App*	*N*

1. Among my favorite sports is trout fishing. _____ _____

2. Uncle Morris has built a cabin near Lava Hot Springs, Idaho. _____ _____

3. Being the first speaker is sometimes a blessing. _____ _____

4. Have you ever gone to the Annual Albuquerque Balloon Fiesta? _____ _____

5. Clinton, having recently completed Columbia Law School, has opened his own practice. _____ _____

6. Every organization needs people who are willing to express their opinions. _____ _____

7. Claude Simon, 1985 Nobel Prize winner, is a French novelist. _____ _____

8. The board will appoint three additional committee members, including a veterinarian. _____ _____

9. Roger will attend the college offering the best scholarship. _____ _____

10. His assignment is to find a good caterer. _____ _____

11. The dictionary was placed on the second shelf. _____ _____

12. Reed's grandmother loved to bake Halloween treats. _____ _____

13. Susie, having failed her driving test again, could not be consoled. _____ _____

14. After I have finished reading this novel, we can leave. _____ _____

15. Those jeans are not appropriate to wear this evening. _____ _____

	Type	Use

16. Rita had fun driving the golf cart. _____ _____

17. Alice's first-grade class went to visit a dairy. _____ _____

18. I did not understand Stanley's leaving so early. _____ _____

19. That warm October day watching a football game seemed
    a waste of time. _____ _____

20. Lawrence Malamud, a graduate assistant, was our phys-
    ics lab instructor. _____ _____

Exercise 25   Phrases

A. Combine the following pairs of sentences, making one sentence a participial phrase. Punctuate each sentence correctly.

Example: Our conference will be held on the Hotel Queen Mary. The Queen Mary is anchored at Pier 1, Long Beach, California.

Our conference will be held on the Hotel Queen Mary, anchored at Pier 1, Long Beach, California

1. James A. Michener wrote *Tales of the South Pacific*. Rodgers and Hammerstein adapted these tales for the musical *South Pacific*.

2. Our new mathematics textbook is well organized. The textbook is overflowing with practical information.

3. Dr. Mifflin taught at the University of Alabama for thirty years. He has decided to retire this year.

4. Alice Walker was awarded a Pulitzer Prize for her novel *The Color Purple*. She currently lives in California.

5. This month's bills are on the desk. They must be paid by the tenth of the month.

6. I was walking down Capitol Avenue. I came upon a group of people marching around the Capitol Building.

7. Joan of Arc was burned at the stake as a heretic. She was later canonized a saint.

8. The governor droned on and on. He was totally unaware of his inattentive audience.

9. Angie and I left the party early. We hoped to see our favorite television show at home.

10. The drama club rehearsed daily for several weeks. The performers waited anxiously for opening night.

B. Combine the following pairs of sentences, making one of the sentences an *appositive* phrase.

Example: Joey is a fraternity brother of mine. He is a brilliant mathematician.
           Joey, a fraternity brother of mine, is a brilliant mathematician.

1. Jack London is the author of many tales of adventure. He wrote *The Iron Heel*.

2. Russell will get us tickets to the Super Bowl. He is a friend of the Commissioner.

3. Mary Alice is a faithful and fanatical fan of the Chicago Bears. She rarely misses a home game.

4. Wilson is a broadcasting major. He wants to own a radio station someday.

5. "A Good Man Is Hard to Find" is a story by Flannery O'Connor. It is a story of a killer and his victims.

6. The Grand Canyon National Park is located in Arizona. It is one of the most frequently visited national parks.

7. Dr. Batler is a professor at Michigan State University. He has a phenomenal grasp of laser technology.

8. Bradford Academy was incorporated in 1820. It was one of the first tuition-free coeducational schools.

9. Mount Everest is the world's highest mountain. It lies between Tibet and Nepal.

10. The Eiffel Tower is a symbol of Paris. It was designed by the French engineer Alexandre Gustave Eiffel.

Exercise 26   Punctuation of Phrases

In the following sentences insert all commas required by the rules stated in Chapter 5. In the blanks write the commas with the words that precede them. When the sentence requires no comma, write **C** in the space.

Example: To make an omelet , one must use eggs.   *omelet,*

1. Trying to improve my serve I spent several hours a day practicing.   _____

2. After attending four different colleges Michael decided to get a job.   _____

3. Not reading directions causes many students to answer questions incorrectly.   _____

4. To be selected as a Rhodes Scholar is a distinct honor.   _____

5. To qualify to take the state bar examination Gail had to submit her application six weeks before the day of the exam.   _____

6. Having exercised for over an hour I felt exhausted.   _____

7. That handsome young man standing by the fireplace is my nephew.   _____

8. Having circled the block for thirty minutes I thought that I would never find a parking space.   _____

9. In *The Pilgrim's Progress* an allegorical narrative   _____
   John Bunyan has his hero travel the road of life.   _____

10. Encouraged by his grade on the latest test Marshall decided to study more.   _____

11. Jeff spends most of his time hanging around the mall.   _____

12. The old photographs torn and faded brought   _____
    back many memories.   _____

13. To find our way to the cabin we had to follow Bill and Gail.   _____

14. Ferrol Sams a physician and novelist has written   _____
    several best sellers.   _____

15. Having acknowledged his error the computer pro- grammer then tried to determine what had gone wrong.   ————————

16. The novel unorganized and incoherent was re- jected by the publisher.   ————————

17. To begin the class Dr. Russ asked her students to summarize the major points in today's assign- ment.   ————————

18. The mail having arrived I was disappointed that the oranges which I had ordered had not come.   ————————

19. To finance the homecoming parade the students sold cakes and washed cars.   ————————

20. Dr. Galligar a professor in the Electrical Engineer- ing Department has accepted a position at Pur- due University.   ————————

6

Independent Clauses

▪ 6a Independent Clauses

A group of words containing a subject and a verb and expressing a complete thought is called a sentence or an **independent clause.** Some groups of words that contain a subject and a verb, however, do not express a complete thought and therefore cannot stand alone as a sentence. Such word groups are dependent on other sentence elements and are called **dependent clauses.**

Sometimes an independent clause stands alone as a sentence. Sometimes two or more independent clauses are combined into one sentence without a connecting word. Then a semicolon is used to connect the independent clauses:

> The day is cold.
>
> The day is cold; the wind is howling.

Sometimes independent clauses are connected by one of the coordinating conjunctions, *and, but, for, or, nor, so,* and *yet.* As these conjunctions do not subordinate, an independent clause beginning with one of them may stand as a complete sentence. Independent clauses joined by a coordinating conjunction are separated by commas. Therefore, to punctuate correctly, you must distinguish between independent clauses and other kinds of sentence elements joined by coordinating conjunctions. In the following examples note that only independent clauses joined by coordinating conjunctions are separated by commas:

> The day was *dark* and *dreary.* [The conjunction *and* joins two adjectives, *dark* and *dreary.* No comma permitted.]
>
> The fallen tree *blocked* the highway and *delayed* travel. [The conjunction *and* joins the two verbs. No comma permitted.]

She ran *up the steps* and *into the house*. [The conjunction *and* joins two phrases. No comma permitted.]

Mrs. Brown caught the fish, and *her husband cooked them*. [The conjunction *and* connects two independent clauses, and these are separated by a comma.]

Sometimes two independent clauses are connected by a **conjunctive,** or **transitional, adverb** such as one of the following:

however	moreover	nevertheless	therefore
then	accordingly	otherwise	thus
hence	besides	consequently	

A semicolon is necessary before any of these words beginning a second clause. After the longer *conjunctive adverbs* a comma is generally used:

We drove all day; *then* at sundown we began to look for a place to camp.

It rained during the afternoon; *consequently,* our trip to the mountains had to be postponed.

Note: Conjunctive adverbs can be distinguished from subordinating conjunctions by the fact that the *adverbs* can be shifted to a later position in the sentence, whereas the *conjunctions* cannot:

It rained during the afternoon; our trip to the mountains, *consequently,* had to be postponed.

Summary of punctuation: From the foregoing discussion and examples we can establish the following rules for the punctuation of independent clauses:

1. *Two independent clauses connected by a coordinating conjunction are separated by a comma:*

   Our goat chewed up the morning paper, *and* Father is angry.

   You should call Hank tonight, *for* he is all alone.

2. *Two independent clauses not connected by a coordinating conjunction are separated by a semicolon.* Remember that this rule also holds true when the second clause begins with a conjunctive adverb:

   Philip is quite strong; he is much stronger than I.

   We both wanted to go to the toboggan race; *however,* Mother had asked us to be home by six.

3. *A semicolon is used to separate independent clauses that are joined by a coordinating conjunction but are heavily punctuated with commas internally:*

   Being somewhat excited and, incidentally, terribly tired, Ellen's two children, Mary and Fred, became unruly; but they went quickly to sleep on the trip home.

4. *Short independent clauses, when used in a series with a coordinating conjunction preceding the final clause, may be separated by commas:*

   The audience was seated, the lights were dimmed, and the curtain was raised.

Note: A series consists of at least three elements.

■ 6b The Comma Splice

Use of a comma between two independent clauses not joined by a coordinating conjunction (Rule 2), is a major error called the **comma splice** (This term comes from the idea of splicing or "patching" together two clauses that should be more strongly separated.):

COMMA SPLICE: I enjoyed his company, I do not know that he enjoyed mine.

CORRECTION: I enjoyed his company, but I do not know that he enjoyed mine. (Rule 1)

I enjoyed his company; I do not know that he enjoyed mine. (Rule 2)

OR

I enjoyed his company; however, I do not know that he enjoyed mine. (Rule 2)

■ 6c The Run-together Sentence

The **run-together sentence** results from omitting punctuation between two independent clauses not joined by a conjunction. Basically the error is the same as that of the comma splice: it shows ignorance of sentence structure:

Twilight had fallen it was dark under the old oak tree near the house.

When you read the sentence just given, you have difficulty in getting the meaning at first because the ideas are run together. Now consider the following sentence:

Twilight had fallen, it was dark under the old oak tree near the house.

The insertion of the comma is not a satisfactory remedy, for the sentence now contains a comma splice. There are, however, four reliable devices for correcting the run-together sentence and the comma splice:

1. Connect two independent clauses by a comma and a coordinating conjunction if the two clauses are logically of equal importance:

   Twilight had fallen, and it was dark under the old oak tree near the house.

2. Connect two independent clauses by a semicolon if they are close enough in thought to make one sentence and you want to omit the conjunction:

   Twilight had fallen; it was dark under the old oak tree near the house.

3. Write the two independent clauses as separate sentences if you wish to give them separate emphasis.

   Twilight had fallen. It was dark under the old oak tree near the house.

4. Subordinate one of the independent clauses:

   When twilight had fallen, it was dark under the old oak tree near the house.

Exercise 27 The Comma Splice and the Run-together Sentence

Mark correct sentences **C**, run-together sentences **R**, and sentences containing a comma splice **CS**.

Example: You are hiding in the closet, Jeff, I saw you go in there.   _CS_

1. The reason that we did not buy a new car last spring is that we like this year's model better.   _____

2. This mahogany table has been in our family for over a hundred years it was built by my great grandfather.   _____

3. On the first day of the tour we visited the Capitol, we spent the second day at Smithsonian.   _____

4. The hotel could not find Scott's reservations, therefore, he had to make other arrangements.   _____

5. Lucille beamed with excitement when she was told that she had won the door prize.   _____

6. To satisfy Dr. Finley is almost impossible, however, students love to take his classes.   _____

7. Diane explained the various periods of art to us we listened intently.   _____

8. No one noticed Chatty's leaving the house we missed her at supper time.   _____

9. What the little boy said is not completely true.   _____

10. That telephone number is their old one, however, I have their new number in my office.   _____

11. The train was ten minutes late, consequently, I was late to work.   _____

12. The guests threw bird seed at the bride and groom because both are avid bird watchers.   _____

13. Even though I did not feel very well today, I went to my morning classes I cut my afternoon biology class.   _____

14. Our family reunion will be next month I will be unable to attend.   _____

15. Most of the students wrote very good essays, however, a few students disregarded all the rules of coherence.   _____

16. Kyle stays in the nursery while his parents work.   _____

17. We checked all the doors and windows and then turned off the lights before we left, when we got home, a light was on upstairs.   _____

18. Adam's vacation plans have been changed he will be here all next
    week.   ———

19. I wish that it were possible for me to go with you I have a meeting
    tomorrow; therefore, I can't leave.   ———

20. Give these tickets to anyone who enjoys the symphony, Marie has de-
    cided not to go.   ———

Name _____   Score _____

Exercise 28   The Comma Splice and the Run-together Sentence

Mark correct sentences **C**, run-together sentences **R**, and sentences containing a comma splice **CS**.

Example: He was not in his room however, his light was burning.   _R_

1. We were excited about winning the game, we forgot about eating supper.   _____

2. The telephone rang several times no one answered.   _____

3. Ron lacked the discipline to study daily, this lack of discipline was the cause of his failure.   _____

4. If I lived on a farm, I would raise horses I would probably raise goats also.   _____

5. Charles Dickens's *David Copperfield* is one of my favorite novels, some scholars think it is somewhat autobiographical.   _____

6. Last month I had a wonderful time visiting my cousin who lives in Switzerland, but I was really glad to get home.   _____

7. The house on the corner is still vacant, we wonder whether it will ever be sold.   _____

8. I was the last passenger to get off the plane I had fallen asleep.   _____

9. Paul worked for a short time as a truck driver, however, he quit his job because he didn't enjoy traveling all the time.   _____

10. Special orientation programs are planned for new employees I did not participate because I had worked at Belk's before.   _____

11. I hope that we have the flexibility to select our own novels, I never like those chosen by the professor.   _____

12. Although reading, fishing, and hiking are my favorite hobbies, I also enjoy an occasional football game.   _____

13. Neither my sister nor my brother will be at home Christmas Eve our family gathering will not be the same without them.   _____

14. Be careful picking up those logs you may hurt your back.   _____

15. Hal's driving makes me nervous, everybody's driving makes me nervous.   _____

16. We worked very hard all quarter on our science project, I hope that Dr. Stelson recognizes our efforts.   _____

17. While at the beach, we sat in the sun too long, I got sunburned.   _____

91

18. All the desserts were beautiful to look at and delicious to taste.   _____

19. I don't think that everyone should go to college, do you?   _____

20. None of the food lost its freshness before the picnic, however, the drinks got a little warm.   _____

21. Some of my neighbors go to the grocery store every day, therefore, they never have left-over food to throw away.   _____

Exercise 29   Punctuation of Independent Clauses

In the following sentences insert all necessary commas and semicolons. Then in the space at the right write the correct punctuation mark with the word that precedes it. Write **C** if the sentence is correct.

Example: Colonel Hill in our Department of Military Science will answer any questions regarding the program , and he will be glad to meet with you personally.   *program,*

1. Professor Christenson has over thirty years of teaching experience she has also developed and published several instructional packages.   _____

2. He stared disbelievingly at the old woman he had not seen his sister in ten years.   _____

3. Day-care services will be available on campus next semester and the fee for the service will be nominal.   _____

4. My father was a kind and gentle man however, he was a firm believer in discipline.   _____

5. I am sending you four photographs of the old home place I hope that you can paint a watercolor of the house for me.   _____

6. Lamar, you really need a haircut I'll never understand why you let your hair get into such a state.   _____

7. He began his career selling farm machinery in Iowa but now he is in manufacturing.   _____

8. An updated list of the committee membership is attached if you need additional information, please call my office.   _____

9. Gwen closed her mind to anything new consequently she was considered narrow-minded.   _____

10. At the next meeting of our study club Myrtle will review James Agee's *Let Us Now Praise Famous Men*, a beautiful book about life in the South.   _____

11. Judge Simmons promised my nephew a clerkship in his office but Van decided to join a law firm.   _____

12. One morning a few weeks ago I met Elizabeth in the market and I hardly recognized her because she had lost so much weight.   _____

13. The children were so excited about going to the circus that they hardly ate their lunch.   _____

14. I remember with pleasure my first day of teaching the students seemed eager to learn.   _____

15. He is without a doubt the dullest person I know I can hardly bear to be around him.   _____

16. Society identifies with those who produce something tangible and useful yet it seldom appreciates those who are thinkers and creators of ideas.   _____

17. I don't know where to begin cleaning my house the children left every room in a mess.   _____

18. The spontaneous laughter of the children caused the old man to smile, remembering happier times.   _____

19. After Clarence had completed the examination, he went back to the dormitory to take a nap he had stayed up all night to study.   _____

20. When you see Arthur today, ask him to call me I need to discuss next week's meeting with him.   _____

7

Dependent Clauses

As you remember, a dependent clause is one that cannot stand alone as a sentence: although it has both a subject and a verb, it does not express a complete thought. Any clause beginning with a subordinating word like *what, that, who, which, when, since, before, after,* or *if* is a **dependent clause.** Dependent clauses, like phrases, function as grammatical units in a sentence — that is, as nouns, adjectives, and adverbs:

> I went to school.   }   [Both clauses are independent.]
> Too much time had elapsed.
>
> *When I went to school,* I studied my lessons. [The first clause is dependent.]
>
> *Since too much time had elapsed,* she remained at home. [The first clause is dependent.]

In the last two sentences *I studied my lessons* and *she remained at home* are complete statements. But the clauses *When I went to school* and *Since too much time had elapsed* do not express complete thoughts. They depend upon the independent statements to complete their meanings. Both of these dependent clauses function as adverbs.

■ 7a Noun Clauses

A **noun clause** is a dependent clause used as a noun, that is, as a subject, complement, object of a preposition, or appositive. Noun clauses are usually introduced by *that, what, why, whether, who, which,* or *how.* Some of these introductory words can introduce both noun and adjective clauses, since the function of the whole clause in the sentence, and not its introductory word, determines its classification. Most sentences containing noun clauses differ from those containing adjective and adverbial clauses in that, with the clause removed, they are no longer complete sentences.

Your *plan* is interesting. [This is a simple sentence, containing no dependent clause. The subject is the noun *plan*. The following example sentences show that dependent noun clauses may be substituted for the word *plan*, and vice versa.]

What you intend to do [your plan] is interesting. [The italicized noun clause is the subject of the verb *is*. Notice that the noun *plan* can be substituted for the clause.]

Tell me *what you intend to do* [your plan]. [The italicized noun clause is the direct object of the verb *tell*.]

That is *what you intend to do* [your plan]. [The italicized noun clause is a predicate nominative.]

I am interested in *what you intend to do* [your plan]. [The italicized noun clause is the object of the preposition *in*.]

The fact *that he had not told the truth* soon became apparent. [The italicized noun clause is in apposition with the noun *fact*.]

Bob's problem, *how he could open the locked door*, seemed insoluble. [The italicized noun clause is in apposition with the noun *problem*.]

Punctuation: *Noun clauses used as nonessential appositives are set off by commas.*

■ 7b Adjective Clauses

An **adjective clause** is a dependent clause that modifies a noun or pronoun. The common connective words used to introduce adjective clauses are the relative pronouns *who* (and its inflected forms *whom* and *whose*), *which, that,* and relative adverbs like *where, when,* and *why*. (*Where* and *when* can introduce all three kinds of clauses.)

The italicized clauses in the following sentences are all adjective clauses:

She is a woman *who is respected by everyone.*

Mr. Johnson, *whose son attends the University of Oklahoma,* is our minister.

He saw the place *where he was born.*

It was a time *when money did not count.*

I know the reason *why I failed the course.*

Adjective clauses are classified as **essential** (restrictive) and **nonessential** (nonrestrictive).

An *essential* clause, as its name indicates, is necessary in a sentence, for it identifies or points out a particular person or thing; a *nonessential* clause adds information about the word it modifies, but it is not essential in pointing out or identifying a person or thing:

Thomas Jefferson, *who was born on the frontier,* became President. [The name *Thomas Jefferson* has identified the person, and the italicized clause is not essential.]

A person *who loves to read* will never be lonely. [The italicized adjective clause is essential in identifying a particular kind of person.]

My father, *who was a country boy,* has lived in the city for years. [Since a person has only one father, an identifying clause is not essential.]

The girl *by whom I sat in class* is an honor student. [The italicized adjective clause is essential to the identification of *girl*.]

To determine whether an adjective clause is essential, you may apply this test: read the sentence leaving out the adjective clause and see whether the removal omits necessary identification. Try this test on the following sentence:

Jet pilots, *who work under a great deal of stress*, must stay in excellent physical condition.

You will see that the removal of the adjective clause does not change the basic meaning of the sentence. The italicized adjective clause is, therefore, nonessential.

Now read the following sentence, leaving out the italicized adjective clause:

Jet pilots *who are not in excellent physical condition* should not be allowed to fly.

If the adjective clause of this sentence is removed, the statement is not at all what the writer meant to say. The adjective clause is, therefore, essential.

Punctuation: *Nonessential adjective clauses are set off from the rest of the sentence by commas.* (See Chapter 19, Section b.)

■ 7c Adverbial Clauses

An **adverbial clause** is a dependent clause that functions exactly as if it were an adverb. Like an adverb it modifies a verb, an adjective, an adverb, or the whole idea expressed in the sentence's independent clause; for example, *As luck would have it*, we missed his telephone call.

An adverbial clause is used to show *time, place, cause, purpose, result, condition, concession, manner,* or *comparison.* Its first word is a subordinating conjunction. Common subordinating conjunctions and their uses are listed below:

1. Time (*when, before, since, as, while, until, after, whenever*)

   I will stay *until you come.*

   When the whistle blew, the laborer stopped.

2. Place (*where, wherever, whence, whither*)

   He went *where no one had ever set foot before.*

   Wherever you go, I will go also.

3. Cause (*because, since, as*)

   Since I had no classes on Saturday, I went home.

   Because he was afraid of being late, Bob ran all the way.

4. Purpose (*in order that, so that, that*)

   My family made many sacrifices *so that I could have an education.*

   Men work *that they may eat.*

5. Result (*so . . . that, such . . . that*)

   The weather was *so* cold *that I decided not to walk to school.*

6. Condition (*if, unless*)

   You will hurt your hand *if you are not careful.*

   Unless you apply at once, your name will not be considered.

7. Concession (*though, although*)

   Although she had no money, she was determined to go to college.

8. Manner (*as, as if, as though*)

   She looked *as though she wanted to laugh.*

   Do *as you like,* but take the consequences.

9. Comparison (*as, than*)

   He is older *than his brother.*

   He is as tall *as his brother.*

Punctuation: *Introductory adverbial clauses are always set off by commas:*

   Although he had tests to take and a term paper to write, he went home for the weekend.

   While I was eating lunch, I had a phone call from my brother.

■ 7d Kinds of Sentences

For the purpose of varying style and avoiding monotony, you may need to be able to distinguish the four basic types of sentences. According to the number and kind of clauses (phrases do not affect sentence type), sentences may be grouped into four types: **simple, compound, complex,** and **compound-complex.**

1. A **simple** sentence is a single independent clause with one subject and one predicate. The one subject, however, may consist of more than one noun or pronoun, and the one predicate may consist of more than one verb.

   Robert has a new car. [Single subject and single predicate.]

   Robert and his *brother* have a new car. [There is one verb, *have,* but the subject consists of two nouns.]

   Robert *washed* and *polished* his new car on Sunday. [There is one subject, *Robert,* but two verbs.]

   Robert and his *brother washed* and *polished* their new car. [The subject consists of two nouns, *Robert* and *brother;* and the predicate consists of two verbs, *washed* and *polished.*]

2. A **compound** sentence contains at least two independent clauses and no dependent clause:

   Mary likes the mountains, but Jackie prefers the seashore.

   A lamp was lighted in the house, the happy family was talking together, and supper was waiting.

3. A **complex** sentence contains only one independent clause and one or more dependent clauses (the dependent clauses are in italics):

The toy truck *that you gave Molly for her birthday* is broken.

Why he refused to contribute to the fund we do not know.

4. A **compound-complex** sentence has at least two independent clauses and one or more dependent clauses (the independent clauses are in italics):

My friend was offended by my attitude, and *I was sorry* that she was hurt.

We spent the morning looking for the home of the woman who paints landscapes, but *we were unable to find it.*

Exercise 30   Clauses

In the following sentences underline each dependent clause. In the space at the right, write **Adj** if the clause is an adjective clause, **Adv** if it is an adverbial clause, and **N** if it is a noun clause. If the sentence contains no dependent clause, leave the space blank.

Example: I did not realize <u>that he is leaving today</u>.   *N*

1. Education is designed to produce individuals who can think and act independently.   _____

2. The North Carolina School of the Arts, which is located in Winston-Salem, was established in the 1960s.   _____

3. The idea that garlic helps prevent blood clotting is not altogether wrong.   _____

4. Dr. Colin Mertz, who is a professor of nutritional biochemistry, will be the guest speaker tonight.   _____

5. Occasionally dancers discover that the stage is not their only love.   _____

6. Inspiring teachers are those who instill in their students the joy and excitement of learning.   _____

7. Our expectations sometimes pose some problems when we are confronted by reality.   _____

8. Even though the survey was conducted three years ago, the findings have only recently been published.   _____

9. My aunt, who lives in Santa Fe, has the tenacity of a Boston terrier.   _____

10. They did not understand why the movie did not start on time.   _____

11. Because he came in late, John missed the most exciting part of the game.   _____

12. The plan that the committee presented has merit.   _____

13. The audience that attended the opening night performance was disappointed to find an understudy in the leading role.   _____

14. As soon as the play was over, they complained to the management.   _____

15. I only recently heard that the Stewarts are moving to Nebraska.   _____

16. Tell us where you will be staying in Los Angeles.   _____

17. April, our boxer, got sick after she had eaten a sack of chocolate chips. _____

18. Randall looked forward to going to college, even though he would be leaving his family. _____

19. As the name of the contest winner was being announced, the auditorium was silent. _____

20. I hope that you will be able to attend the Blue Key awards dinner. _____

21. The film raised questions about how electronic devices are affecting our lives. _____

22. When you are ready, I will go with you to the park. _____

23. The man who is standing by the window is Pam's brother. _____

24. The truth is that I really like Eugene O'Neill's plays. _____

25. Metropolitan Opera star Timothy Jenkins, who was born in Oklahoma, will give a recital at the University next month. _____

26. The exhibition hall, which covers six thousand square feet, is the largest in the state. _____

27. Our physics class made an animated display, demonstrating how instant color film works. _____

28. Wichita State University, where Melvin is studying mechanical engineering, is an urban university, enrolling seventeen thousand students. _____

29. I think that I will be late leaving the office. _____

30. We will not begin studying until you get here. _____

Exercise 31 Clauses

Give the function of each of the *italicized* clauses by writing the proper abbreviations in the space at the right:

S for subject,   **OP** for object of a preposition,
DO for direct object,   **Adj** for adjective modifier,
PN for predicate nominative,   **Adv** for adverbial modifier.

Example: He is an intelligent man *who thinks seriously about his life and his career.* _*Adj*_

1. *When I travel,* I eat hardly anything. _____

2. The story *that Dolores told* is obviously fiction. _____

3. *If we don't do our laundry tonight,* we won't have any clean clothes to wear. _____

4. Please don't pick the apples from that tree *until they ripen.* _____

5. Tomorrow night I will introduce you to my roommate, *who plays the piano for the symphony.* _____

6. *That Aaron had undertaken too many projects* was evident to everyone around him. _____

7. The young man *who is sitting on the side of the pool* is the state tennis champion. _____

8. I did not know *that your brother is an airline pilot.* _____

9. The freeway route *that was suggested by the highway department* was rejected by the neighborhood. _____

10. The truth of the matter is *that I do not enjoy cooking for a crowd.* _____

11. Our organization gave a great deal of thought to *what your report said.* _____

12. *What Professor Elliott has asked the class to read* will take several weeks. _____

13. The fertilizer *that I used on my roses* is too high in nitrogen. _____

14. We could not decide *where we should go for the holidays.* _____

15. Anita is a person *who is loved* by all *who know her.* _____
_____

16. *Unless we go early,* we may not get a good seat *since there is no reserve seating for this puppet show.* _____
_____

17. I have not read *what this morning's paper had to say about the mayoral race.* _____

18. Although not everyone likes animals, psychologists are finding *that pets fulfill special needs for many people.* _____

19. *Why Gerry retired early* was a mystery to all of us. _____

20. *While we were in London,* Carl spent several days doing research at the British Museum. _____

21. Our fraternity is giving a prize to *whoever collects the most money for the Empty Stocking Fund.* _____

22. The fact is *that no one wanted to attend the special session of the legislature.* _____

23. *Because I was not prepared for class yesterday,* I was embarrassed *when Dr. Thomas asked me to discuss the character of Hamlet.* _____ _____

24. After tasting caviar, I cannot say *that I really like it.* _____

25. *That Ralph is uncomfortable in large crowds* was obvious to all of us. _____

Exercise 32 Review of Clauses

In the following sentences enclose the dependent clauses in parentheses. In the spaces at the right indicate the number of independent and dependent clauses in each sentence. Be able to tell the function of each of the dependent clauses. (Note that some sentences may not contain a dependent clause.)

	Ind.	Dep.
Example: Lucille, (who is my first cousin,) lives in Tacoma, Washington.	_1_	_1_

1. Before we met Marie, we had never heard of Mount Holyoke College; consequently, neither of us applied for admission. _____ _____

2. Jerry, a member of the National Intercollegiate Rodeo Association, attends Blue Mountain Community College, which is located in Oregon. _____ _____

3. Steve was educated in England, where he attended lectures at Oxford and Cambridge. _____ _____

4. As long as you are here, will you help me paint? _____ _____

5. I don't remember another July when it was so cold. _____ _____

6. The little dog jumped excitedly when its master removed the leash from the hook because it knew that they were going for a walk. _____ _____

7. If you will wait a few minutes, I will go with you; however, if you want to go ahead, it's all right with me. _____ _____

8. Although karate is practiced by many, there are other martial arts such as judo, kung-fu, and tae kwan. _____ _____

9. Eureka Springs, which is surrounded by the Ozark Mountains, is a quaint town with old-fashioned charm. _____ _____

10. Although the young man has much to learn, the committee thinks that his previous experience has prepared him for the position of senior researcher. _____ _____

11. When Godfrey was a little boy, he and his father spent several weeks each summer fly-fishing on Deschutes River, which is located in Oregon. _____ _____

12. Irene worked in an industrial plant while she attended night school. _____ _____

13. When I finished the test, I thought that I had answered all the questions correctly. _____ _____

14. What causes a student to choose one college over another is not easy to determine. _____ _____

15. After we had finished our shopping, we went to René's New York Style Delicatessen. _____ _____

16. As far as the committee was concerned, the report was finished when it was submitted to the president. _____ _____

17. The first thing that strikes the reader of Eudora Welty's novels is that her characters are real people. _____ _____

18. My father never understood why my brother Ned wanted to tour Europe on a bicycle. _____ _____

19. Let's take a walk after we finish dinner; I want to drop by Aunt Ellie's house to pick up a recipe. _____ _____

20. We were very lucky on our vacation; it rained only one day. _____ _____

21. I like to think that Jay did the best that he could do on his final examination, but I'm not sure that he read every assignment carefully. _____ _____

22. If you are bored, you may not have enough to do. _____ _____

23. High school dropouts who later decide to continue their education frequently find that they spend many hours in remedial courses. _____ _____

24. There are a number of reasons why I cannot attend the Hawthorne lecture next Tuesday. _____ _____

25. Because he spends so much time talking on the telephone, we are giving Jake a gold one when he retires. _____ _____

Exercise 33   Clauses

Complete each of the sentences below by writing in the spaces an *adjective clause,* an *adverbial clause,* or a *noun clause* as indicated above each space.

(adverbial clause)

Example: *If we are going to fly to Toronto next week* _____, we need to make our reservations at once.

(adjective clause)

1. Everybody seemed to enjoy the blueberry pancakes _____

_____

(noun clause)

2. _____ is a mystery to all of us.

(adverbial clause)

3. Nancy has flowers all year _____

_____

(noun clause)

4. Dad told us quite plainly _____

(adjective clause)

5. The carry-on bag _____ fits easily under the seat.

(noun clause)

6. From many years of experience the Woffords know _____

_____

(adverbial clause)

7. You may take the newspaper with you _____

_____

(adjective clause)

8. This is the time of year _____

_____

(adverbial clause)

9. _____ we decided to paint the
walls pale yellow.

(noun clause)

10. The idea _____ was my
mother's.

Exercise 34   Punctuation of Clauses

In the following sentences supply commas and semicolons where they are needed. In the spaces at the right, write the marks of punctuation with the words that precede them. Write **C** if the sentence is correct.

Example: Although my grandfather thinks that the price of the Sunday newspaper is outrageous , he always buys one.   _outrageous,_

1. After the sun comes out Murphy's Carwash is one of the most popular spots in town. _____

2. Dr. Gonzalez who teaches astronomy explained to the audience how comets are named. _____

3. The English language is always changing for instance a fast-food restaurant was once called a drive-in. _____

4. Because he could not fully understand her poetry Steve looked in the library for a critical discussion of Sylvia Plath's work. _____

5. The congressman who appeared on *Firing Line* proved to be a good match for William Buckley. _____

6. *The New York Times* described Helen MacInnes who was the author of twenty-one novels as the "queen of international espionage fiction." _____

7. Many historic documents were printed on paper that is now disintegrating consequently they are being reproduced on microfilm. _____

8. We thought that we would have a hard time finding a parking place but one was right in front of the church. _____

9. Did you know that the U.S. Army which wore khaki uniforms for more than eighty years now wears green ones? _____

10. The gallery became very quiet as the tournament leader addressed the ball. _____

11. Once the ball had rolled across the green and had finally dropped into the cup the crowd roared in approval. _____

12. The reader is on a table in the reference room and the microfiche are filed in the cabinet next to the table.   _____

13. The small town turned out to celebrate the visit of its favorite son who had received a Nobel Prize.   _____

14. The cosmetic firm has its headquarters in Chicago and regional offices in several other cities in the United States and Canada.   _____

15. Marie had to wake me up for I had forgotten to pack my alarm clock.   _____

16. None of us are interested in going to the basketball tournament tomorrow however all of us want to find tickets for the finals on Friday.   _____

17. While Sue was recuperating from her accident she read detective novels and worked crossword puzzles.   _____

18. The television star's schedule is so crowded that he scarcely has time to enjoy his fame.   _____

19. Edith ran to the grocery store I straightened up the apartment and we made the lasagna together.   _____

20. That hat is not becoming to Ms. Winchell as anyone can see.   _____

21. The construction company building the town houses is small but it has an excellent reputation.   _____

22. Please answer the telephone I'm sure it's for you.   _____

23. We walked all the way to Colony Square then we had lunch and took the bus back home.   _____

24. Did you knit that sweater yourself or is it one of those from the Needleworks?   _____

25. She thinks that letter writing as an art form is almost a thing of the past and she believes that the same may be said of keeping diaries and journals.   _____

Exercise 35 Kinds of Sentences

Identify the type of sentence by writing one of the following abbreviations in the space at the right:

S if the sentence is simple, **Cx** if the sentence is complex,
Cp if the sentence is compound, **Cp-Cx** if the sentence is compound-complex.

Example: Peggy is a teller at the branch bank that opened last week in Washington Mall. _*Cx*_

1. Kenneth has been broadcasting football games for a decade. _____

2. The colors in the Oriental carpet were rich, and the pattern was complex. _____

3. Although the politician denied that he intended to run for the presidency, he behaved as if he might. _____

4. John Roberts has been an insurance agent ever since he graduated from college. _____

5. My father rejected the notion that weekends are meant for relaxation; he worked seven days a week. _____

6. Charles was determined to find a way to buy a personal computer. _____

7. The nicest feature of my schedule for winter quarter is that on three mornings a week I have no classes before ten o'clock. _____

8. No comment has been made by the President's press secretary, nor is he expected to make one. _____

9. The members of the City Council announced that they wanted to renovate their offices at City Hall. _____

10. Because it was raining, the three of us decided to go to a movie instead of the fair. _____

11. Some who have seen *Macbeth* found the elaborate sets distracting; others liked them very much. _____

12. The differences between labor and management were many, but both sides recognized the importance of avoiding a strike. _____

13. David and I ordered the croissants, which proved to be absolutely delicious with orange marmalade. _____

14. The ring of the telephone interrupted me for the third time; there seemed to be no way to finish the last chapter of *Sophie's Choice* before class. _____

15. Mother's pound cake has always been something of a problem for me: I can eat a piece any time of day or night. _____

16. Her brownies, furthermore, have consistently interfered with my intention to lose five pounds. _____

17. Seemingly, it is impossible for us to agree upon the proper role of government in the lives of private citizens. _____

18. The outcome of the basketball game was affected because Bert Jacobson, our leading scorer, was injured in the second half. _____

19. As we were climbing the hill from the stadium, we met the Corbins, old friends from Greenville. _____

20. This bus goes down Edwards Street and then turns left into Mills Avenue. _____

21. Scott has been interested in stamps since he was a boy, and he is still collecting them. _____

22. The administration is concerned over the parking problem; in fact, it has asked a student-faculty committee to explore ways of solving it. _____

23. The helicopter flew low over the forest, spotting the missing hunters just before dark. _____

24. The rag doll, with her pink cheeks and yellow hair, charmed the small child who was standing on the other side of the plate glass window. _____

25. The weather is more like that of April than of December; nevertheless, when I dropped by the gift shop, I found my friend Susan hanging gold ornaments on a Christmas tree. _____

8

Agreement of Subject and Verb

The verb in every independent or dependent clause must agree with its subject in person and number. (There are **three persons:** the **first person** is the speaker, the **second person** is the person spoken to, and the **third person** is the person or thing spoken about. There are **two numbers:** the **singular,** denoting one person or thing, and the **plural,** denoting more than one person or thing.) A careful study of the conjugation of the verb in Chapter 1 will show you that a verb can change form not only in *tense* but also in *person* and *number.* If you can recognize the subject and the verb, you should have no trouble making the two agree. Although there is ordinarily no problem in doing so, certain difficulties need special attention.

■ 8a Intervening Expressions

The number of the verb in a sentence is not affected by any modifying phrases or clauses standing between the subject and the verb but is determined entirely by the number of the subject:

> The *evidence* that they submitted to the judges *was* [not *were*] convincing. [*Evidence* is the subject of the verb *was.*]

> The new *library* with its many books and its quiet reading rooms *fills* [not *fill*] a long-felt need. [*Library* is the subject of the verb *fills;* the phrase *with its many books . . .* has nothing to do with the verb.]

> A *list* of eligible candidates *was* [not *were*] posted on the bulletin board. [*List* is the subject of the verb *was posted.*]

Our big pine tree as well as a small oak *was* [not *were*] damaged by the high winds. [*Tree* is the subject of the verb *was damaged;* the intervening phrase *as well as a small oak* is not a part of the subject.]

The famous golfer along with his many fans *was* [not *were*] heading toward the ninth green. [*Golfer* is the subject of the verb *was heading; along with his many* fans is not a part of the subject.]

My father, together with my two brothers, *is* [not *are*] planning to build a cabin at the lake. [*Father* is the subject of the verb *is planning.* The phrase that comes between the subject and the verb is not a part of the subject.]

■ 8b Verb Preceding the Subject

In some sentences the verb precedes the subject. This reversal of common order frequently leads to error in agreement:

There *is* [not *are*] in many countries much *unrest* today. [*Unrest* is the subject of the verb *is.*]

There *are* [not *is*] a *table,* two *couches,* four *chairs,* and a *desk* in the living room. [*Table, couches, chairs,* and *desk* are the subjects of the verb *are.*]

Where *are* [not *is*] *Bob* and his *friends going*? [*Bob* and *friends* are subjects of the verb *are going.*]

■ 8c Indefinite Pronouns

The indefinite pronouns or adjectives *either, neither,* and *each;* the adjective *every;* and such compounds as *everybody, anybody, everyone, anyone* are always singular. *None* may be singular or plural. The plural usage is more common:

Each of the plans *has* [not *have*] its advantages.

Everyone who heard the speech *was* [not *were*] impressed by it.

Every bud, stalk, flower, and seed *reveals* [not *reveal*] a workmanship beyond the power of man.

Is [not *Are*] *either* of you ready for a walk?

None of the men *have* brought their wives.

None of the three *is* [*are*] interested.

None — no, not one — *is* prepared.

■ 8d Compound Subjects

Compound subjects joined by *and* normally require a plural verb:

Correctness and *precision are* required in all good writing.

Where *are* the *bracelets* and *beads*?

Note: When nouns joined by *and* are thought of as a unit or actually refer to the same person or thing, the verb is normally singular:

> The *sum* and *substance* of the matter *is* [not *are*] hardly worth considering.
>
> My *friend* and *coworker* Mr. Jones *has* [not *have*] gone abroad.

■ 8e Subjects Joined by *Or* and *Nor*

Singular subjects joined by *or* or *nor* take a singular verb. If one subject, how-ever, is singular and one plural, the verb agrees in number and person with the nearer one:

> Either the *coach* or the *player was* [not *were*] at fault.
>
> Neither the *cat* nor the *kittens have* been fed. [The plural word *kittens* in the compound subject stands next to the verb *have been fed.*]
>
> Neither the *kittens* nor the *cat has* been fed. [The singular subject *cat* stands next to the verb, which is therefore singular.]
>
> Neither my *brothers* nor *I am* going. [Note that the verb agrees with the nearer subject in person as well as in number.]

■ 8f Nouns Plural in Form

As a general rule use a singular verb with nouns that are plural in form but singular in meaning. The following nouns are usually singular in meaning: *news, economics, ethics, physics, mathematics, gallows, mumps, measles, shambles, where-abouts:*

> The *news is* reported at eleven o'clock.
>
> *Measles is* a contagious disease.

The following nouns are usually plural: *gymnastics, tactics, trousers, scissors, athletics, tidings, acoustics, riches, barracks:*

> *Athletics attract* him.
>
> The *scissors are* sharp.
>
> *Riches* often *take* wing and *fly* away.

Plural nouns denoting a mass, a quantity, or a number require a singular verb when the subject is regarded as a unit.

> Five *dollars is* too much for her to pay.
>
> Fifty *bushels was* all the bin would hold.

Though usage is mixed, phrases involving addition, multiplication, subtrac-tion, and division of numbers preferably take the singular:

> *Two and two is* [are] four.
>
> *Two times three is* six.
>
> *Twelve divided by six is* two.

■ 8g Determining Modifiers

In expressions like *some of the pie(s)*, *a percentage of the profit(s)*, *all of the money*, *all of the children*, the number of *some*, *percentage*, and *all* is determined by the number of the noun in the prepositional phrase:

> *Some* of the pie *is* missing.
>
> *Some* of the pies *are* missing.

Whether to use a singular or plural verb with the word *number* depends on the modifying article. *The number* requires a singular verb; *a number*, a plural one.

> *The number* of students at the art exhibit *was* small.
>
> *A* small *number* of students *were* at the art exhibit.

■ 8h The Subject of Some Form of *To Be*

When one noun precedes and another follows some form of the verb *to be*, the first noun is the subject, and the verb agrees with it and not with the complement even if the complement is different in number:

> The only *fruit* on the market now *is* peaches.
>
> *Peaches are* the only fruit on the market now. [In the first sentence *fruit* is the subject; in the second, *peaches*.]

■ 8i Relative Pronoun as Subject

When a relative pronoun (*who*, *which*, or *that*) is used as the subject of a clause, the number and person of the verb are determined by the antecedent of the pronoun, the word to which the pronoun refers:

> This is the student *who is* to be promoted. [The antecedent of *who* is the singular noun *student*; therefore, *who* is singular.]
>
> These are the students *who are* to be promoted. [The antecedent of *who* is the plural noun *students*.]
>
> Should I, *who am* a stranger, be allowed to enter the contest? [*Who* refers to *I*; *I* is first person, singular number.]
>
> She is one of those irresponsible persons *who are* always late. [The antecedent of *who* is *persons*.]

If sentences such as the last one give you trouble, try beginning the sentence with the "of" phrase, and you will readily see that the antecedent of *who* is *persons* and not *one:*

> Of those irresponsible *persons who are* always late she is one.

■ 8j Collective Nouns

Some nouns are singular in form but plural in meaning. They are called **collective nouns** and include such words as *team, class, committee, crowd,* and *crew.* These nouns may take either a singular or a plural verb: if you are thinking of the group as a unit, use a singular verb; if you are thinking of the individual members of the group, use a plural verb:

> The *crew is* striking for higher pay. [The crew is acting as a unit.]
>
> The *crew are* writing reports of the wreck. [The members of the crew are acting as individuals.]

■ 8k Nouns with Foreign Plurals

Some nouns retain the plural forms peculiar to the languages from which they have been borrowed: *alumni, media, crises.* Still other nouns occur with either their original plural forms or plural forms typical of English: *aquaria* or *aquariums, criteria* or *criterions.* If you are in doubt as to the correct or preferred plural form of a noun, consult a good dictionary.

Note: Be careful not to use a plural form when you refer to a singular idea. For instance, write *He is an alumnus of Harvard,* not *He is an alumni of Harvard.*

Exercise 36   Subject-Verb Agreement

Write the correct form of the *italicized* verb in the space at the right.

Example: Neither of the cars parked at Wendy's
(*belong, belongs*) to Fred.   _____*belongs*_____

1. The foreman along with two other employees (*have, has*)
   been asked to discuss working hours with the plant
   manager.   _____

2. When I arrived at school, there (*were, was*) only a desk, a
   chair, and a bed in my dorm room.   _____

3. Each of these china patterns (*are, is*) a reproduction of
   one used in the colonial town of Williamsburg.   _____

4. The sum and substance of the debate concerning the
   United Nations (*are, is*) discussed in this editorial.   _____

5. Two dollars (*were, was*) all I had left after my day at the
   races.   _____

6. I believe that either she or her brother (*are, is*) a member
   of the Branchville Volunteer Fire Department.   _____

7. Some of the books (*were, was*) suitable for children of almost any age.   _____

8. Where (*do, does*) Interstate 85 and Interstate 95 meet?   _____

9. My landlord and my neighbor who lives across the hall
   (*are, is*) planning to watch the bowl games most of the
   weekend.   _____

10. None of the vegetables at the market (*seem, seems*) quite
    fresh enough for a salad.   _____

11. The whereabouts of the Turners, who are touring the
    West in a camper, (*are, is*) unknown.   _____

12. According to the saleswoman $19.95 (*are, is*) an excellent
    price for this sweater.   _____

13. Margie has difficulty remembering whether nine times six
    (*are, is*) fifty-four or fifty-six.   _____

14. Grandmother reminds us that riches often (*prove, proves*)
    to be more of a problem than a pleasure.   _____

15. Not one of us, however, (*are, is*) willing to take her word
    for it.   _____

16. Under the bed (*were, was*) an odd bedroom slipper, an overdue library book, and my long-lost pen.   _____

17. The economic news for the last three quarters of the year (*have, has*) been surprisingly good.   _____

18. What (*are, is*) the criteria for the governorship of this state?   _____

19. Surely every man, woman, and child (*know, knows*) that Washington is preparing for the visit of royalty.   _____

20. I daresay that it will be one of those events that (*consume, consumes*) the interest of the American people.   _____

Exercise 37   Subject-Verb Agreement

Write the correct form of the *italicized* verb in the space at the right.

Example: Either of the restaurants that you have suggested
(*are, is*) fine with me.   *is*

1. Neither of the traffic lights on Mason Street (*are, is*) working.   _____

2. The list of groceries that I will need for the weekend (*are, is*) on
   the refrigerator door.   _____

3. The jacket fits nicely, but these trousers (*are, is*) positively baggy.   _____

4. The data in the *Statesman's Year-Book* (*are, is*) the most recent we
   have concerning Peru.   _____

5. Engrossed in their inspection of the Honda's motor (*were, was*)
   Jenkins and his crony T. J.   _____

6. The only rock group my mother can recognize (*are, is*) the Beatles.   _____

7. Can you believe that one hundred dollars a month (*are, is*) all that
   Yugoslavian auto workers receive?   _____

8. No matter how often he protests to Julia, athletics (*are, is*)
   Horace's first love.   _____

9. Beyond the second stop sign (*are, is*) a shopping center on the
   right and an apartment house on the left.   _____

10. Although some of the horses (*have, has*) been rubbed down, I am
    not sure about Star Wars.   _____

11. At the bottom of the stairs (*are, is*) a door that opens into the
    laundry room and another that leads to the furnace.   _____

12. I believe that every man, woman, and child in town (*have, has*)
    turned out to see the fireworks.   _____

13. At least a dozen gallons of milk (*were, was*) squeezed into the
    dairy case at the convenience store.   _____

14. Six dollars (*seem, seems*) to be more than one should have to pay
    for a paperback novel.   _____

15. There (*are, is*) a word processor as well as a printer in the office
    next to Mr. Rainwater's.   _____

16. None of the people on our tour of the Napa Valley (*have, has*)
    been to California.   _____

17. At the far end of the path (*were, was*) a statue of a soldier, flanked on either side by benches and shrubbery.   _____

18. Either Miss Meyer or her assistants (*need, needs*) to be responsible for locking the warehouse at night.   _____

19. The union (*represent, represents*) the interests of some but not all employees at the printing firm.   _____

20. Rico is one of those friends who (*are, is*) always willing to stand up for me.   _____

Exercise 38   Subject-Verb Agreement

Write the correct form of the *italicized* verb in the space at the right.

Example: My favorite winter supper (*are, is*) a bowl of hot chili
and a green salad.   *is*

1. In the waiting room at Dr. Davenport's office (*were, was*) an attractive Oriental woman along with her two children.
   _____

2. The whole crowd at the concert (*were, was*) enthusiastic about the opening group.
   _____

3. It is one of those damp spring days that (*make, makes*) one doubt that warm weather will ever come.
   _____

4. Do you know the alumna who (*are, is*) to represent Converse College at Dr. Link's inauguration?
   _____

5. Only a small percentage of the apples (*were, was*) to be shipped to the market in Atlanta.
   _____

6. The criteria for the job (*have, has*) not been listed in the want ad.
   _____

7. My close friend and cousin (*live, lives*) in the same apartment house but on a different floor.
   _____

8. The percentage of the graduating class (*continue, continues*) to be divided almost equally between men and women.
   _____

9. My calculator lets me know in short order that eight times $3.35 (*equal, equals*) $26.80.
   _____

10. The shambles left by a hurricane (*last, lasts*) long after the headlines.
    _____

11. Vanilla ice cream topped with strawberries or peaches (*make, makes*) a heavenly concoction.
    _____

12. You realize that eighteen holes (*are, is*) considered one round of golf.
    _____

13. Because the number of registered students (*are, is*) too small, the Dean has canceled Tapdancing 101.
    _____

14. Neither his father nor his brothers (*have, has*) a true Newfoundland accent.
    _____

15. Haven't you read that economics (*are, is*) the underlying cause of all modern wars?
    _____

16. The U.S. Senate (*have, has*) debated foreign aid bills ever since my parents can remember.
    _____

17. Every one of the television networks (*devote, devotes*) an increasing amount of time to weather forecasting.   _____

18. A number of articles about the standards of living in other countries (*are, is*) on our reading list.   _____

19. Bennie's Discount Shoes (*are, is*) located off the interstate at Exit 38.   _____

20. There are those who believe that the mass media (*serve, serves*) to weaken our distinctive dialects.   _____

Exercise 39   Subject-Verb Agreement

Write the correct form of the *italicized* verb in the space at the right.

Example: (*Are, Is*) the salt and pepper still in the picnic basket?   *Are*

1. Billy as well as his mother (*were, was*) anticipating the first day of school.   _____

2. In the late afternoon a pair of doves usually (*arrive, arrives*) at the bird feeder.   _____

3. The European ballet troupe (*have, has*) appearances scheduled for Dallas, San Francisco, and Chicago.   _____

4. In a memo from the dean's office (*are, is*) a list of the students visiting WSB-TV tomorrow.   _____

5. The phenomena of creativity (*are, is*) analyzed in Dr. Berger's recently published essay.   _____

6. Neither Larry nor the other members of the soccer team (*know, knows*) that he is to receive the best-player award.   _____

7. Either the full committee or its chairwoman (*are, is*) sure to be at the meeting of the zoning commission.   _____

8. (*Are, Is*) Mother or Father aware that you are going to Florida for spring break?   _____

9. Beth's usual breakfast (*are, is*) a cup of coffee and two pieces of buttered toast.   _____

10. Folklore suggests that the number of fogs in August (*indicate, indicates*) the number of snows during the coming winter.   _____

11. To Uncle Al's delight neither of the children (*were, was*) interested in going to the carnival.   _____

12. Sitting in a booth at the far end of Sonny's Diner (*were, was*) Guy and two or three of his friends.   _____

13. Janice together with her two roommates (*are, is*) planning to go to the homecoming game next weekend.   _____

14. Imagine how much time and effort (*are, is*) spent trying to produce a research paper without time and effort.   _____

15. Finally every piece of the jigsaw puzzle (*were, was*) in place.   _____

16. A number of the dogs from this kennel (*have, has*) not been shown before.   _____

17. Marie is one of those women who (*feel, feels*) equally at home in the kitchen and the boardroom.   _____

18. The nuclei of the book collections (*are, is*) much the same in all the branch libraries.   _____

19. None of the banks in town (*open, opens*) before nine o'clock.   _____

20. The medium that most interests Jan (*are, is*) film.   _____

Exercise 40   Subject-Verb Agreement

Write the correct form of the *italicized* verb in the space at the right.

Example: A large percentage of the oranges (*were, was*)
damaged by the late freeze.   *were*

1. The crowd that gathered at the airport to see the rock stars (*were, was*) large and enthusiastic.   _____

2. Each spring the alumni (*are, is*) honored at a reception in Gaither Hall.   _____

3. Neither my friends nor I (*are, am*) interested in subscribing to still another magazine.   _____

4. The four quarts of oil on the shelf in the garage (*belong, belongs*) to Dad.   _____

5. The long and short of the matter (*are, is*) that we should have attended Dr. Cohen's lectures.   _____

6. Two tablespoons of flour (*are, is*) all that you will need for the cream sauce.   _____

7. The green velvet chair was one of those pieces of furniture that (*are, is*) handsome but impractical.   _____

8. Everybody who (*play, plays*) handball or racquetball will be interested in the classes being offered at the YMCA.   _____

9. The glad tidings announced at the noon convocation (*are, is*) that the cafeteria is under new management.   _____

10. Mumps (*were, was*) the last childhood disease that Abe and his brothers had.   _____

11. Either of those routes into Danville (*are, is*) recommended by most commuters.   _____

12. A series of workshops concerning the preservation of local history (*are, is*) on the summer schedule.   _____

13. The military tactics of Civil War generals (*are, is*) still a subject for study.   _____

14. The inevitable shambles of a spend-the-night party always (*annoy, annoys*) the children's mother.   _____

15. Twenty percent of the houses in our community (*were, was*) damaged when the river overflowed its banks.   _____

16. A pick-up truck piled high with chairs of every description (*have,* *has*) parked in front of Miss Bigby's house.   _____

17. Can I, who (*is, am*) on such a limited budget, possibly manage a trip to Colorado?   _____

18. The news going around campus (*are, is*) that Dr. Andrews will be the next Dean of Students.   _____

19. The orchestra performing at the state capitol (*have, has*) come from various places.   _____

20. Each of the Christmas catalogs (*were, was*) thoroughly studied and then added to the stack on the table.   _____

9

Agreement of Pronoun and Antecedent

Pronouns, as you saw in Chapter 1, are words that are used in the place of nouns when repetition of a noun would be awkward. *The dog hurt the dog's foot* is clearly an unnatural expression. Usually a pronoun has a definite, easily recognized *antecedent* (the noun or pronoun to which it refers), with which it agrees in *person, number,* and *gender.* The *case* of a pronoun, however, is not dependent on the case of its antecedent.

■ 9a Certain Singular Antecedents

Use singular pronouns to refer to singular antecedents. The indefinite pronouns *each, either, neither, anyone, anybody, everyone, everybody, someone, somebody, no one, nobody* are singular, and pronouns referring to them should be singular:

> *Each* of the girls has *her* own car.
>
> *Neither* of the boys remembered *his* poncho.
>
> Does *everyone* have *his* or *her* ticket?
>
> Does *everyone* have *his* ticket?

Note: The last two sentences illustrate a current usage dilemma prompted by a limitation of English: the language has no third person singular form of the personal pronoun that refers to persons of either sex. By definition a dilemma has no satisfactory solution; nevertheless, you will need to be aware of and sensitive to the different viewpoints. Some writers use *he or she, his or her,* and *him or her,* although such expressions are awkward. Others use the masculine pronouns (or possessive adjectives) in a universal sense, a practice based on long tradition but one objected to by

those who perceive it to be sexist. On many occasions, however, you can avoid the
problem by rephrasing the sentence:

> Does *everyone* have *a* ticket?
>
> Do *we* all have *our* tickets?
>
> *Who* doesn't have *a* ticket?

■ 9b Collective Nouns as Antecedents

With *collective nouns* use either a singular or a plural pronoun according to the
meaning of the sentence. Since collective nouns may be either singular or plural,
their correct usage depends upon (1) a decision as to meaning (see Chapter 8,
Section 8i) and (2) consistency:

> The *team* has elected Jan as *its* captain. [The team is acting as a unit and therefore
> requires the singular possessive pronoun *its*.]
>
> The *team* quickly took *their* positions on the field. [Here each member of the team is
> acting individually.]

Exercise 41 Agreement of Pronoun and Antecedent

From the *italicized* forms in parentheses choose the correct pronoun for each sentence and write it in the space at the right.

Example: The coach commended the debate team for (*their*, *its*) stunning victory. _____*its*_____

1. Because Dr. Bass is particularly interested in business ethics, he will discuss (*them*, *it*) at the management seminar. _____

2. Each of the horses was led around the paddock by (*their*, *its*) groom. _____

3. Of course not every member of the cast can have (*their*, *his*) own dressing room. _____

4. No one on our hall has received (*their*, *her*) telephone bill this month. _____

5. Aunt Marie has misplaced her scissors again in spite of (*their*, *its*) orange handles. _____

6. Do you know whether the Carroll County Arts Council publishes (*their*, *its*) annual calendar in December or January? _____

7. During yesterday's windstorm the barracks across from the post library lost (*their*, *its*) roof. _____

8. I suppose that it is human nature for everyone to want (*their*, *his*) own way. _____

9. The alumnae will submit (*their*, *her*) fund-raising proposal at the next meeting of the executive committee. _____

10. Often all three of the popular news magazines feature the same story on (*their*, *its*) covers. _____

11. My uncle and favorite car dealer opened (*their*, *his*) used-car lot last Saturday. _____

12. Did either of the candidates at the forum discuss (*their*, *her*) ideas concerning day care? _____

13. Each of the mail boxes in the apartment complex must be labeled with (*their*, *its*) owner's name. _____

14. Every man working on the highway crew should be wearing (*their*, *his*) helmet at all times. _____

15. Yesterday Baskin-Robbins opened (*their*, *its*) second shop on this side of town. _____

16. After Dr. Crump began teaching mathematics, I changed my attitude toward (*them, it*). _____

17. In the beginning each of us in our investment club considered (*ourselves, herself*) a rank amateur. _____

18. You can imagine how pleased everybody was to receive (*their, his*) Christmas bonus early in December. _____

19. Neither Joe's car nor mine has (*their, its*) original paint job. _____

20. Once a person is interested in politics, he seldom loses his fascination for (*them, it*). _____

Exercise 42 Agreement of Pronoun and Antecedent

In the following sentences underline each pronoun or possessive adjective incorrectly used; then write the correct form and, if necessary, the correct form of the verb in the space at the right. Write **C** if the sentence is correct.

Example: The data would have been more valuable had it

been more timely. _____*they*_____

1. After midterms everybody begins thinking about their research
papers and projects. _____

2. Someone driving a silver-gray Subaru has left their headlights on. _____

3. This year the alumnae will hold their book fair in the spring. _____

4. The U.S. Weather Bureau gives each hurricane a name of their
own. _____

5. That phenomena discussed by Dr. Hill in her book is seldom
the subject of biological study. _____

6. The crew of the racing shell knows that its success depends in
large measure upon a spirit of cooperation. _____

7. For a long time prior to departure the crew of the *Calypso*
knew what its individual responsibilities would be. _____

8. In the Western that I saw last night on Channel 4 the gallows
sat squarely in the middle of town, where everyone could see
them. _____

9. Have either of the accountants offered their suggestions as to
how you should set up the books for your shop? _____

10. The party leaders are afraid that this latest crises could cause
the government to fall. _____

11. Neither of my brothers knows what they want to do after
graduation. _____

12. None of the consultants have submitted their proposals to the
Board of Trustees. _____

13. Unfortunately no one was allowed to have any electric appli-
ance in their dorm room. _____

14. Because economics ultimately involves people, they must be
considered an inexact science. _____

15. The news published in that magazine is always current, but it also is analyzed carefully and treated in depth. _____

16. I don't know of anybody who claims to know themselves completely. _____

17. Either Will or Bernie have left their bicycle lying in the front walk. _____

18. Although German measles may be highly contagious, young children are seldom seriously ill with them. _____

19. Dr. Karl not only teaches physics, but he also eats, sleeps, and breathes them. _____

20. Everybody taking weaving will have to bring their own yarn. _____

10

Reference of Pronouns

The word to which a pronoun refers should always be clear to the reader; that is, a **pronoun** and the **antecedent** to which it refers must be instantly identified as belonging together. Even when a pronoun agrees properly with its antecedent in person and number, it may still be confusing or misleading if there is more than one possible antecedent. Therefore, it is sometimes necessary to repeat the antecedent or to reword the whole sentence for the sake of clarity.

■ 10a Ambiguous Reference

Sometimes a sentence contains more than one word to which a pronoun may grammatically refer (the term *ambiguous* means "capable of more than one interpretation"). The sentence should be written in such a way that the reader has no doubt which word is the antecedent:

> Albert told his uncle that his money had been stolen. [The first *his* is clear, but the second *his* could refer to either *Albert* or *uncle*.]

> Albert told his uncle that Albert's money had been stolen. [The meaning is clear, but the sentence is unnatural and awkward.]

To avoid the ambiguous reference of the first sentence and the awkward repetition of the second, reword the sentence:

> Albert said to his uncle, "My money has been stolen."

Another kind of ambiguous reference (sometimes called *divided* or *remote* reference) occurs when a modifying clause is misplaced in a sentence:

> INCORRECT: The colt was almost hit by a car that jumped over the pasture fence.

> CORRECT: The colt that jumped over the pasture fence was almost hit by a car.

Note: A relative pronoun should always be placed as near as possible to its antecedent. (See Chapter 15.)

■ 10b Broad Reference

Usually a pronoun should not refer broadly to the whole idea of the preceding clause:

> She avoided using slang, which greatly improved her speech. [*Which* has no clearly apparent antecedent but refers broadly to the whole idea in the first clause.]

> She talked endlessly about her operation, and this was tiresome.

A method often used to improve such sentences is to supply a definite antecedent or to substitute a noun for the pronoun:

> She avoided using slang, a practice that greatly improved her speech.

> She talked endlessly about her operation, and this chatter was tiresome.

As you can see, these sentences are awkward, adding unnecessary words. A better method is to get rid of the pronoun and make a concise, informative sentence that says everything in one clause:

> By avoiding slang, she greatly improved her speech.

> Her endless talk about her operation was tiresome.

■ 10c Weak Reference

A pronoun should not refer to a word that is merely implied by the context. Nor, as a common practice, should the pronoun refer to a word used as a modifier:

> INCORRECT: My father is a chemist. *This* is a profession I intend to follow. [The antecedent of *This* should be *chemistry*, which is implied in *chemist* but is not actually stated.]

> CORRECT: My father is a chemist. Chemistry is the profession I intend to follow.

> ALSO CORRECT: My father's profession of chemistry is the one I intend to follow.

> INCORRECT: When she thrust a stick into the rat hole, it ran out and bit her. [*Rat* in this sentence is the modifier of *hole*.]

> CORRECT: When she thrust a stick into the rat hole, a rat ran out and bit her.

■ 10d Impersonal Use of the Personal Pronoun

Remember that pronouns are frequently used impersonally and when so used do not have antecedents. Notice the correct impersonal use of *it* in statements about *weather, time,* and *distance:*

It looks like rain. [Reference to weather.]

It is now twelve o'clock. [Reference to time.]

How far is *it* to the nearest town? [Reference to distance.]

Avoid the use of *you* and *your* unless you are directing your statement specifically to the reader. Instead, use an impersonal word like *one* or *person*. Also note that the pronoun *you* can never refer to an antecedent in the third person:

> INCORRECT: If *you* want to excel in athletics, *you* should watch your diet. [Incorrect when referring to athletes in general.]

> CORRECT: If *one* wants to excel in athletics, *he* should watch his diet.

> INCORRECT: When a woman marries, *you* take on new responsibilities. [Here *you* refers incorrectly to *woman*, an antecedent in the third person.]

> CORRECT: When a woman marries, *she* takes on new responsibilities.

> INCORRECT: All those planning to attend the meeting should get *your* registration fees in on time. [Here *your* incorrectly refers to the third person plural antecedent *those*.]

> CORRECT: All those planning to attend the meeting should get *their* registration fees in on time.

A rewording of the sentence often produces a clearer and more emphatic sentence while eliminating the problem of the correct pronoun to use:

> CORRECT: Those who wish to excel in athletics should watch their diets.

> CORRECT: To marry is to take on new responsibilities.

> CORRECT: Registration fees must be in on time for those who plan to attend the meeting.

Exercise 43   Reference of Pronouns

Write **R** after each sentence that contains an error in the reference of a pronoun. Then rewrite the sentence correctly. Notice that some sentences may be corrected in more than one way. Write **C** if the sentence is correct.

Example: Rick is an excellent car salesman, but he knows very little about them.   _____R_____

Rick is an excellent car salesman, but he knows very little about automobiles.

1. The weather is extremely hot, which has forced Coach Williams to shorten football practice.   _____

2. I was not surprised when Ellen won the tennis match; she had practiced it for hours on end.   _____

3. After one has become accustomed to an air-conditioned office, you hate to leave it for the steamy sidewalks.   _____

4. It always seems farther going to Oceanside than it does coming home.   _____

5. The Hope Diamond is on display in the Smithsonian, which weighs more than forty-four carats.   _____

6. The reruns of *Gunsmoke* have been moved to seven o'clock, which irritates some of us in the six o'clock lab.   _____

7. Mr. Harris has received a grant that he will use to develop a stimulating course in freshman composition.   _____

8. Such a breakthrough will be nothing short of miraculous, which countless students will applaud.   _____

9. Because Miriam has had experience with crowd control, they will not faze her at the museum this weekend.   _____

10. Foster told Lewis that he would do well to forget about the red-headed vocalist at the Lantern Inn.   _____

11. A helicopter was searching for the missing campers, which flew just above the treetops.   _____

12. Neither of us had a watch; this made keeping track of time difficult.   _____

Exercise 44 Reference of Pronouns

Write **R** after each sentence that contains an error in the reference of a pronoun. Then rewrite the sentence correctly. Notice that some sentences may be corrected in more than one way. Write **C** if the sentence is correct.

Example: If anyone is planning to go to the baseball game tomorrow night, you should get your ticket today.   _R_

All those planning to go to the baseball game tomorrow night should get their tickets today.

1. My muscles were stiff and sore, which happened after I had washed the windows and the front porch.   _____

2. The commuter train ran just back of our house, which we heard passing several times a day.   _____

3. Kevin is trying to learn to play the cornet, and this is taking a great deal of his time.   _____

4. Last night I drove from Columbia, which was all the more tiring because of the fog.   _____

5. The meteorologist reports that it has turned extremely cold all across the Northwest.   _____

6. Herbert told Bryan that he thinks that he will be eligible for a track scholarship.   _____

7. The child's room was small and full of toys and books; that made cleaning difficult.   _____

8. My grandfather carved the Thanksgiving turkey, who was something of an expert.   _____

9. If a student can get through registration, you can survive the rest of the semester.   _____

10. Shop at the fish market down by the wharf if you want to be sure it is fresh.   _____

11. The conference took place in Geneva, Switzerland, which seems to attract many kinds of meetings.   _____

12. I am not in the least surprised that Ted is a good cook; he learned it from his father.   _____

Exercise 45   Reference of Pronouns

Write **R** after each sentence that contains an error in the reference of a pronoun. Then rewrite the sentence correctly. Notice that some sentences may be corrected in more than one way. Write **C** if the sentence is correct.

Example: The telephone rang shrilly in the middle of the night,
which woke me with a start.   _R_

*The telephone's shrill ring in the middle of the night woke me
with a start.*

1. My mother has been an amateur photographer for years, and recently my brother and I have also developed an interest in it.   _____

2. If one is interested in Creole cooking, you should certainly visit Louisiana.   _____

3. Margaret told Susan that she should call AMTRAK's toll-free number to make her reservation.   _____

4. The surf was very rough, and this made swimming difficult.   _____

5. It was after midnight before we had washed the dishes, straightened up the living room, and climbed into bed.   _____

6. The reviews of the musical were enthusiastic, which undoubtedly ac-counted for the immediate increase in ticket sales.   _____

7. I really can't say which television network I prefer; as a matter of fact, I don't watch it often. _____

8. That year retail prices rose only slightly, which was welcome news to Perry and me. _____

9. In the middle of the block is the Sandwich Basket, where one can order a light but nutritious lunch. _____

10. My Aunt Carrie gets up every morning at five o'clock; this is a habit that I know I will never cultivate. _____

11. If anyone in this class wishes to go with Mr. Cary to the Mariner's Museum, you must make reservations by Thursday. _____

12. The chess tournament will be held in the student union building, which is open to players only with certain ratings. _____

11

Case of Pronouns

Nouns and pronouns have three case functions: the **nominative,** the **objective,** and the **possessive.** Except in the possessive, nouns do not show case by change of form and consequently do not present any problems of case. The chief difficulties are in the correct use of personal and relative pronouns.

■ 11a The Nominative Case

The **nominative case** is used (1) as the subject of a verb (*I* shall come); (2) as the complement after *is, are,* and the other forms of the verb *to be* (It is *I*); or (3) as an appositive of the subject or of the complement after forms of the verb *to be* (Two of us — *he* and *I* — called). Ordinarily the case of a pronoun that comes before a verb presents no difficulties, for we naturally write "I am going," not "Me am going." But all constructions requiring the nominative case are not so simple as this one. Study carefully the following more difficult constructions:

1. A clause of comparison introduced by *as* or *than* is often not written out in full; it is elliptical. The verb is then understood. The subject of this understood verb is in the nominative case:

No one can do the work as well as *he* (can).

He knows more about the subject than *she* (does).

2. After forms of the linking verb *to be,* nouns and pronouns used to identify the subject agree in case with the subject. Nouns and pronouns used in this way

are called **predicate nominatives** and are in the nominative case:

It was *they* [not *them*].

The persons mentioned were *she* and Rob [not *her*].

He answered, "It could not have been *I* [not *me*]."

3. Pronouns are frequently combined with a noun or used in apposition with a noun. If they are thus used in the subject of the sentence or with a predicate nominative, they are in the nominative case:

We boys will be responsible for the equipment.

Two photographers — *you* and *he* — must attend the convention.

My friend and *I* went to town. [Not *Me* and my friend went to town.]

If you read these sentences omitting the nouns, you will see at once the correct form of the pronoun.

4. The position of the relative pronoun *who* often causes confusion, especially if it follows a verb or a preposition. The role of the relative pronoun within the dependent clause determines its case. Thus if *who* is the subject of the verb in the dependent clause, it is in the nominative case:

You know *who* sent the money. [Since *who* is the subject of the verb *sent* and not the object of *know*, it must be in the nominative case. The whole clause *who sent the money* is the object of *know*.]

Give the praise to *whoever* deserves it. [*Whoever* is the subject of *deserves*. The whole clause *whoever deserves it* is the object of the preposition *to*.]

5. Parenthetical expressions such as *you think, I believe, I suppose,* and *he says* often stand between a verb and the pronoun that is the subject. The pronoun must still be in the nominative case:

Who do you think called me last night? [The expression *do you think* has nothing to do with the case of *who*. Leave it out, or place it elsewhere in the sentence, and you will see that *who* is the subject of *called*.]

The man *who* Jim says will be our next governor is in the room. [Leave out or place elsewhere *Jim says*, and you will see that *who* is the subject of *will be*.]

■ 11b The Objective Case

The **objective case** of a pronoun is used when the pronoun is the direct or indirect object of a verb, the object of a preposition, or an appositive of an object:

1. Compound objects present a special difficulty:

He wrote a letter to Mary and *me*. [Both words *Mary* and *me* are objects of the preposition *to* and therefore in the objective case. Omit *Mary and* or shift *me* to the position of *Mary*, and the correct form is at once apparent.]

She gave George and *him* the list of names. [*Him* is part of the compound indirect object.]

They invited William and *me* to the barbecue. [*Me* is part of the compound direct object.]

2. You will also have to watch the case of a pronoun, in combination with a noun, that serves as an object or the appositive of an object.

The Dean spoke candidly to *us* boys.

The chairman appointed three of us girls — Mary, Sue, and *me* — to the subcommittee.

Note: In the sentence *The Dean spoke candidly to us boys, boys* is an appositive of *us. Boys* renames *us*. Here both words are substantives. The following sentence may appear similar to this one, but actually its structure is different:

The Dean spoke candidly to *them* boys.

This sentence mistakenly uses a personal pronoun when a demonstrative adjective is needed. First-person speakers do not need to point out themselves; a second person is spoken to directly and needs no pointing out. Only a noun or pronoun in the third person must be pointed out; therefore, use of a demonstrative adjective is called for to modify that noun or pronoun. *Those* is the word needed to modify *boys*. Once the correction is made, you can see that the prepositional phrase in this sentence contains a substantive and a demonstrative adjective, not two substantives.

3. *Whom,* the objective case of *who,* deserves special consideration. Its use, except after a preposition, is declining in colloquial or informal usage (see Chapter 21). Formal usage, however, still requires *whom* whenever the relative pronoun serves as an object:

Whom were you talking to? [To *whom* were you talking?]

He is the boy *whom* we met on the plane. [*Whom* is the object of the verb *met.* The subject of *met* is *we.* Remember that the case of the relative pronoun is determined by its role within the dependent clause.]

Whom do you think we saw last night? [The parenthetical expression does not change the fact that *whom* is the object of *saw.*]

■ 11c Case of Pronouns Used with Infinitives

An infinitive phrase, as you have learned already, can have both an object and adverbial modifiers. In addition, an **infinitive** may have a subject. There are rules governing the case of pronouns when they are subjects or complements of infinitives:

1. When a pronoun is the subject of an infinitive, it will be in the objective case:

We want *him* to be elected.

2. If the infinitive is a form of the verb *to be* and if it has a subject, its complement will also be in the objective case:

She took him to be *me*.

3. If the infinitive *to be* does not have a subject, its complement will be in the nominative case:

The best player was thought to be *he*.

■ 11d The Possessive Case

Personal pronouns and the relative pronoun *who* have **possessive case** forms, which may be used with a noun or a gerund.

1. When the possessive forms *my, our, your, her, his, its,* and *their* modify nouns or gerunds, they are classified as **possessive adjectives:**

My book is on the table. [*My* is a possessive adjective, modifying *book.*]

We appreciate *your* giving to the Community Chest. [Not *you giving.* The object of the verb *appreciate* is the gerund *giving*; therefore, *your* is merely the possessive adjective modifying the gerund.]

2. Personal and relative pronouns form their possessives without the apostrophe:

The boy *whose* car is in the driveway works here.

The dog chewed *its* bone.

Note: Notice the difference between *its,* the possessive form, and *it's,* the contraction of *it is:*

It's time for your car to have *its* oil changed.

Name _____ Score _____

Exercise 46 Case of Pronouns

In the following sentences underline each pronoun that is used incorrectly, and then write the correct form in the space at the right. Write **C** if the sentence is correct.

Example: Between you and I there are no easy answers to the
downtown parking problems. _____*me*_____

1. You will never guess who was sitting across from Gus and I on the train into town. _____

2. No one in the conference can run the mile faster than him. _____

3. Three of us — Ted, Mary and me — are making plans to take the boat trip to Nantucket tomorrow. _____

4. Could it have been him who was behind the counter at McDonald's? _____

5. Doug found us girls where he thought he would: visiting over coffee at the drugstore. _____

6. Sitting on the front steps were her and Tom, talking about tomorrow's political science test. _____

7. Madame Benét will not be pleased to hear about them cutting French class to watch the soap operas. _____

8. The only stockbroker in town is thought to be him. _____

9. At six this morning we were up, getting ready to drive she and Al to the airport. _____

10. The birthday cake was a thing of beauty, but it's taste left something to be desired. _____

11. Him planning to teach is certainly news to me. _____

12. The pictures that Bob took of she and Tony, standing in front of St. Patrick's, are splendid. _____

13. Tell Joan to ask for either of us, Stan or I. _____

14. The managing editor said that us three could all be on next year's annual staff. _____

15. Very often we discover that experts are no different from you and I. _____

149

16. We've taken a vote and concluded that no one can create a better
    pizza than him.   _____

17. The two persons standing beside me on the subway were her and
    the woman in the plaid jacket.   _____

18. Its absolutely necessary for me to find some shoes that fit better
    than the ones I have on.   _____

19. Did you ask Stephanie and him to come to the open house after
    the game?   _____

20. I know of no other children as well behaved as them.   _____

Name _____ Score _____

In the following sentences underline each pronoun that is used incorrectly, and then write the correct form in the space at the right. Write **C** if the sentence is correct.

Example: Many of my friends think that my cousin is older

than <u>me</u>.   *I*

1. The governor's choice for administrative assistant is believed to be
   her.   _____

2. Between you and I, spending a weekend on Cumberland Island
   sounds like a better idea than going duck hunting.   _____

3. Saturday morning me and Jim are planning to try out for the
   baseball team.   _____

4. I believe that the coach is interested in him playing second base.   _____

5. With a batting average like mine I am not sure that he is interested in my playing anything.   _____

6. The ticket agent assured Jean and I that we could get tickets for
   the matinee.   _____

7. No one can drive this old car as well as her.   _____

8. In fact, it was she who persuaded Grandfather not to trade for a
   new Corvette.   _____

9. Mabel will have to accept the fact that Leonard is just one of we
   boys.   _____

10. Neither Luke nor me could find the ball in the sand trap or in the
    rough.   _____

11. No one can tell a bigger fish story than him.   _____

12. In fact, it is him who claims to be the best fisherman on the lake.   _____

13. At least one of the sales representatives — either him or Louisa —
    needs to be at the convention.   _____

14. Someone must send he and Catherine directions to the farm, or
    they will never find the picnic.   _____

15. Its not easy to explain how to get to the farm, even to Catherine,
    who has a good sense of direction.   _____

16. What would you think of us waiting until five o'clock and taking them with us?   _____

17. An old friend asked Nancy and I to have dinner with him at the Italian restaurant on Tenth Street.   _____

18. You cannot drive the car with one of it's turn signals out of order.   _____

19. When the doorbell rang, my mother thought the electrician to be I.   _____

20. If you need help raking your lawn, call one of us — Nick, Joe, or I.   _____

Exercise 48   Case of Pronouns

In the space at the right, write the correct form of the pronoun *who* (*whoever*).

Example: (*Who, Whom*) do you think manages the concession
stand at the basketball games?   <u> *Who* </u>

1. I don't remember (*who, whom*) owns the hardware store on Tindall
Street.   _____

2. Would you return these books to (*whoever, whomever*) is at the cir-
culation desk.   _____

3. A young woman (*who, whom*) Flo said had an excellent voice sang
"The Star-Spangled Banner."   _____

4. It is absolutely essential that any soloist (*who, whom*) undertakes
the national anthem have an excellent voice.   _____

5. (*Who, Whom*) has Mrs. Fuller asked to help in the computer lab?   _____

6. Finding a house sitter (*who, whom*) I have confidence in has not
been easy.   _____

7. I believe that you can leave the flowers with (*whoever, whomever*) is
at the reception desk.   _____

8. (*Who, Whom*) will you ask to help you deliver the baskets of fruit?   _____

9. (*Who's, Whose*) going to chop the onions and peppers for the spaghetti sauce?   _____

10. Ask (*whoever, whomever*) you want to bring the ice and lemonade.   _____

11. As I was going into Macy's, (*who, whom*) do you think I saw?   _____

12. (*Who, Whom*) did you say is calling?   _____

13. (*Who, Whom*) was Bob talking about when we sat down at the
table?   _____

14. (*Whose, Who's*) turn is it to go for the mail?   _____

15. (*Whoever, Whomever*) does go needs to take an umbrella.   _____

16. The person (*who, whom*) everyone says is the best cabinet maker in
town is Mae Jones.   _____

17. Can you imagine (*who, whom*) just called me from St. Paul?   _____

18. To (*who, whom*) should we address this letter?   _____

19. I sent a résumé to anyone (*who, whom*) I thought would be the least bit interested in a super salesman.   _____

20. Perhaps some of those (*who, whom*) you sent a résumé to will appreciate a man of great confidence.   _____

Name _____ Score _____

Exercise 49 Review of Agreement and Case

Underline each word that is incorrectly used. Then write the correct word in the space at the right. Write **C** if the sentence is correct.

Example: You can depend on <u>him</u> being here on time.   *his*

1. Seated in the pew near the front of the church was the bride's aunt and two cousins from St. Louis.   _____

2. Neither of the candidates were willing to admit that there are two sides to the issue.   _____

3. I am certain that the person who wrote the letter to the editor was either her or her sister.   _____

4. Harry, Fred, and me plan to go hunting Thanksgiving weekend.   _____

5. The data appearing in the current edition of the *Statistical Abstract of the United States* is usually the latest available.   _____

6. The girl whom I think is Albert's fiancée is sitting near the window.   _____

7. The commanding general along with his aides were in that car that just drove by.   _____

8. The idea of you riding a bike on that thoroughfare is not worth considering.   _____

9. The travel agent told Marvin and I that we will have to fly to London by way of New York.   _____

10. No one can charm an audience as completely as him.   _____

11. Each of the window washers came at eight o'clock and had completed his work by the middle of the afternoon.   _____

12. Are either of the circuit judges available to speak at the luncheon on Law Day?   _____

13. A politician and historian are to lead a discussion of arms control after we see the documentary film.   _____

14. The media is aware that the President plans to stop over in Miami on his way back from South America.   _____

15. Mack tells me that it is him and not Ralph who has agreed to organize the class reunion.   _____

155

16. Everybody has their own idea of how to study for an exam.   _____

17. Marcia is one of those people who knows the secret of operating a successful restaurant.   _____

18. Just between you and I there is a good chance that Bert will get a job at Yellowstone Park this summer.   _____

19. The young man whom we saw talking to the bus driver is to be our guide today.   _____

20. Neither my sister nor I are the talented pianist that Mother is.   _____

21. The forest between here and the coastal plain consist chiefly of scrub oaks and long-leaf pines.   _____

22. According to the clerk in the bookshop $15.00 are not an unreasonable price for this book.   _____

23. No smoking, drinking, or eating are allowed in the auditorium.   _____

24. Because it was almost dark, the security guard took Peter to be I.   _____

25. Marilyn Lawson is the person whom I believe repairs electronic equipment at the store in Thompson Plaza.   _____

26. Every one of our cats have had a distinctive personality.   _____

27. Chris along with his old friend Dan Mason are heading down the Appalachian Trail as soon as spring breaks.   _____

28. Have you noticed that Jim Austen's son looks exactly like him?   _____

29. The front-runner in the race for student-body president is reported to be her.   _____

30. Whose glasses are these on the dashboard?   _____

31. Us girls are going to pack tonight and leave for Houston the first thing in the morning.   _____

32. Deciding to go on a diet and actually doing it is two entirely different things.   _____

33. Please ask whomever is at the cash register for my car keys.   _____

34. Him and Agnes have been dating for at least two years.   _____

35. Do either of the doctors suggest that burning the candle at both ends might be the cause of Alison's poor health?   _____

36. Who do you think might be willing to make the posters for Clean Campus Week?   _____

37. Sarah Ann explained the reason for her black eye to whoever she met. _____

38. Neither the meteorologist nor my great-uncle Albert have ventured to predict when we will see the last of this hot, humid weather. _____

39. Between we two, the owner of Cedric's Used Cars should not appear in his own television commercials. _____

40. However, who at the station has nerve enough to tell him? _____

12

Adjectives and Adverbs

Adjectives and adverbs, as you saw in Chapter 1, are words that modify, describe, or add to the meaning of other words in a sentence. It is important to remember the special and differing functions of these two kinds of modifier; *adjectives* modify only nouns and other substantives; *adverbs* modify verbs, adjectives, adverbs, and certain phrases and clauses.

■ 12a Adjective and Adverb Forms

An adverb is frequently formed by adding *-ly* to the adjective form of a word: for example, the adjectives *rapid, sure,* and *considerate* are converted into the adverbs *rapidly, surely,* and *considerately* by this method. But there are numerous exceptions to this general rule. Many common adverbs, like *well, then,* and *quite,* do not end in *-ly;* moreover, there are many *adjectives* that do end in *-ly,* like *manly, stately, lonely,* or *unsightly.*

Sometimes the same form is used for both adjective and adverb: *fast, long,* and *much,* for example. (There are no such words as *fastly, longly,* or *muchly.*) Certain adverbs have two forms, one being the same as the adjective and the other ending in *-ly: slow, slowly; quick, quickly; loud, loudly;* etc. The first form is often employed in short commands, as in the sentences *Drive slow* and *Speak loud.*

■ 12b Predicate Adjectives

In any sentence that follows a "subject-verb-modifier" pattern, you must be careful to determine whether the modifier is describing the subject or the verb:

John talks *intelligently*.

John is *intelligent*.

In the first sentence the modifier clearly describes how John talks — that is, it modifies the verb *talks;* consequently, the adverb *intelligently* is needed. But in the second sentence the modifier describes the subject *John;* therefore, an adjective is used. In this construction the adjective following the linking verb *is* is called the **predicate adjective.**

The term **linking verb,** as you learned from Chapter 1, refers to certain intransitive verbs that make a statement not by expressing action but by expressing a condition or state of being. These verbs "link" the subject of the sentence with some other substantive that renames or identifies it or with an adjective that describes it. Any adjective that appears after a subject-linking verb construction is called the **predicate adjective.** The verbs most commonly used as linking verbs are the following:

appear	become	remain	stay
be	grow	seem	feel (as an emotion)

Along with these are the five "sense" verbs, which are usually linking verbs:

look	feel	smell	taste	sound

The following sentences illustrate the use of predicate adjectives:

The little dog was *glad* to be out of his pen. [*Glad,* a predicate adjective, follows the linking verb *was* and describes *dog.*]

Father appeared *eager* to drive his new car.

Laurie became *angry* at being put to bed.

Jackie seems *happy* in her new job.

Remain *quiet,* and I will give you your seat assignments. [*Quiet,* the predicate adjective, describes the subject, *you,* understood.]

The day grew *dark* as the clouds gathered.

Peggy looks *sporty* in her new tennis outfit.

I feel *confident* that Ty will win his case.

That cinnamon bread smells *delicious.*

The rain sounds *dismal* beating on the roof.

Almond toffee ice cream tastes *marvelous.*

This warm robe feels *comfortable.*

A practical test to follow in determining whether to use an adjective or an adverb is to try to substitute some form of the verb *to be* for the verb in the sentence. If the substitution does not substantially change the meaning of the sentence, then the verb should be followed by an adjective. For instance, *She is smart in her new uniform* has essentially the same meaning as *She looks smart in her new uniform;* therefore, the adjective *smart* is the correct modifier.

Occasionally, one of the "sense" verbs is followed by an adverb because the verb is being used not as a *linking* verb but as an *action* verb: *He looked nervously for his keys. Nervously* describes the act of looking, so the adverb is used to express how the looking was done. The substitution test would show immediately that an adjective would be incorrect in the sentence.

■ 12c Misuse of Adjectives

Using an adjective to modify a verb is a common error but a serious one. The sentence *The doctor spoke to the sick child very kind* illustrates this error. *Kind* is an adjective and cannot be used to modify the verb *spoke;* the adverb *kindly* must be used.

Four adjectives that are frequently misused as adverbs are *real, good, sure,* and *some.* When the adverbial form of these words is needed, the correct forms are *really, well, surely,* and *somewhat:*

> The mountain laurel is *really* (or *very,* not *real*) colorful.
>
> You did *well* (not *good*) to stop smoking so quickly.
>
> I *surely* (not *sure*) hope to see him before he leaves.
>
> I feel *somewhat* (not *some*) better today.

Note: Remember that *well* can also be an adjective, referring to a state of health, as in *I feel well now, after my long illness.*

■ 12d Comparison of Adjectives and Adverbs

When you wish to indicate to what extent one noun has a certain quality in comparison with that of another noun, change the form of the modifying adjective that describes the quality: My dog is *bigger* than your dog. My dog is the *biggest* dog in town.

Descriptive adverbs, like adjectives, may be compared in the same way:

> We awaited the holidays *more eagerly* than our parents did.
>
> The shrimp and the oysters were the foods *most rapidly* eaten at the party.

Adjectives and adverbs show or imply comparison by the use of three forms, called **degrees:** the **positive, comparative,** and **superlative degrees.**

Positive Degree

The **positive degree** of an adjective or adverb is its regular form:

> He is a *fine* man.
>
> John took notes *carefully.*

Comparative Degree

The **comparative degree** of an adjective or adverb compares two things, persons, or actions:

> He is a *finer* man than his brother.
>
> John took notes *more carefully* than Bob did.

Superlative Degree

The **superlative degree** compares three or more persons, things, or actions:

> He is the *finest* man I know.
>
> John took notes *most carefully* of all the boys in his class.

The comparative degree is regularly formed by adding *-er* to the positive form of an adjective or adverb or by using *more* or *less* before the positive form. The superlative degree is formed either by adding *-est* to the positive or by using *most* or *least* before the positive. The number of syllables in the word determines which of these forms must be used:

	Positive	Comparative	Superlative
	strong	stronger	strongest
Adj.	pretty	prettier	prettiest
	difficult	more difficult	most difficult
	quietly	more quietly	most quietly
Adv.	easily	more easily	most easily
	fast	faster	fastest

The comparison of some words is irregular, as of *good* (*good, better, best*) and *bad* (*bad, worse, worst*).

Be careful not to use the superlative form when only two persons, groups, objects, or ideas are involved:

> Tom is the *healthier* (not *healthiest*) of the two brothers.

Certain adjectives and adverbs such as *perfect, unique, round, square, dead,* and *exact* cannot logically be used in the comparative or superlative degrees, and most should not be modified by words like *quite* or *very*. These words in their simplest forms are absolute superlatives, incapable of being added to or detracted from:

> ILLOGICAL: Samuel is the *most unique* person I know.
>
> LOGICAL: Samuel is a unique person.
>
> ALSO LOGICAL: Samuel is an *almost unique* person.

ILLOGICAL: Beth's engagement diamond is the *most perfect* stone I've seen in years.

LOGICAL: Beth's engagement diamond is a *perfect* stone.

ALSO LOGICAL: Beth's engagement diamond is the *most nearly perfect* stone I've seen in years.

ILLOGICAL: The figures that Ben used in his report are *less exact* than they should be.

LOGICAL: The figures that Ben used in his report are not exact, though they should be.

■ 12e Incomplete Comparisons

When using the comparative degree of an adjective or adverb, be sure that both items being compared are included; for example, do not say, *Using a paint roller is quicker*. Your reader will ask, "Quicker than what?" The unknown answer might even be *Using a paint roller is quicker than daubing paint on with one's fingers.* Always complete a comparison by including both items: *Using a paint roller is quicker than using a brush.*

Exercise 50   Adjectives and Adverbs

Underline the word or words modified by the *italicized* adjective or adverb. Then in the space at the right, write **Adj** if the italicized word is an adjective, **Adv** if it is an adverb.

Example: In the spring the river *frequently* <u>overflows</u> its banks.   *Adv*

1. The wind shifted *suddenly*, bringing with it a torrent of rain. _____

2. I am the first to admit that Mrs. Brown's coconut cake tastes *better* than mine. _____

3. The old actor *seldom* appears on stage any more. _____

4. The factory whistle sounded unusually *loud* that quiet, gray morning. _____

5. A representative from the Chamber of Commerce meets *regularly* with our committee. _____

6. Is anyone *ready* for a cup of tea? _____

7. Your car runs *smoothly* since you have had the wheels realigned. _____

8. Once it is greased and the oil is changed, it will run even *better*. _____

9. *Not* one of the children was interested in the suggestion that we leave the playground. _____

10. Uncle Arthur feels *well* enough to walk two miles a day. _____

11. The attorney was young and inexperienced, but he argued the case *convincingly*. _____

12. I was *not* surprised to hear that Felicia is an excellent swimmer. _____

13. Run *fast*, and you can catch that bus! _____

14. Because it had belonged to a former governor, the book collection was *especially* significant. _____

15. Do you think that those are *real* flowers in that arrangement? _____

16. I'll have to return this coat; it seems *tight* across the shoulders. _____

17. Furthermore, the sleeves are *too* short. _____

18. I'm going to make a *fast* trip to Dunkin' Donuts before my nine o'clock class. _____

19. Outside the courtroom the two lawyers have a *friendly* relationship. _____

20. Warren is *sure* that Mother will be here in time for lunch.   _____

21. Paul says that he is *somewhat* interested in going to Montana with us.   _____

22. The snow covered the lawn, the sidewalk, and *finally* the street.   _____

23. Dorothy remains the sweetest of the three sisters.   _____

24. Despite the incessant rain our spirits were *good*.   _____

25. I'm *surely* glad, because a rainy weekend in the mountains can be
    depressing.   _____

26. *Never* have I waited so long in a doctor's office.   _____

27. Some of the patients were *totally* absorbed in their reading.   _____

28. Others chatted *casually* with friends and acquaintances.   _____

29. The sports page contains the *liveliest* prose in the newspaper.   _____

30. By the time that Nick had mowed the whole yard, he was *really*
    weary.   _____

Exercise 51   Adjectives and Adverbs

Underline any adjective or adverb that is incorrectly used. Then write the correct form at the right. Write **C** if the sentence is correct.

Example: I <u>sure</u> wish that I knew someone who would
help me paint the fence.   *surely*

1. The whistle blew so shrill that all of us on the platform were startled. _____

2. The tree in front of Morris Hall would make the most perfect Christmas tree. _____

3. The young man spoke sharp to the two boys who persisted in scuffling in the back of the bus. _____

4. Is this typewriter or that one the best? _____

5. Warm apple pie tastes absolutely delectable with a wedge of sharp cheese. _____

6. The driver switched lanes sudden when he realized that he was on his way to South Boston. _____

7. Just for a moment the crow perched uncertain on the branch of the poplar tree. _____

8. I feel real good about Dr. Moses's midterm exam. _____

9. The President's wife usually wears a special designed gown to the Inaugural Ball. _____

10. We muchly appreciated the opera tickets that Walter gave us. _____

11. The fog grew thickly as I drove toward the bridge. _____

12. Turn left just beyond the sign that reads "Drive Slow." _____

13. Duncan came down the ladder careful, still remembering the time he had fallen. _____

14. Julia, that's the tallest tale that I have ever heard. _____

15. Despite Alec's best intentions the toast was burned bad and the eggs were hard boiled. _____

16. Clair drove steady all afternoon, arriving in Rockingham well before dark. _____

17. The Powells seem really happy with their new camper. _____

18. Does this map or that one have the most detail? _____

19. Tina sure was nervous on opening night but has seemed quite calm ever since. _____

20. If you are going to have enough money to go to Spain, you will have to watch your nickels and dimes closer. _____

21. Year after year my father and Uncle Ben laughed hearty at each other's jokes. _____

22. Norman reads good for a child of seven. _____

23. The old fairy tale says that Hansel and Gretel wandered deep into the forest. _____

24. With your background you will find trigonometry more easy than you think. _____

25. I feel badly about losing my new yellow sweater. _____

26. His heart beating rapid, the runner nearly stumbled as he reached the finish line. _____

27. Please sit up straightly in your seat. _____

28. If you want me to make the trifle, you will have to give me the most exact instructions. _____

29. Of all the horses on the Hargraves's farm, Blue Moon is the faster. _____

30. Having leaned back in his chair, the lawyer began reading very slow the fine print of the contract. _____

Name _____   Score _____

Exercise 52   Adjectives and Adverbs

Select the correct form of the word in parentheses, and write it in the space at the right.

Example: These bananas are (*some, somewhat*) riper than those.   *somewhat*

1. As he was waiting for a table, Weatherby chatted (*casual, casually*) with the couple standing behind him.   _____

2. Which of these three Japanese cars gets the (*better, best*) mileage?   _____

3. Its whistle sounding as (*mournful, mournfully*) as ever, the freight train made its way across the prairie.   _____

4. Mrs. Quincy frequently speaks (*grand, grandly*) about her illustrious ancestors.   _____

5. I will always remain (*wary, warily*) of Buster Crump, our neighborhood bully.   _____

6. Although we had climbed (*steady, steadily*) all morning, we still had not reached the campsite by mid-afternoon.   _____

7. Sue Ellen glanced (*anxious, anxiously*) at her watch: Roger was late again.   _____

8. Determined to be in shape for spring practice, Guy exercises (*vigorous, vigorously*) every morning.   _____

9. The river flowed (*rapid, rapidly*) through the long, rocky gorge.   _____

10. I believe that Sheba is the (*lazier, laziest*) of the two cats.   _____

11. The grocery clerk thumped the watermelon (*sound, soundly*), hoping to find a ripe one.   _____

12. The whipped cream tastes too (*sweet, sweetly*) for me.   _____

13. The Russian visitors looked (*brief, briefly*) at the courthouse and then drove on to the museum.   _____

14. I've heard that Heathrow is the (*busier, busiest*) of all the international airports.   _____

15. The view of the bridge from Stuart's office is one of the (*prettiest, most pretty*) I have seen.   _____

16. The baby slept (*quiet, quietly*) even though the stereo was going full blast downstairs.   _____

17. If you will look out this porthole, you can see the shoreline (*clear, clearly*). _____

18. Mr. Sims goes to the Farmers' Market (*regular, regularly*) to buy produce for his grocery store. _____

19. Once my fever was gone, I soon felt (*good, well*) again. _____

20. The trapeze artist balanced (*precarious, precariously*) on the high wire. _____

21. Can one buy gasoline (*cheaper, more cheaply*) now than six months ago? _____

22. When the child fell from the swing, he hit the ground (*hard, hardly*). _____

23. Mr. Christopher twirled his mustache as he talked (*important, importantly*) about his latest success on Wall Street. _____

24. Our whole neighborhood felt (*good, well*) about the decision to reopen Bruce Elementary School. _____

25. As the discussion progressed, the panelists grew less (*objective, objectively*) in their comments. _____

26. The photography collection in the New Orleans museum is the (*finer, finest*) of the two. _____

27. Senator Bullard seems (*adamant, adamantly*) in his opposition to the proposed dam. _____

28. In fact, he argued (*ardent, ardently*) against it at the oyster bake. _____

29. The hammock swung (*lazy, lazily*) back and forth, and Hugh was soon asleep. _____

30. Edgar (*sure, surely*) is glad that he has been asked to join the orchestra. _____

13

Tense, Voice, Mood

In Chapter 1 you found that a single verb may be classified according to **tense, voice,** and **mood;** therefore, it is not surprising that choosing the appropriate verb form occasionally presents difficulty.

■ 13a Principal Parts of Verbs

There are three **principal parts** of a verb. These are (1) **the first person singular, present indicative;** (2) **the first person singular, past indicative;** (3) **the past participle.** The first two of these provide the basic forms of the present, past, and future tenses; the third is used as the basis for the three perfect tenses:

Principal parts: *begin, began, begun*		
Present:	I begin	
Past:	I began	
Future:	I will (shall) begin ——————	(This form based on present tense *begin*)
Present Perfect:	I have begun	(These forms based on past participle *begun*)
Past Perfect:	I had begun	
Future Perfect:	I will (shall) have begun	

If you know the principal parts of a verb and the way to form the various tenses from them, you should never make a mistake such as the one contained in the following sentence: "The play had already began when I arrived." If the speaker had known that the principal parts of *begin* are *begin, began, begun* and that the past perfect tense is formed by using *had* with the past participle, he would have known that the correct form is *had begun*.

Regular verbs — that is, those verbs that form their past tense and past participle by adding *-d* or *-ed* to the present tense — rarely cause difficulty. It is the **irregular verbs** that are most frequently used incorrectly. When necessary, consult a dictionary for their principal parts. The following list contains the principal parts of certain especially troublesome verbs. Learn these forms:

Present	Past	Past participle	Present	Past	Past participle
ask	asked	asked	know	knew	known
bite	bit	bitten	lead	led	led
blow	blew	blown	ride	rode	ridden
break	broke	broken	ring	rang (rung)	rung
burst	burst	burst	run	ran	run
choose	chose	chosen	see	saw	seen
come	came	come	shake	shook	shaken
dive	dived (dove)	dived	sing	sang (sung)	sung
do	did	done	speak	spoke	spoken
drag	dragged	dragged	steal	stole	stolen
draw	drew	drawn	sting	stung	stung
drink	drank	drunk	suppose	supposed	supposed
drown	drowned	drowned	swim	swam	swum
eat	ate	eaten	swing	swung	swung
fall	fell	fallen	take	took	taken
fly	flew	flown	tear	tore	torn
freeze	froze	frozen	throw	threw	thrown
give	gave	given	use	used	used
go	went	gone	wear	wore	worn
grow	grew	grown	write	wrote	written

Note that the past tense and the past participle of the verbs *ask, suppose,* and *use* are regularly formed by the addition of *-ed* (or *-d*) to the present tense. Possibly because the *d* is not always clearly sounded in the pronunciation of the past tense and the past participle of these verbs, people frequently make the mistake of writing the present-tense form when one of the other forms is required:

I have *asked* (not *ask*) him to go with me.

I was *supposed* (not *suppose*) to do that job.

He *used* (not *use*) to be my best friend.

■ 13b Two Troublesome Pairs of Verbs

Lie and *lay* and *sit* and *set* are frequent stumbling blocks to correct writing. These verbs need not be confusing, however, if the following points are remembered:

1. Each verb has a distinguishing meaning. *Lay* and *set*, for instance, are clearly distinguished from *lie* and *sit* by their meanings: both *lay* and *set* usually mean *place* and are correctly used when the verb *place* can be substituted for them.

2. *Lay* and *set* are always transitive verbs; that is, they require an object to complete their meaning when they are used in the active voice. *Lie* and *sit* are intransitive verbs and hence do not take an object.

3. Although *lay* and *lie* share the form *lay*, they use it in different tenses. The remaining principal parts are clearly distinguishable.

These three points may be graphically shown:

Principal parts	
Intransitive (takes no object)	Transitive (takes an object)
lie lay lain, *recline, remain in position*	lay laid laid, *place*
sit sat sat, *be in a sitting position*	set set set, *place*

Look at a few sentences that illustrate these distinguishing characteristics. Is it correct to say *I set the box on the table* or *I sat the box on the table*? To answer the question, try substituting *placed* for *set* and also see whether a direct object follows the verb. You can see at once that *placed* can be substituted for *set* and that *box* is the direct object of the verb; therefore, the first sentence, employing *set*, is the correct one. But in the sentence *I left the box sitting on the table*, the correct form is *sitting*, not *setting*, since *placing* cannot be substituted for *sitting* and since there is no direct object after *sitting*:

I *laid* (that is, *placed*) the book by the bed and *lay* (past tense of *lie*) down to rest.

Do not fall into the error of thinking that only animate things can stand as subjects of intransitive verbs. Note the following sentences in which inanimate objects are used as subjects of the intransitive verbs:

The book *lies* on the table.

The house *sits* near the road.

■ 13c Tense Sequence

Tense sequence demands that a logical time relationship be shown by the verbs in a sentence. Through force of habit we generally indicate accurate time relationships. A few cautions, however, should be stressed:

1. Use the present tense in the statement of a timeless universal truth or a customary happening:

I wonder who first discovered that the sun *rises* (not *rose*) in the east. [The fact that the sun rises in the east is a universal truth.]

Joe said that the class *begins* (not *began*) at 10:30. [The clause *that the class begins at 10:30* states a customary happening.]

2. Use the present tense of an infinitive or the present participle if the action it expresses occurs at the same time as that of the governing verb:

Yesterday I really wanted *to go.* [Not *to have gone.* The governing verb *wanted* indicates a past time. At that past time I wanted to do something *then* — that is, yesterday — not at a time prior to yesterday.]

Skipping along, she hummed a merry tune. [The skipping and the humming occur at the same time.]

3. When necessary for clarity, indicate time differences by using different tenses:

INCORRECT: I told him that I *finished* the work just an hour before.

CORRECT: I told him that I *had finished* the work just an hour before. [The verb *told* indicates a past time. Since the work was finished before the time indicated by *told,* the past perfect tense *had finished* must be used.]

INCORRECT: *Making* my reservations, I am packing to go to Cape Cod.

CORRECT: *Having made* my reservations, I am packing to go to Cape Cod. [The perfect participle *having made* must be used to denote an action before the time indicated by the governing verb *am packing.*]

■ 13d Voice

Transitive verbs always indicate whether the subject is acting or is being acted upon. When the subject is doing the acting, the verb is said to be in the **active voice:**

I *laid* the book on the table. [*Laid* is in the active voice because the subject *I* is doing the acting.]

When the subject is being acted upon or receiving the action, the verb is in the **passive voice:**

The book *was laid* on the table. [*Was laid* is in the passive voice because the subject *book* is being acted upon.]

Note: The passive voice verb always consists of some form of the verb *to be* plus a past participle: *is seen, was laid, have been taken.*

In general, the active voice is more emphatic than the passive and therefore should normally be used in preference to the passive voice:

WEAK: The automobile *was driven* into the garage.

MORE EMPHATIC: She *drove* the automobile into the garage.

When, however, the receiver of the action should be stressed rather than the doer, or when the doer is unknown, the passive voice is appropriate.

Class officers *will be elected* next Thursday. [The receiver of the action should be stressed.]

The dog *was found* last night. [The doer is unknown.]

Generally speaking, one should not shift from one voice to the other in the same sentence:

AWKWARD: John *is* the best athlete on the team, and the most points *are scored* by him.

BETTER: John *is* the best athlete on the team and also *scores* the most points.

AWKWARD: After Dr. Lovett *was conferred* with, I *understood* the assignment.

BETTER: After I *conferred* with Dr. Lovett (OR After *conferring* with Dr. Lovett), I *understood* the assignment.

■ 13e Mood

In Chapter 1, Section 1d defined the indicative, imperative, and subjunctive moods. Through force of habit we usually select the correct verb forms for the first two moods but sometimes have difficulty choosing the correct forms for the subjunctive mood.

The **subjunctive mood** is most frequently used today to express a wish or to state a condition contrary to fact. In both types of statement the subjunctive *were* is used instead of the indicative *was*. Tenses in the subjunctive do not have the same meaning as they do in the indicative mood. For example, the past subjunctive form points toward the present or future, as seen in the sentence *If I WERE you, I would give his suggestion strong consideration.* The present subjunctive form usually points toward the future with a stronger suggestion of hopefulness than does the past subjunctive. (*I move that John Marshall BE named chairman of our committee.*) The present subjunctive form of the verb *to be* is invariably *be* for all persons, and the past subjunctive form of the verb *to be* is invariably *were*. In all other verbs the subjunctive form varies from the indicative only in that in the present tense the third person singular ending is lost, as in *I suggest that he TAKE the subway to his friend's house.* Note the following examples of verbs in the subjunctive mood:

I wish that I *were* (not *was*) going with you to Hawaii this summer.

If I *were* (not *was*) king, I couldn't be happier.

The subjunctive mood may also be used in the following instances:

If the report *be* true, we will have to modify our plans. [To express a doubt or uncertainty.]

She commanded that the rule *be* enforced. [To express a command.]

Even though he *disagree* with me, I will still admire him. [To express a concession.]

It is necessary that he *see* his parents at once. [To express a necessity.]

I move that the proposal *be* adopted. [To express a parliamentary motion.]

Exercise 53 — Tense and Mood

A. In the space at the right, write the correct form of the verb that appears in parentheses.

Example: Elsie has (*begin*) knitting a scarf for Mark's
birthday.   *begun*

1. If you had (*take*) the other route to Hampton, you would
   have saved at least twenty minutes.   _____

2. All winter long the brown leaves have (*cling*) to the oak trees
   in front of the bank.   _____

3. Although the wind (*blow*) most of the night, it died down a
   bit just before dawn.   _____

4. During the recent holidays the quartet (*sing*) at several parties.   _____

5. Immediately after the sun had (*sink*), the sky appeared gray-
   ish-green.   _____

6. The candidate for sheriff must have (*shake*) a thousand hands
   today.   _____

7. Everyone (*stand*) when the judge entered the courtroom.   _____

8. The icy rain (*sting*) my cheeks as I hurried from the office to
   my car.   _____

9. When we move, what are we (*suppose*) to do with our telephone?   _____

10. Although the children had been told not to play in the attic,
    they (*steal*) up there that rainy afternoon.   _____

11. I have not (*see*) Lucy Meadows since last summer at the
    music festival.   _____

12. Who on earth could have (*tear*) the coffee coupon from the
    morning paper?   _____

13. The balloon (*burst*), startling everyone on the bus.   _____

14. I am certain that Joel (*use*) to wear glasses.   _____

15. You are right, but he has recently (*get*) contact lenses.   _____

B. Underline all verbs in the following sentences. Then write the past tense of the underlined verbs in the space at the right.

Example: Miriam usually <u>wears</u> a bright, engaging smile.   _____*wore*_____

1. The temperature rises swiftly once the sun comes up.   _____

2. The quarterback throws the football to Red Mason, who invariably catches it.   _____

3. The lifeguard blows his whistle when the children go beyond the sand bar.   _____

4. Professor Blankenship not only writes poetry but also reads it to her classes.   _____

5. Marion dives into the lake and swims out to the raft.   _____

C. Select the correct form of the verb in parentheses, and write it in the space at the right.

Example: I wish that I (*was, were*) able to spend the day skiing.   _____*were*_____

1. It is necessary that at least two persons (*are, be*) witnesses to this document.   _____

2. (*Running, Having run*) all the way down the platform, I scrambled up the steps and onto the train.   _____

3. A member of the centennial committee moved that the proposed calendar of events (*was, be*) adopted.   _____

4. If I (*was, were*) Harold, I would certainly consider the trip to Thailand.   _____

5. The innkeeper told Anna that breakfast (*was, is*) served at eight o'clock every day except Sunday.   _____

Exercise 54 Tense and Mood

In the space at the right write the correct form of the verb that appears in parentheses.

Example: How many times has Dad (*speak*) to you about
leaving the gas tank empty? _____*spoken*_____

1. Although Gail has (*write*) most of her essay, she hasn't
   found anyone to type it for her. _____

2. The boy's jeans were (*tear*) as he was climbing the pecan
   tree. _____

3. We studied the map and concluded that the road from Johnson to Apple Creek (*be*) not paved. _____

4. When the children were small, the Merediths (*use*) to go
   downtown for the tree-lighting ceremony. _____

5. Before the first play had even begun, the referee (*blow*) his
   whistle. _____

6. The wind having come up, we (*fly*) kites most of the afternoon. _____

7. Sam regretted that he had (*throw*) his bat to the ground. _____

8. By the time I arrived, Bert had (*swim*) several lengths of the
   pool. _____

9. Angela has (*wear*) that magenta tam and scarf for three or
   four winters. _____

10. Because we have (*drink*) all the milk, someone will have to
    drop by the Quick-Stop on the way home. _____

11. Before using any of the computers in the lab, one is (*sup-
    pose*) to get permission from Ms. West. _____

12. Ever since I can remember, roses have (*grow*) along that
    fence. _____

13. Uncle David has decided that the children have (*swing*)
    enough. _____

14. Dolly wishes that she (*be*) able to get a summer job in Van-
    couver. _____

15. The architect has (*draw*) some preliminary sketches of the
    proposed student union building. _____

16. (*Finding*) a seat on the subway, Frances rummaged in her
    tote bag for a book to read. _____

17. Evidently, Maude has never been (*give*) any instructions in cake baking. _____

18. Well, I have (*lend*) her several cookbooks. _____

19. On my way to work I noticed that the fountain in front of the synagogue on Sixth Street was (*freeze*). _____

20. Even though the boys had never tasted Mexican food, they (*eat*) the tacos with relish. _____

21. When Robert was a child, his chief ambition was to (*be*) an engineer on the Norfolk and Western. _____

22. Of course, he (*know*) very little about what the job entailed. _____

23. Has anyone (*speak*) to Dr. Lindsay about changing the date of the geology test? _____

24. On very cold mornings Liza is (*accustom*) to having a cup of hot chocolate. _____

25. I turned on the television set and (*sink*) down on the couch to watch the last round of the golf tournament. _____

26. The telephone (*ring*) repeatedly, but I could not unlock the door in time to answer it. _____

27. Although Isabel did not need another piece of cake, she (*take*) one anyway. _____

28. Neither of the horses had (*run*) in a major race. _____

29. Although I admire the car when it passes me on the expressway, I have never (*drive*) a Porsche. _____

30. It is necessary that we (*be*) on time if we want to take the ferry back to the mainland. _____

31. We could not count the times we had (*drag*) the sleds to the top of the hill. _____

32. Ernest hoped to (*finish*) his art project last week. _____

33. Thursday night I was so tired that I was in bed by nine o'clock and had (*fall*) asleep soon afterward. _____

34. Have you (*see*) Mystery on Channel 8? _____

35. When a murder occurs, I can never figure out who (*do*) it. _____

36. (*Catching*) the four-thirty train, she thought she would be at the Martins' house in time for dinner. _____

37. Everybody in the hall has (*get*) an invitation to Fred and Nell's wedding. _____

38. I am sure that I would not have (*dive*) off that board when I was his age.   _____

39. The woman who moved that the Ways and Means Committee (*be*) adjourned represents Maxwell County.   _____

40. If I (*be*) you, I would bring along a sweater for the boat ride.   _____

41. Albert has (*ask*) a dozen times about your plans for next fall.   _____

42. Before Leslie (*hang*) up the telephone, she reminded Mother that we were going shopping after lunch.   _____

43. The full moon had (*rise*), lighting the field that lay behind the house.   _____

44. My brother wishes that he (*be*) able to operate a printing service.   _____

45. Either someone (*steal*) the beach towels, or Ginger took them back to the cottage.   _____

46. In many an old sea story the pirates are (*hang*) from the yardarm.   _____

47. After putting on the coffee, Julie (*raise*) the blinds in the kitchen.   _____

48. The sun (*shine*) in through the windows, brightening both the room and my sister's spirits.   _____

49. When have you (*ride*) up Interstate 75?   _____

50. Because that freeway is being widened, I have (*drive*) another way home lately.   _____

Exercise 55 Two Troublesome Pairs of Verbs

Select the correct form of the verbs in parentheses, and write it in the space at the right.

Example: The two girls (*lay*, *laid*) on the deck, soaking up the sun.   ___*lay*___

1. (*Sitting*, *Setting*) on the counter was an array of irresistible desserts. _____

2. We (*sat*, *set*) in the airport most of the morning while we waited for the snowplow to clear a runway. _____

3. A forthright man, Donald has always (*lain*, *laid*) his cards on the table. _____

4. (*Lying*, *Laying*) the carpet proved to be more of a job than Stanley expected. _____

5. With time running out, the hockey players (*sat*, *set*) despondently on the bench. _____

6. Several small cottages had been (*sat*, *set*) in the woods near the path that led to the falls. _____

7. The stone wall surrounding the condominiums had been (*lain*, *laid*) by a master mason. _____

8. I had read most of the magazines (*lying*, *laying*) on the table in the doctor's waiting room. _____

9. The small girl (*sat*, *set*) gingerly on the back of the Irish pony. _____

10. The pitcher (*lain*, *laid*) his fast ball across the plate. _____

11. Invariably, her passport (*lies*, *lays*) at the bottom of her voluminous pocketbook. _____

12. Our old collie delighted in (*lying*, *laying*) in the flower bed at the bottom of the back steps. _____

13. Mother always (*lies*, *lays*) the mail on the table in the front hall. _____

14. After (*sitting*, *setting*) the child in the car seat, Margaret remembered that she had left the grocery list on the kitchen counter. _____

15. The computer will (*sit*, *set*) here, and Betty's desk will be over there. _____

16. Because Grandmother has (*lain*, *laid*) down for a nap, we will need to be quiet. _____

17. When his bridge partner (*lay, laid*) down her hand, Ray knew that they had a grand slam.   _____

18. Colonel Compton's trophies had been carefully (*sat, set*) in a cabinet behind his desk.   _____

19. The rusty fan, droning as it moved back and forth, was (*sitting, setting*) in the corner of the kitchen.   _____

20. Having (*lain, laid*) in bed until noon, Sophie could not decide whether it was time for breakfast or lunch.   _____

21. The driver has taken the luggage from the trunk of his cab and has (*sat, set*) it on the curb.   _____

22. Every afternoon the cats (*lie, lay*) on the front steps, waiting for Father to come home.   _____

23. Marsha's clothes were scattered all over the room: they were (*lying, laying*) on the chairs, on the bed, and on the floor.   _____

24. Before (*lying, laying*) his brick walk, Neil consulted several of his friends.   _____

25. The gardener spent most of the day (*sitting, setting*) out geraniums in Aragon Park.   _____

26. Marilyn (*sat, set*) her best cups and saucers on the carefully polished tray.   _____

27. All week the children had collected shells, (*sitting, setting*) them one by one on the gray railing.   _____

28. Any Monday night one can find C.J. (*lying, laying*) on the couch watching television.   _____

29. The Sunday paper (*lay, laid*) unopened on the recliner in the den.   _____

30. (*Lying, Laying*) his packages by the door, Tim searched through his pockets for the apartment key.   _____

Exercise 56 Voice

Revise the following sentences, using verbs in the active voice and eliminating unnecessary verbs.

Example: A trip to the West Coast was suggested by Hal.

Hal suggested a trip to the West Coast.

1. The marketing plan had been evaluated and updated by the Office of Public Relations and Development.

2. The performance of *Cinderella* was sponsored by the City Ballet Company, which was organized by a group of citizens several years ago.

3. The rate of foreign exchange is published regularly by *The Wall Street Journal;* this information is often needed by persons traveling abroad.

4. The football was fumbled by the tight end immediately after he was tackled by Mick Kerry.

5. The cover of the magazine's July issue was designed by an illustrator who was selected by the art director.

6. This morning Mother was driven to the station by David because her car was being repaired by Joe Elliott.

7. A million dollars was quickly earned by the superstar, but a million dollars was also quickly spent by her.

8. The moderator was ignored by the partisans, and their discussion was soon turned into a shouting match.

9. After the golden retriever had been found at Roosevelt Square by Terry and me, an ad was placed by the two of us in the lost-and-found column of the newspaper.

10. The tax bill was debated at length by the General Assembly, which had been called into emergency session by the Governor.

11. Edward was reminded by Ms. Murdock that his car would be towed away by the campus police.

12. The credit card has been lost by my sister, despite the frequent warnings that were given her by Mother.

13. The story "The Old Forest" was written by Peter Taylor and was first published by *The New Yorker*.

14. Stratford-on-Avon was visited by my parents, who have been interested in Shakespeare for a long time.

15. The waltzes were composed by Frederic Chopin and often are played by concert pianists.

14

Dangling Modifiers

A **modifier** must always have a word to modify. This fact seems almost too obvious to warrant discussion. And yet we frequently see sentences similar in construction to this one: "Hearing a number of entertaining stories, our visit was thoroughly enjoyable." *Hearing a number of entertaining stories* is a modifying phrase. But where in the sentence is there a word for it to modify? Certainly the phrase cannot logically modify *visit*: it was not our visit that heard a number of entertaining stories. Who did hear the stories? *We* did. Since, however, the word *we* does not appear in the sentence for the phrase to modify, the phrase is said to "dangle." Any modifier dangles, or hangs unattached, when there is no obvious word to which it is clearly and logically related. (Note the similarity of this problem of modifiers and the problem of pronouns and their antecedents.)

■ 14a Recognizing Dangling Modifiers

It is important that you recognize dangling modifiers when you see them. Such modifiers usually appear as two types of constructions — as *verbal phrases* and as *elliptical clauses*. (An elliptical clause, as applicable to this lesson, is a dependent clause in which the subject and/or verb are omitted.)

> *Hearing a number of entertaining stories*, our visit was thoroughly enjoyable. [Dangling participial phrase.]
>
> *On entering the room*, refreshments were being served. [Dangling gerund phrase.]
>
> *To play tennis well*, the racket must be held properly. [Dangling infinitive phrase.]
>
> *When only three years old*, my father took me to a circus. [Dangling elliptical clause.]

In each of the examples given above, the dangling modifier stands at the beginning of the sentence. If the modifier were *not* dangling — that is, if it were correctly used — it would be related to the subject of the sentence. In none of these sentences, however, can the introductory modifier logically refer to the subject. If the error is not immediately apparent, try placing the modifier just after the subject. The dangling nature of the modifier becomes easily recognizable because of the illogical meaning that results when you say, "Our visit, *hearing a number of entertaining stories, . . .*" or "Refreshments, *on entering the room, . . .*"

Dangling modifiers frequently appear at the end as well as at the beginning of sentences. The participial phrase dangles in the sentence "The dog had only one eye, *caused by an accident.*"

At this point an exception to the rules governing the recognition of dangling modifiers should be noted: some introductory verbal phrases are general or summarizing expressions and therefore need not refer to the subject that follows:

CORRECT: *Generally speaking,* the boys' themes were more interesting than the girls'.

CORRECT: *To sum up,* our vacation was a disaster from start to finish.

■ 14b Correcting Dangling Modifiers

Sentences containing dangling modifiers are usually corrected in one of two ways. One way is to leave the modifier as it is and to reword the main clause, making the subject a word to which the modifier logically refers. Remember that when modifiers such as those discussed in this lesson stand at the beginning of the sentence, they must always clearly and logically modify or be related to the subject of the sentence:

Hearing a number of entertaining stories, *we* thoroughly enjoyed our visit.

On entering the room, *I* found that refreshments were being served.

To play tennis well, *one* must hold the racket properly.

When only three years old, *I* was taken to a circus by my father.

You may test the correctness of these sentences, as you tested the incorrectness of the others, by placing the modifier just after the subject. Then see whether the sentence reads logically; if it does, the modifier has been correctly used. The following sentence, though awkward, is clear and logical: "We, hearing a number of entertaining stories, thoroughly enjoyed our visit."

The other way to correct sentences containing dangling modifiers is to expand the modifiers into dependent clauses:

Since we heard a number of entertaining stories, our visit was thoroughly enjoyable.

When I entered the room, refreshments were being served.

If one wishes to play tennis well, he must hold the racket properly.

When I was only three years old, my father took me to a circus.

Exercise 57 Dangling Modifiers

Rewrite in correct form all sentences containing dangling modifiers. Write **C** if a sentence is correct.

Example: After raining all night, the lawn was covered with leaves.
After it rained all night, the lawn was covered with leaves.

1. When completed, the four of us will enjoy the new tennis courts.

2. Darting from one lane to another, the traffic jam seemed to have little effect on the driver of the sports car.

3. While waiting at the bus stop, reading a paperback occupied my time.

4. Before buying a condominium, the agreement should be studied closely.

5. To drive an eighteen-wheeler, skill as well as strength is required.

6. Upon reaching the stage, the opening-night audience stood to applaud the play-wrights.

7. Having failed to sell all the Valentine candy, it was drastically reduced on February 15.

8. To be able to take a picture at a moment's notice, the camera was always by the tourist's side.

9. Generally speaking, fishing here is better than it is at River Point.

10. If unoccupied, please drive to the next pump.

11. Loaded with firewood, it was difficult for the pick-up truck to make the steep hill.

12. To work effectively in a tropical climate, air conditioning is a definite help.

13. Surrounding the radio tower, the chain-link fence served as protection from the curious and the malicious.

14. Having hung from the rear-view mirror for weeks, Clarence scarcely noticed the bobbling foam-rubber dice.

15. After creeping along the freeway for twenty minutes, a break in the traffic suddenly occurred.

16. Although made from beautiful material, Ruby could have selected a more becoming dress.

17. Laughing and shouting as the clowns paraded in, the circus tent was filled with children.

18. To have prize-winning roses, constant attention is needed.

19. Since taking two aspirins, my headache has disappeared.

20. Hiding under the bed, Aunt Susie could not coax the cat to eat its supper.

Exercise 58   Introductory Modifiers

Using the following phrases and elliptical clauses as introductory modifiers, write complete sentences.

Example: Continuing down the hall, *Dudley finally found the registrar's office.*

1. Looming in the distance, _____

   _____

2. Having neglected to call home, _____

   _____

3. Upon returning to the store, _____

   _____

4. Technically speaking, _____

   _____

5. While searching through the want ads, _____

   _____

6. Bouncing across the unplowed field, _____

   _____

7. When riding my bicycle to work, _____

   _____

8. After stumbling out of bed, _____

   _____

9. When first noticed by the talent scout, _____

   _____

10. Groping for a solution to the problem, _____

    _____

11. Browned well on both sides, _____

    _____

12. To sum up, _____

    _____

13. While rummaging through the old trunk, _____

    _____

14. Scattered all over the lawn, _____

    _____

15. Before becoming a parachutist, _____

    _____

16. To read *Moby Dick* from cover to cover, _____

    _____

17. After having rung the doorbell several times, _____

    _____

18. By leaving the shop at four-thirty every afternoon, _____

    _____

19. Having promised myself never to procrastinate again, _____

    _____

20. Since buying a new bathing suit, _____

    _____

21. To close the suitcase, _____

    _____

22. Though forgotten by most of us, _____

_____

23. Not having heard the morning news, _____

_____

24. Without considering the consequences, _____

_____

25. Looking for an adventure, _____

_____

15

Misplaced Modifiers

Modifiers must always be so placed that there will be no uncertainty about the words they modify. A modifier should, in general, stand as close as possible to the word that it modifies. This does not mean, however, that in every sentence there is only one correct position for a modifier. The following sentence, in which the adverb *today* is shifted from one position to another, is equally clear in any one of these three versions:

> *Today* she arrived in Chicago.
>
> She arrived *today* in Chicago.
>
> She arrived in Chicago *today*.

The position of the modifier *today* can be shifted because, no matter where it is placed, it clearly modifies the verb *arrived*.

■ 15a Misplaced Phrases and Clauses

When, however, a modifier can attach itself to two different words in the sentence, the writer must be careful to place it in a position that will indicate the meaning intended:

> They argued the subject while I tried to study *at fever pitch*.

This sentence is illogical as long as the phrase *at fever pitch* seems to modify *to study*. The phrase must be placed where it will unmistakably modify *argued*:

> CORRECT: They argued the subject *at fever pitch* while I tried to study.
>
> ALSO CORRECT: *At fever pitch* they argued the subject while I tried to study.

A relative clause — that is, a clause introduced by a relative pronoun — should normally follow the word that it modifies:

ILLOGICAL: A piece was played at the concert *that was composed of dissonant chords.*

CORRECT: A piece *that was composed of dissonant chords* was played at the concert.

■ 15b Ambiguous Modifiers

When a modifier is placed between two elements so that it may be taken to modify either element, it is **ambiguous.** These ambiguous modifiers are sometimes called **squinting modifiers:**

The girl who had been dancing *gracefully* entered the room.

Does the speaker mean that the girl had been dancing gracefully or that she entered the room gracefully? Either of these meanings may be expressed with clarity if the adverb *gracefully* is properly placed:

The girl who had been *gracefully* dancing entered the room. [*Gracefully* modifies *had been dancing.*]

The girl who had been dancing entered the room *gracefully.* [Here *gracefully* modifies *entered.*]

■ 15c Misplaced Words Like *Only, Nearly,* and *Almost*

Words such as *only, nearly,* and *almost* are frequently misplaced. Normally these modifying words should immediately precede the word they modify. To understand the importance of properly placing these modifiers, consider in the following sentences the different meanings that result when *only* is shifted:

Only I heard John shouting at the boys. [*Only* modifies *I.* Meaning: I was the only one who heard John shouting.]

I *only* heard John shouting at the boys. [*Only* modifies *heard.* Implied meaning: I heard but didn't see John shouting.]

I heard *only* John shouting at the boys. [*Only* modifies *John.* Meaning: John was the only one whom I heard shouting.]

I heard John *only* shouting at the boys. [*Only* modified *shouting.* Possible implied meaning: I didn't hear John hitting the boys — I heard him only shouting at them.]

I heard John shouting at the boys *only.* [*Only* modifies *boys.* Possible implied meaning: The boys were the ones I heard John shouting at — not the girls.]

Misplacing *only, nearly,* or *almost* will frequently result in an illogical statement:

ILLOGICAL: The baby *only* cried until he was six months old.

CORRECT: The baby cried *only* until he was six months old.

ILLOGICAL: Since his earnings amounted to $97.15, he *nearly* made a hundred dollars.

CORRECT: Since his earnings amounted to $97.15, he made *nearly* a hundred dollars.

ILLOGICAL: At the recent track meet Ralph *almost* jumped six feet.

CORRECT: At the recent track meet Ralph jumped *almost* six feet.

■ 15d Split Infinitives

A **split infinitive** is a construction in which the sign of the infinitive *to* has been separated from the verb with which it is associated. *To vigorously deny* and *to instantly be killed* are split infinitives. Unless emphasis or clarity demands its use, such a construction should be avoided:

AWKWARD: He always tries *to efficiently and promptly do* his work.

CORRECT: He always tries *to do* his work *efficiently and promptly*.

CORRECT: We expect *to more than double* our sales in April. [Placing the modifiers *more than* anywhere else in this sentence would result in ambiguity or changed meaning.]

Exercise 59   Misplaced Modifiers

Place **M** or **C** in the space at the right to indicate whether each sentence contains a misplaced modifier or is correct. Underline the misplaced words and indicate their proper position by means of a caret (∧). Use additional carets if there is more than one correct position.

Example: Someone has <u>nearly</u> eaten∧all the raspberry sherbet.   __M__

1. My mother read the latest book written by Anne Tyler while under the hair dryer.   _____

2. I make a serious mistake to under any circumstances debate Harvey.   _____

3. The first mountain climber reaching the summit breathlessly exclaimed at the view.   _____

4. We decided to hang the mirror on this wall that once belonged to Aunt Eliza.   _____

5. Although I have read both chapters, I have only taken notes on the first one.   _____

6. A review of the play is in today's *Globe*, which opened last week in Philadelphia.   _____

7. My friend who works in Canton now wants to find a job in San Francisco.   _____

8. The cat scooted out of the car and up the tree, nearly reaching the top in less than a minute.   _____

9. My brother enjoys any film starring John Wayne, who goes to Utah State.   _____

10. The rug is in the upstairs bedroom that my father brought from China.   _____

11. Ruth went to Bridgeport High School for only one year.   _____

12. Will you be able to deliver the balloons to my friend who is in the infirmary that I have selected?   _____

13. To further deal with the crisis, my parents called a meeting of the family council.   _____

14. The books were brought to the librarian that needed cataloging.   _____

15. The skater who slipped on the ice suddenly winced with pain.   _____

16. The house sold very quickly; it was just on the market a month.   _____

17. Because Amelia scarcely ate a bite of the pecan pie, I do believe that she is dieting again.   _____

18. They decided to avoid the road in need of paving for a while.   _____

19. The rain dripping from the eaves slowly lulled me to sleep.   _____

20. When driving on the New Jersey Turnpike, I hesitate to even for a moment take my eyes off the road.   _____

Exercise 60 Misplaced Modifiers

Place **M** or **C** in the space at the right to indicate whether each sentence contains a misplaced modifier or is correct. Underline the misplaced words and indicate their proper position by means of a caret (ʌ). Use additional carets if there is more than one correct position.

Example: On these winter afternoons one <u>just</u> gets homeʌbefore dark.   *M*

1. Sitting around the bonfire, we almost sang every camping song we knew.   _____

2. The cookbook says that we are to quickly brown the chops.   _____

3. Did you read the feature story about the shipwreck in this magazine?   _____

4. The woman who was humming quietly rocked her baby.   _____

5. The dog barked at the passing cars sitting in the back of the pick-up truck.   _____

6. Mr. Tyler disputed my estimation of Herbert Hoover, relaxed in his chair before the fire.   _____

7. The photocopier is out of order in the library.   _____

8. Those of us who played soccer consistently defended our right to the field on Saturday mornings.   _____

9. The three Christmas stockings were hung from the mantel, which had been knitted many years ago.   _____

10. I am glad to once and for all understand the requirements for graduation.   _____

11. Stewart often enjoyed feeding peanuts to the elephant at the zoo when he was a child.   _____

12. The grounds were landscaped by my friend in front of the mansion.   _____

13. Neither train stops for more than a minute in Gainesville.   _____

14. To reach his apartment, Norman only has to climb one flight of stairs.   _____

15. The watercolor that you saw was painted by a folk artist hanging at the top of the stairs.   _____

16. The shuttle bus stood in front of the hotel that was scheduled to leave in five minutes.   _____

17. Most of the afternoon my roommates listened to Bach and Beethoven, who have a music appreciation test tomorrow.   _____

18. Mr. Fernandez almost sees every movie that is shown at the Ritz Theater.   _____

19. The first day at sea she spent the morning reading the poems of Browning sitting in a deck chair.   _____

20. The reservations for dinner should only be made by one member of the committee.   _____

16

Parallelism

Frequently in writing and speaking you need to indicate equality of ideas. To show this equality, you should employ **parallel** grammatical constructions. In other words, convey parallel thought in parallel language; and conversely, use parallel language only when you are conveying parallel thoughts.

■ 16a Coordinate Elements

In employing parallelism, balance nouns against nouns, infinitives against infinitives, prepositional phrases against prepositional phrases, adjective clauses against adjective clauses, etc. Never make the mistake of saying, "I have always liked swimming and to fish." Because the object of *have liked* is two parallel ideas, you should say:

I have always liked *swimming* and *fishing*. (*And* joins two gerunds.)

OR

I have always liked *to swim* and *to fish*. (*And* joins two infinitives.)

Parallel prepositional phrases are illustrated in the following sentence. The parallel elements appear immediately after the double bar:

Government ‖ of the people,
            by the people,
and ‖ for the people shall not perish from the earth.

Next we see an illustration of parallel noun clauses:

He said ||| that he would remain in the East,
        ||| that his wife would travel through the Northwest,
   and || that his son would attend summer school in the South.

The following sentence contains parallel independent clauses:

||| I came;
||| I saw;
|| I conquered.

Parallel elements are usually joined either by simple coordinating conjunctions or by correlative conjunctions. The most common coordinating conjunctions used with parallel constructions are *and, but, or.* Whenever one of these connectives is used, you must be careful to see that the elements being joined are coordinate or parallel in construction:

FAULTY: Ann is a girl with executive ability and who therefore should be elected class president.

This sentence contains faulty parallelism, since *and* is used to join a phrase (*with executive ability*) and a dependent clause (*who therefore should be elected class president*). To correct the sentence, (1) expand the phrase into a *who* clause, or (2) make an independent clause of the *who* clause:

CORRECT: Ann is a girl ||| who has executive ability
           and ||| who therefore should be elected class president.

Note: A safe rule to follow is this: *And who* or *and which* should never be used unless preceded by another *who-* or *which*-clause.

ALSO CORRECT: ||| Ann is a girl with executive ability;
             || she therefore should be elected class president.

A common error results from making a construction appear to be parallel when actually it is not:

Mr. Lee is honest, intelligent, and works hard.

The structure of the sentence suggests an *a, b,* and *c* series; yet what we have is not three parallel elements but two adjectives (*honest, intelligent*) and a verb (*works*). The sentence can be corrected in two ways: we can use three adjectives in a series or two independent clauses in parallel construction, thus:

CORRECT: Mr. Lee is ||| honest,
               ||| intelligent,
         and || industrious.
ALSO CORRECT: ||| Mr. Lee is honest and intelligent,
       and || he works hard.

■ 16b Use of Correlative Conjunctions

Correlative conjunctions are used in pairs: *either . . . or . . . ; neither . . . nor . . . ; both . . . and . . . ; not only . . . but also . . . .* When these conjunctions are employed in a sentence, they must be followed by parallel constructions:

> INCORRECT: I hope *either* to spend my vacation in Mexico *or* Hawaii. [In this sentence *either* is followed by an infinitive, *or* by a noun.]

> CORRECT: I hope to spend my vacation either ‖ in Mexico
> or ‖ in Hawaii.

> ALSO CORRECT: I hope to spend my vacation in either ‖ Mexico
> or ‖ Hawaii.

> INCORRECT: She knew *not only* what to say, *but also* she knew when to say it.

> CORRECT: She knew not only ‖ what to say
> but also ‖ when to say it.

■ 16c Repetition of Certain Words

In order to make parallel constructions clear, you must sometimes repeat an article, a preposition, an auxiliary verb, the sign of the infinitive (*to*), or the introductory word of a dependent clause. Three of these types of necessary repetition are illustrated in the sentences that follow:

> OBSCURE: He must counsel all employees who participate in sports and also go on recruiting trips throughout the Southwest.

> CLEAR: He must counsel all employees who participate in sports and *must* also go on recruiting trips throughout the Southwest.

> OBSCURE: The instructor wants to meet those students who enjoy barber-shop harmony and organize several quartets.

> CLEAR: The instructor wants to meet those students who enjoy barber-shop harmony and *to* organize several quartets.

> OBSCURE: He thought that economic conditions were improving and the company was planning to increase its dividend rate.

> CLEAR: He thought that economic conditions were improving and *that* the company was planning to increase its dividend rate.

■ 16d *Than* and *As* in Parallel Constructions

Than and *as* are frequently used to join parallel constructions. When these two connectives introduce comparisons, you must be sure that the things compared are similar. Don't compare, for instance, a janitor's salary with a teacher. Compare a janitor's salary with a teacher's salary:

> INCORRECT: A janitor's salary is frequently larger than a teacher.
>
> CORRECT: ||| A janitor's salary is frequently larger
>   than ||| a teacher's (salary).

■ 16e Incorrect Omission of Necessary Words

A very common kind of faulty parallelism is seen in the following sentence:

> I always have and always will *remember* to send my first-grade teacher a Christmas card.

In this sentence *remember* is correctly used after *will,* but after *have* the form needed is *remembered.* Consequently, *remember* cannot serve as the understood participle after *have:*

> CORRECT: I ||| always have *remembered*
>   and ||| always will remember   to send my first-grade teacher
>   a Christmas card.

Other sentences containing similar errors are given below:

> INCORRECT: I *was* mildly surprised, but all of my friends gravely shocked. [After *all of my friends* the incorrect verb form *was* seems to be understood.]
>
> CORRECT: I was mildly surprised, but all of my friends *were* gravely shocked.
>
> INCORRECT: He gave me an apple and pear. [Before *pear* the incorrect form *an* seems to be understood.]
>
> CORRECT: He gave me an apple and *a* pear.
>
> INCORRECT: I was interested and astounded *by* the story of his latest adventure.
>
> CORRECT: I was ||| interested *in*
>   and ||| astounded by   the story of his latest adventure
>
> INCORRECT: She is as tall if not taller *than* her sister.
>
> CORRECT: She is as tall *as* her sister, if not taller. [The reader understands *than her sister.*]
>
> ALSO CORRECT: She is as tall *as,* if not taller than, her sister.

■ 16f Correct Use of "Unparallel" Constructions

A caution should be added to this lesson. Parallelism of phraseology is not always possible. When it is not, do not hesitate to use natural, "unparallel" constructions:

> CORRECT THOUGH "UNPARALLEL": He spoke *slowly* and *with dignity.*

Here *slowly* and *with dignity* are parallel in a sense: they are both adverbial modifiers.

Exercise 61 Parallelism

Rewrite in correct form all sentences that contain faulty parallelism. Note that some sentences may be corrected in more than one way. Write **C** if a sentence is correct.

Example: Tony is sensitive, artistic, and a gifted pianist.

Sensitive and artistic, Tony is a gifted pianist.

1. The chandelier in the foyer of the theater was large, handsome, and made of brass.

2. Pam is a fan of all jazz musicians but who especially enjoys Wynton Marsalis.

3. By five o'clock the manager's secretary is harried, tired, and wants to go home.

4. If we are going to use this recipe, you will have to buy a pepper, onion, and bunch of celery.

5. The magazine article traced not only the actor's career but also related some incidents from his childhood.

6. The parade began at the Civic Center, wound down Naples Boulevard, and then it turned into Brighton Park.

7. Always interested and concerned about others, Julia is a good friend to many people.

8. This band is as loud, if not louder, than any I have ever heard.

9. When we come back from skating, let's either make mulled cider or spiced tea.

10. Our postman is an interesting person: he writes limericks, plays the guitar, and he is a native Californian.

11. Gus hopes to major in marketing and after graduation that he will find a job in New York.

12. Isn't Hazel's telephone number similar to Roy?

13. While I was in Europe, I neither sent a card to Alice Ann nor to Eileen.

14. The sunroom has pale green walls, large windows, and opens into the garden.

15. I always have and always will prefer pistachio ice cream to any other kind.

16. Kelly wrote to tell me what the weather was like and the clothes to bring.

17. Did you know that Alfredo's caters for parties and serves both lunch and dinner?

18. I agree that Dick's tie looks better than Arnold.

19. Dr. Taylor should let all of us know that tonight's class has been canceled and tell us whether we will meet on Thursday night.

20. The winner of the cake-baking contest was very pleased with the judge, but the losers rather unhappy with him.

Exercise 62   Parallelism

Complete each of the following sentences by adding a construction that is parallel to the *italicized* construction.

Example: The car that drew up to the curb was *old, rusty,* and *dilapidated.*

1. Fashion authorities have predicted *that women's hats are coming back* _____

   _____

2. I have already heard about *John's interest in rock climbing* and _____

   _____

3. Ike not only *skis on Lake Lanier* but also _____

   _____

4. In spite of the heavy snow *the carolers ventured out,* and _____

   _____

5. At the back of my locker were *a notebook, a key to something or other,* and _____

   _____

   _____

6. Please *turn up the television* or _____

   _____

7. Not only *are Winifred's shelves filled with books,* but also _____

   _____

8. The reporter's knowledge of Mongolia was *negligible* and _____

   _____

9. Physical exercise is a subject *that Americans are increasingly interested in* and _____

   _____

10. In the marketplace the shopkeepers haggled *shrewdly* and _____

_____

17

Subordination

Parallelism enables you to indicate equality of ideas. More often, however, your writing will include sentences in which some ideas are more important than others. The main device for showing the difference between major and minor emphasis is **subordination:** reserve the independent clause for the main idea and use dependent clauses, phrases, and single words to convey subordinate ideas:

> In our garden there is a birdbath *that is carved from marble.* [Subordinate idea placed in a dependent clause.]

> In our garden there is a birdbath *carved from marble.* [Subordinate idea reduced to a participial phrase.]

> In our garden there is a *marble* birdbath. [Subordinate idea reduced to a one-word modifier.]

■ 17a Primer Style

It is necessary to understand the principle of subordination, for without subordination you would be unable to indicate the relative importance of ideas or their various shades of emphasis in your thinking. The following group of sentences is both childish and monotonous because six dissimilar ideas have been presented in six simple sentences and thus appear to be of equal importance:

> A pep meeting was held last Friday night. Memorial Stadium was the scene of the meeting. The meeting was attended by thousands of students. Over a hundred faculty members were there too. It rained Friday night. There was also some sleet.

As you know, coordinating conjunctions are used to join ideas of equal importance; consequently, the six sentences given above would not be improved if they were joined by such conjunctions. As a matter of fact, a type of sentence that you should avoid is the long, stringy one tied together by *and, but, so,* or *and so*. Instead of using this kind of sentence, weigh the relative importance of your several ideas, and show their importance by the use of main and subordinate sentence elements. Notice how the six ideas can be merged into one clear sentence:

> Despite rain and some sleet the pep meeting held last Friday night at Memorial Stadium was attended by thousands of students and over a hundred faculty members.

In combining the six sentences, the writer has chosen to use the fact about student and faculty attendance as the main idea. Another writer might have chosen otherwise, for there will not always be complete agreement as to which idea can be singled out and considered the most important. You may be sure, however, that if your sentence reads with emphasis and effectiveness you have chosen a correct idea as the main one.

■ 17b Upside-down Subordination

When there are only two ideas of unequal rank to be considered, you should have no difficulty in selecting the more important one:

1. He showed some signs of fatigue.
2. He easily won the National Open Golf Tournament.

Of these two sentences the second is undoubtedly the more important. Hence, when the two sentences are combined, the second should stand as the independent clause, and the first should be reduced to a dependent clause or even a phrase. If you made an independent clause of the first sentence and a subordinate element of the second, your sentence would contain upside-down subordination:

> FAULTY (upside-down subordination): Though he easily won the National Open Golf Tournament, he showed some signs of fatigue.
>
> CORRECT: Though he showed some signs of fatigue, he easily won the National Open Golf Tournament.

■ 17c Choice of Subordinating Conjunctions

In introducing a subordinate element, be sure that you choose the right subordinating conjunction. The following sentences illustrate the correct use of certain conjunctions:

> I don't know *whether* (or *that*; not *as* or *if*) I can see you tomorrow.
>
> *Although* (not *while*) she isn't a genius, she has undeniable talent.
>
> I saw in the autobiography of the actor *that* (not *where*) there is a question about the exact date of his birth.

(See Glossary of Faulty Diction in Chapter 22 for further discussion of accurate word choice.)

Exercise 63 Subordination

Combine the ideas in each of the following groups of sentences into one effective simple or complex sentence.

Example: Joseph Conrad was a novelist.
He was born in Poland.
He chose to write in English.

Although the novelist Joseph Conrad was born in Poland, he chose to write in English.

1. Edward Hopper was an American painter.
   He was born in 1882.
   He died in 1967.
   His most famous painting is possibly *Nighthawks*.

2. Thirty-two states comprise the United States of Mexico.
   The Distrito Federal has the largest population.
   It covers the smallest area.
   Its capital is Mexico City.

3. There is a modern flower identified as the "hyacinth."
   It is native to countries surrounding the Mediterranean Sea.
   It is not the same flower that honored the slain Hyacinthus.
   Hyacinthus is a youth in Greek mythology.

4. Robert Zimmerman is a musician and songwriter.
   He is better known as Bob Dylan.
   He selected his stage name because of his admiration for Dylan Thomas.
   Dylan Thomas was a Welsh writer.

5. The American Quarter Horse Association keeps a registry of quarter horses.
   It was founded in 1940.
   Quarter horses were first developed in the American colonies.
   Their name is derived from their special ability to run a quarter-mile course.

6. *A Farewell to Arms* is a novel written by Ernest Hemingway.
   Its principal female character is Catherine Barkley.
   She is an English nurse.
   She falls in love with Lt. Frederic Henry.
   He is a driver with an Italian ambulance unit.

7. The Kingdom of Saudi Arabia occupies a large portion of the Arabian Peninsula.
   Mecca is in Saudi Arabia.
   It is the second most populous city of the country.
   It is the birthplace of Muhammad.
   It is the holy city of Islam.

8. Sandra Day O'Connor is an associate justice on the United States Supreme Court.
   She is the first woman to serve on the Supreme Court.
   She was appointed by Ronald Reagan.

9. George Gallup was at one time a college professor.
   Then he was a director of marketing.
   He founded the American Institute of Public Opinion.
   It has become known as the Gallup Poll.

Exercise 64   Subordination

Combine the ideas in each of the following groups of sentences into one effective simple or complex sentence.

Example: Gemini is the name of a constellation.
It contains the stars Castor and Pollux.
It is also the name of the third sign of the zodiac.

Gemini, the name of a constellation containing the stars Castor and Pollux, is also the name of the third sign of the zodiac.

1. The snow leopard lives in the mountains of Central Asia.
This large cat is also known as an "ounce."
It has white fur with black spots.

2. Henry Ford was principally responsible for the design of the Model T car.
The first one appeared in 1908.
The last one was produced in 1927.
During this period fifteen million Model T's were sold.

3. Barbara Jordan is from Texas.
She served three terms in the United States House of Representatives.
She is a professor in the Lyndon B. Johnson School of Public Affairs.
The school is a part of the University of Texas.

4. John Peter Zenger was the printer and publisher of the New York *Weekly Journal.*
He was tried for seditious libel in August, 1735.
He was successfully defended by Andrew Hamilton.
Andrew Hamilton was an outstanding Philadelphia lawyer.

5. The Indian Ocean is the third-largest body of water on earth.
   Its deepest area runs parallel to the islands of Sumatra and Java.
   This area is known as the Java Trench.

6. George Stewart is the author of a book entitled *American Place Names.*
   In it he notes that "Los Angeles" is Spanish for "the angels."
   He also points out that "Los Angeles" is the shortened form of "Our Lady of the Angels of the Little Portion."

7. The Guggenheim Museum is in New York City.
   Its building was designed by Frank Lloyd Wright.
   The museum is noted for this building.
   It is also noted for its collections of Impressionist and Neo-Impressionist paintings.

8. Historians are not certain where playing cards originated.
   Perhaps they were first used in the Near East.
   Perhaps they originated in the Far East.
   Historians do agree that Tarots or Tarot cards were the forerunners of our modern deck of cards.

9. Barbara McClintock is an American geneticist.
   She was educated at Cornell University.
   She received the Nobel Prize for Medicine or Physiology in 1983.
   At the time she was eighty-one years old.

Exercise 65 Subordination

The following sentences contain upside-down subordination or too much coordination. Rewrite each sentence to make it an effective simple or complex sentence.

Example: It was New Year's Eve, and I had a date with Jim Ridley, and we went to a party at the Levins' house.

On New Year's Eve Jim Ridley and I went to a party at the Levins' house.

1. Beginning to enjoy her first solo flight, the pilot gained confidence.

2. Watching the canoe make its way up the river, Tarzan stood on the bluff.

3. I have a Japanese friend, and she is in my economics class, and she has explained the Japanese monetary system to me.

4. Crossing the finish line in almost record time, Carl was well ahead of the other runners.

5. Margaret Atwood is from Canada, and she is a noted novelist, and she is also well known for her poetry.

6. The Department of Math and Science has bought a word processor, and I am going to learn to use it, and then I will not have to retype long reports.

7. Paul Douglas, who taught economics at the University of Chicago and represented Illinois in the United States Senate, was born in Salem, Massachusetts.

8. As the pair searched for the sunken vessel, they dived again and again into the cold waters.

9. Gabrielle Chanel was a French fashion designer, and she died in 1971, but her influence is still seen in women's clothes.

10. Talking as loudly as possible, Benito recognized that the woman asking directions was deaf.

Exercise 66 Subordination

The following sentences contain upside-down subordination or too much coordination. Rewrite each sentence to make it an effective simple or complex sentence.

Example: When I saw the terrible accident, I was driving to class.

When driving to class, I saw the terrible accident.

1. Trying desperately to keep from drowning, I flailed my arms about in the water.

2. We walked cautiously through the heavily wooded area, and we tried not to make a sound, for we didn't want to give away our presence.

3. After I learned that I had won the thousand-dollar lottery, I went to lunch.

4. The author of dozens of excellent mystery novels, Agatha Christie was an Englishwoman.

5. Running out of gas when I was halfway home, it was about ten o'clock.

6. As she told us the exciting news of her engagement, Margot smiled broadly.

7. Shaking the weeping child, the exasperated mother seemed very tired.

8. When I heard a loud scream from inside the house, I was knocking on the front door.

9. Having a picture taken by the school photographer, our entire class stood there on the steps.

10. The thunderstorm, which delayed our arrival at the hotel by about two hours, had started just after we left home.

18

Illogical Comparisons and Mixed Constructions

Correctness and clarity are essential to good writing. To reach these goals, you must know the rules of grammar and punctuation. But further, you must think logically and find the exact words in which to express your thoughts. Nothing is more bothersome to a reader than inexact, illogical, or confusing sentences. Some of the lessons that you have already studied have shown how to avoid errors that produce vagueness or confusion in writing; among these errors are faulty reference of pronouns, dangling or misplaced modifiers, and upside-down subordination. This lesson will consider certain other errors that obstruct clarity of expression.

■ 18a Illogical Comparisons

When you make comparisons, you must be sure not only that the things compared are similar (a matter considered in the lesson on parallelism) but also that all necessary elements of the comparison are included.

Note the following sentence:

Harold is taller than any boy in his class.

Since *Harold,* the first term of the comparison, is included in the classification *any boy in his class,* the comparison is obviously illogical: the sentence might be interpreted to mean *Harold is taller than Harold.* The first term of the comparison must, therefore, be compared with a second term or classification that excludes the first term, thus:

CORRECT: Harold is taller than any *other* boy in his class.

ALSO CORRECT: Harold is taller than any *girl* in his class.

When the superlative is followed by *of*, the object of *of* must be plural:

ILLOGICAL: Harold is the tallest of any other boy in his class.

CORRECT: Harold is the tallest of *all the boys* in his class.

ALSO CORRECT: Harold is the *tallest boy* in his class.

Ambiguity results from a comparison like this one:

I helped you more than Jim.

Does the sentence mean *I helped you more than I helped Jim* or *I helped you more than Jim did*? The writer should use one sentence or the other, according to whichever meaning is intended.

The type of incomplete comparison illustrated by the following vague sentences is particularly popular with writers of advertising copy and with careless speakers:

VAGUE: Eastern Rubber Company makes a tire that gives 20 percent more mileage.

CLEAR: Eastern Rubber Company makes a tire that gives 20 percent more mileage *than any tire it made ten years ago.*

ALSO CLEAR: Eastern Rubber Company makes a tire that gives 20 percent more mileage *than any other tire made in the United States.*

VAGUE: Litter is more of a problem in cities.

CLEAR: Litter is more of a problem in cities *than in small towns.*

ALSO CLEAR: Litter is more of a problem in cities *than it used to be.*

■ 18b Mixed or Confused Constructions

Mixed constructions are frequently the result of some sort of shift in a sentence. Through ignorance or forgetfulness the writer starts a sentence with one type of construction and then switches to another. Notice the shift of construction in the following sentence:

She bought an old, dilapidated house, which having it extensively repaired converted it into a comfortable home.

The sentence reads correctly through the relative pronoun *which*. The reader expects *which* to introduce an adjective clause; however, he is unable to find a verb for *which*. Instead, he finds that the sentence is completed by a construction in which a gerund phrase stands as the subject of the verb *converted*. The sentence may be corrected in various ways. Two correct versions follow:

She bought an old, dilapidated house, which after extensive repairs was converted into a comfortable home.

By means of extensive repairs she converted into a comfortable home an old, dilapidated house which she had bought.

Other examples of mixed constructions are given below:

MIXED: Bob realized that during the conference how inattentive he had been. [This sentence is confusing because *that* as used here is a subordinating conjunction and should introduce a noun clause. However, the *that*-construction is left incomplete. Further on, *how* introduces a noun clause. What we find then is only one noun clause but two words, *that* and *how*, used to introduce noun clauses. Obviously, only one such word should introduce the one dependent clause.]

CORRECT: Bob realized that during the conference he had been inattentive.

ALSO CORRECT: Bob realized how inattentive he had been during the conference.

MIXED: Because she had to work in the library kept her from attending the party. [A dependent clause introduced by *because* is always adverbial; hence such a clause can never be used as the subject of a sentence.]

CORRECT: Having to work in the library kept her from attending the party.

ALSO CORRECT: Because she had to work in the library, she could not attend the party.

MIXED: He pulled a leg muscle was why he failed to place in the broad jump. [He *pulled a leg muscle* is an independent clause used here as the subject of *was*. An independent clause, unless it is a quotation, can never be used as the subject of a sentence.]

CORRECT: Because he pulled a leg muscle, he failed to place in the broad jump.

MIXED: By attending the reception as a guest rather than as a butler was a new experience for him. [The preposition *by* introduces a modifying phrase, and a modifying phrase can never be used as the subject of a sentence.]

CORRECT: Attending the reception as a guest rather than as a butler was a new experience for him.

ALSO CORRECT: By attending the reception as a guest rather than as a butler, he enjoyed a new experience.

MIXED: A pronoun is when a word is used in the place of a noun. [Never use *is when* or *is where* in defining a word. Remember that an adverbial *when-* or *where*-clause cannot be used as a predicate nominative.]

CORRECT: A pronoun is a word used in the place of a noun.

MIXED: I was the one about whom she was whispering to my father about. [To correct this sentence, omit either *about*.]

MIXED: We know that if he were interested in our offer that he would come to see us. [To correct this sentence, omit the second *that*. The first *that* introduces the noun clause *that . . . he would come to see us. If he were interested in our offer* is an adverbial clause within the noun clause.]

MIXED: The reason I didn't play well at the recital was because I had sprained my little finger. [This very common error again illustrates the incorrect use of a dependent adverbial clause, introduced by *because*, as a predicate nominative. To correct the mistake, use a noun clause, introduced by *that*.]

CORRECT: The reason I didn't play well at the recital was that I had sprained my little finger.

Exercise 67 — Illogical Comparisons and Mixed Constructions

The following sentences contain illogical or ambiguous comparisons and mixed constructions. Rewrite each sentence in a correct form. (Notice that some sentences permit more than one correct interpretation.)

Example: Horace's Irish setter has the shiniest coat.

Horace's Irish setter has a shiny coat.

Horace's Irish setter has the shiniest coat of all the dogs I have seen.

1. St. Augustine is a quaint and beautiful city and which is on Florida's East Coast.

2. I told you, Suzanne, that after walking to class and home again how tired you would be.

3. Hospitality is when a host is friendly and generous in the entertainment of guests.

4. After trying for two hours to get Helen on the phone was when I suddenly remembered that she was out of town for the day.

5. Tom needn't think that just because his father knows the professor that he can neglect his assignments.

6. Hank had a really grand vacation, and it was much longer than Jake or Donna.

7. Stanley says that, oddly enough, he is closer to his cousin than his sister.

8. By using a drop cloth will save cleaning up when you finish painting.

9. Marcia has learned computer science faster than anyone in her class.

10. Because Fred would not help me with the dishes was why I didn't get to the meeting on time.

11. Foster says that he is the brainiest of any other English major.

12. Bragging all the time is the reason why Foster has fewer friends.

13. Tim remarked that he had always felt like that success is not necessarily a matter of money.

14. The mysterious woman was dressed all in purple and whom no one at the party seemed to know.

15. Edwin confessed that all his life how he had wanted to perform on television.

16. If you use that curved knife, Gloria, you can get more mayonnaise from the bottom of the jar.

17. My first experience at skiing was like most beginners.

18. That day on the slopes I learned that I was not the best of any athlete I know.

19. For the beginning skier, humility is when one loses all dignity after dozens of tumbles.

20. We saw Marian pedaling her bicycle toward town and who we had thought was home in bed.

21. A round-trip ticket to Chicago is much cheaper, Joan.

22. Ted and Diana are the couple about whom I was telling you about.

23. The reason why I called so late last night is because I wanted you to be ready to leave by seven o'clock today.

24. The makers of margarine have often stated that their product has fewer calories.

25. I admire you more than anyone.

19

Punctuation

Punctuation depends largely upon the grammatical structure of a sentence. In order to punctuate correctly, you must therefore understand grammatical elements. For this reason, rules of punctuation in this text have been correlated, whenever applicable, with your study of grammar and sentence structure. You learned, for instance, how to punctuate certain phrases when you studied the phrase as a sentence unit.

In order that this chapter may present a reasonably complete treatment of punctuation, you will find on the pages that follow a summary of the rules already studied, as well as reference by chapter to additional rules. The rules given below have become to a large extent standardized; hence they should be clearly understood and practiced. Following the principle of punctuating "by ear" or of using a comma wherever there is a vocal pause results in an arbitrary and frequently misleading use of punctuation.

■ 19a Terminal Marks

The terminal marks of punctuation — that is, those marks used to end a sentence — are the period, the question mark, and the exclamation mark.

Use a period after a declarative sentence, an imperative sentence, or an indirect question:

DECLARATIVE: John answered the telephone.

IMPERATIVE: Answer the telephone.

INDIRECT QUESTION: She asked whether John had answered the telephone.

Note: A request that is stated as a polite question should be followed by a period. Such a request frequently occurs in business correspondence:

Will you please send me your special summer catalog.

Use a period also after most abbreviations:

Mr., Ms., Dr., B.S., Jr., i.e., viz., etc., A.D., B.C., A.M., P.M.

Use three periods to indicate an omission of a word or words within a quoted sentence, three periods plus a terminal mark to indicate an omission at the end of a quoted sentence:

"Fourscore and seven years ago our fathers brought forth . . . a new nation . . . ."

Use a question mark after a direct question:

Did John answer the telephone?

"Have you finished your work?" she asked.

Use an exclamation mark after an expression of strong feeling. This mark of punctuation should be used sparingly:

"Halt!" he shouted.

How disgusting!

There goes the fox!

■ 19b The Comma

1. Use a comma to separate independent clauses when they are joined by the coordinating conjunctions *and, but, or, nor, for, so,* and *yet.* (See Chapter 6.)

The game was over, but the crowd refused to leave the park.

If the clauses are long or are complicated by internal punctuation, use a semicolon instead of a comma. (See 19c, Rule 3.)

2. Use a comma to separate words, phrases, and clauses written as a series of three or more coordinate elements. This rule covers short independent clauses when used in a series, as shown in the third example sentence below.

A trio composed of Marie, Ellen, and Frances sang at the party.

Jack walked into my office, took off his hat, and sat down.

I washed the dishes, I dried them, and I put them away.

3. Use a comma to separate two or more coordinate adjectives that modify the same noun:

The noisy, enthusiastic freshman class assembled in Section F of the stadium. [*Noisy* and *enthusiastic* are coordinate adjectives; therefore they are separated by a comma. But *freshman,* though an adjective, is not coordinate with *noisy* and *enthusiastic;*

actually *noisy* and *enthusiastic* modify not just *class* but the word group *freshman class*. Hence no comma precedes *freshman*.]

To determine whether adjectives are coordinate, you may make two tests: if they are coordinate, you will be able (1) to join them with *and* or (2) to interchange their positions in the sentence. You can certainly say *the noisy and enthusiastic freshman class* or *the enthusiastic, noisy freshman class;* thus *noisy* and *enthusiastic* are clearly coordinate. However, to say *the noisy and freshman class* or *the freshman noisy class* would be absurd; thus *freshman* is not structurally parallel with *noisy*:

a blue wool suit [Adjectives not coordinate.]

an expensive, well-tailored suit [Adjectives coordinate.]

a new tennis court [Adjectives not coordinate.]

a muddy, rough court [Adjectives coordinate.]

4. Use a comma to separate sharply contrasted coordinate elements:

He was merely ignorant, not stupid.

5. Use commas to set off all nonessential modifiers. Do not set off essential modifiers. (See Chapter 5 for a discussion of essential and nonessential phrases; see Chapter 7 for a discussion of essential and nonessential clauses.)

NONESSENTIAL CLAUSE: Sara Sessions, *who is wearing red shorts today*, was voted the most versatile girl in her class.

NONESSENTIAL PHRASE: Sara Sessions, *wearing red shorts today*, was voted the most versatile girl in her class.

ESSENTIAL CLAUSE: The girl *who is wearing red shorts today* is Sara Sessions.

ESSENTIAL PHRASE: The girl *wearing red shorts today* is Sara Sessions.

6. Use a comma after an introductory adverbial clause, verbal phrase, or absolute phrase. (See Chapter 7 for a discussion of dependent clauses, Chapter 5 for a discussion of phrases).

INTRODUCTORY ADVERBIAL CLAUSE: *When he arose to give his speech*, he was greeted with thunderous applause.

INTRODUCTORY PARTICIPIAL PHRASE: *Being in a hurry*, I was able to see him only briefly.

INTRODUCTORY GERUND PHRASE: *On turning the corner*, Tom ran squarely into a police officer.

INTRODUCTORY INFINITIVE PHRASE: *To get a seat*, we have to arrive by 7:30 P.M.

INTRODUCTORY ABSOLUTE PHRASE: *My schedule having been arranged*, I felt like a full-fledged college freshman.

7. Use commas to set off nonessential appositives. (See Chapter 5.)

Tom, *the captain of the team*, was injured in the first game of the season.

Sometimes an appositive is so closely "fused" with its preceding word that it constitutes an essential element in the sentence and thus is not set off by commas:

William *the Conqueror* died in 1087.

The poet *Keats* spent his last days in Italy.

The word *bonfire* has an interesting history.

8. Use commas to set off items in dates, geographical names, and addresses and to set off titles after names:

July 22, 1977, was a momentous day in his life.

Birmingham, Alabama, gets its name from Birmingham, England.

Do you know who lives at 1600 Pennsylvania Avenue, Washington, D.C.?

Alfred E. Timberlake, Ph.D., will be the principal speaker.

9. Use commas to set off words used in direct address:

It is up to you, *Dot*, to push the campaign.

I think, *sir*, that I am correct.

You, *my fellow Americans*, must aid in the fight against inflation.

10. Use a comma after a mild interjection and after *yes* and *no*:

Oh, I suppose you're right.

Yes, I will be glad to go.

11. Use a comma to separate an independent clause from a question dependent on the clause:

You will try to do the work, won't you?

12. Use commas to set off expressions like *he said* or *she replied* when they interrupt a sentence of direct quotation. (But see Rule 1 under The Semicolon, below.)

"I was able," *she replied*, "to build the bookcase in less than an hour."

13. Use commas to set off certain parenthetic elements:

I was, *however*, too tired to make the trip.

My hopes, *to tell the truth*, had fallen to a low ebb.

14. Use a comma to prevent the misreading of a sentence:

Above, the mountains rose like purple shadows.

To John, Harrison had been a sort of idol.

■ 19c The Semicolon

1. Use a semicolon to separate independent clauses when they are not joined by *and*, *but*, *or*, *nor*, *for*, *so* or *yet*. (See Chapter 6.)

Wade held the ball for an instant; then he passed it to West.

"He is sick," she said; "therefore, he will not come."

2. Use a semicolon to separate coordinate elements that are joined by a coordinating conjunction but that are internally punctuated:

His tour included concert appearances in Austin, Texas; Little Rock, Arkansas; Tulsa, Oklahoma; and Kansas City, Kansas.

3. Use a semicolon to punctuate independent clauses that are joined by a coordinating conjunction in sentences that are heavily punctuated with commas internally:

Having invited Sara, Susan, and Leon to my party, I began, at long last, to plan the menu; but I could not decide on a dessert.

■ 19d The Colon

1. Use a colon after a clause that introduces a formal list. Do not use a colon unless the words preceding the list form a complete statement:

INCORRECT: The poets I like best are: Housman, Yeats, and Eliot.

CORRECT: The poets I like best are these: Housman, Yeats, and Eliot.

ALSO CORRECT: The poets I like best are Housman, Yeats, and Eliot.

INCORRECT: The basket was filled with: apples, oranges, and bananas.

CORRECT: The basket was filled with the following fruits: apples, oranges, and bananas.

ALSO CORRECT: The basket was filled with apples, oranges, and bananas.

2. Use a colon after a statement that introduces an explanation or amplification of that statement:

One characteristic accounted for his success: complete honesty. [A dash, which is less formal than the colon, may be substituted for the colon in this sentence.]

There was only one way to solve the mystery: we had to find the missing letter.

3. Use a colon after expressions like *he said* when they introduce a long and formal quotation:

The speaker rose to his feet and said: "Students and teachers, I wish to call your attention to . . . ."

4. Use a colon after the formal salutation of a letter, between the hour and minute figures in time designations, between a chapter and verse reference from the Bible, and between a title and subtitle:

Dear Sir:

8:40 P.M.

John 3:16

Victorian England: Portrait of an Age

■ 19e The Dash

1. Use a dash to indicate an abrupt shift or break in the thought of a sentence or to set off an informal or emphatic parenthesis:

Harvey decided to go to — but you wouldn't be interested in that story.

Mary told me — would you believe it? — that she preferred a quiet vacation at home.

At the age of three — such is the power of youth — Mary could stand on her head.

2. Use dashes to set off an appositive or a parenthetic element that is internally punctuated:

Her roommates — Jane, Laura, and Ruth — are spending the weekend with her.

■ 19f Quotation Marks

1. Use quotation marks to enclose direct quotations, but do not use them to enclose indirect quotations:

INCORRECT: He said that "I was old enough to know better."

CORRECT: He said, "You are old enough to know better."

ALSO CORRECT: He said that I was old enough to know better.

If a direct quotation is interrupted by an expression like *he said*, use quotation marks to enclose only the quoted material. This necessitates the use of two sets of quotation marks:

INCORRECT: "It's just possible, Mary responded, that I'll get up before six in the morning."

CORRECT: "It's just possible," Mary responded, "that I'll get up before six in the morning."

If there are two or more consecutive sentences of quoted material, use only one set of quotation marks to enclose all the sentences, not one set for each sentence:

INCORRECT: Ruby shouted, "Wait for me." "I'll be ready in two minutes."

CORRECT: Ruby shouted, "Wait for me. I'll be ready in two minutes."

Use single marks to enclose a quotation within a quotation:

The instructor asked, "Who said, 'Change the name of Arkansas? Never!'?"

Place the comma and the period inside the quotation marks, the semicolon and colon outside. Place the question mark and exclamation mark inside the quotation marks when they apply to the quoted material, outside when they apply to the entire sentence:

"Of course," he replied, "I remember you." [Comma and period inside the quotation marks.]

Her favorite poem was Kipling's "If."

Several times the witness said, "I swear to the truth of my statement"; yet the jury remained unconvinced. [Semicolon outside the quotation marks.]

He asked, "Where are you going?" [The question mark comes within the quotation marks because only the quoted material is a question.]

Did she definitely say, "I accept your invitation"? [The question mark comes outside the quotation marks because the entire sentence is a question.]

2. Use quotation marks to enclose the titles of short works (short stories, short poems, articles, one-act plays, songs, and speeches) and of smaller units of books. (See Rule 3 under Italics, Chapter 20, Section b.)

Benét's story "The Devil and Daniel Webster" was first published in the *Saturday Evening Post*.

The kindergarten children sang "America" for us.

"Who Will Be the New Bishop?" is the title of the first chapter of *Barchester Towers*.

3. Use quotation marks to enclose words taken from special vocabularies or used in a special sense:

All the money he had won on the quiz program was invested in "blue chips."

In certain sections of the United States a man who is both honest and good-natured is known as a "clever man."

■ 19g Parentheses

Use parentheses to enclose certain parenthetic elements. From a study of the preceding marks of punctuation you will remember that commas and dashes are also used to set off parenthetic material. There are no clearly defined rules by which you can always determine which marks to use. In general, however, commas are used to set off a parenthetic element that is fairly closely connected with the thought of the sentence. Dashes are used to set off a loosely connected element such as an abrupt break in the thought of the sentence; they tend to emphasize the element set off. Parentheses are used to enclose (1) material that is supplementary or explanatory and (2) figures repeated to ensure accuracy or used to designate an enumeration. An element enclosed by parentheses is usually even more loosely connected with the sentence than one set off by dashes; and parentheses, unlike dashes, tend to minimize the element set off:

The *Ville de Nantes* (see Plate 5) is a large, semidouble, red and white camellia.

I am enclosing a check for thirty-five dollars ($35.00).

Please write on the card (1) your full name, (2) your home address, and (3) a parent's or guardian's full name.

■ 19h Brackets

Use brackets to enclose any interpolation, or insertion, that you add to material being quoted. (You will note that in this text brackets are used to enclose explanations that follow illustrative sentences.)

In September, 1793, Robert Burns wrote a letter that included this sentence: "So may God ever defend the cause of truth and liberty as he did that day [the day of Bruce's victory over Edward II at Bannockburn]."

If one parenthetical expression falls within another, then brackets replace the inner parentheses:

Thomas Turner, a member of the Class of 1981 (Mr. Turner was his class valedictorian [See Athens *Banner-Herald* story, May 16, 1981] and class president), has been named a Rhodes Scholar.

Exercise 68 The Comma

In the following sentences insert commas wherever they are needed or remove them if they are not needed. If a sentence is punctuated correctly, mark it **C**.

Example: Well ∧ John ∧ you should have warned me that a thunder-storm was on the way.

1. After you have caught the lobsters the next step is to remove them from the trap without getting nipped.

2. You and Barry have already signed up for Computer Science 201 haven't you Pauline?

3. You will see the point I am trying to make once you fully understand the problem.

4. Being hungry and out of sorts I answered you rather rudely I'm afraid.

5. My mother who has always been very shy surprised us when she spoke up so positively during the argument.

6. Fran Eloise and Hope spent their vacation together on the Outer Banks of North Carolina.

7. My new red jogging suit is warm and comfortable.

8. Sally you should walk not run up that steep hill to the waterfall.

9. Before mixing the cake batter remember to preheat the oven.

10. The youngest Little League player Timmy Franklin is easily our best hitter.

11. Mary Sue decided to see the movie through again but I went to bed.

12. After all we have both seen *Casablanca* about six times.

13. When Bogart says "Here's looking at you kid" I admit it's a touching moment.

14. Of course there is a haunting quality about the song "As Time Goes By."

15. New Orleans Louisiana is a fascinating city with its French Quarter its marvelous food and its jazz musicians.

16. To be honest I do not think that your plan is advisable Frank.

17. Below the snow-capped Rockies were clearly visible from my seat in the plane.

18. Many people say that Thomas Hardy's novel *The Return of the Native* is the book most likely to put them to sleep.

19. The Hardy novel is certainly a worthy candidate but I would have to cast my vote for Dickens's *Hard Times*.

20. Jerry bought his soft drink opened it and drank the whole thing in just one swallow.

21. On January 25 1985 the University of Georgia celebrated its bicentennial.

22. The neat attractive girl was applying for a job in the new fast-food restaurant near the campus.

23. Why whoever told you that I am leaving school is badly mistaken.

24. The word *don't* has very little meaning for a two-year-old.

25. The Reverend Michael Fox D.D. will speak at our parish meeting on Thursday night.

26. To avoid hitting the dog I had to swerve sharply almost hitting a large oak tree.

27. Her beautiful blue cashmere coat has a satin lining.

28. My Aunt Martha who plays the piano by ear has decided to join a Dixieland band.

29. I can't wait to hear her tear into that wonderful old Dixieland tune "Yellow Dog Blues."

30. I know that Jim is planning to go to law school yet who can be sure at this point?

31. The man who taught me Latin is now ninety-one years old.

32. Without knowing who will show up for the party I find it hard to plan refreshments.

33. Eric the Red was an early Scandinavian explorer who discovered and colonized Greenland.

Exercise 69 The Comma

In the following sentences insert commas wherever they are needed or remove them if they are not needed. If a sentence is punctuated correctly, mark it **C**.

Example: After running five miles∧Ted took a hot shower and went to bed.

1. William upset over moving to another town felt that he would never make new friends as good as his old ones.

2. Mississippi author Eudora Welty has a fine comic touch in all her fiction.

3. The shifty-eyed shabbily dressed stranger moved furtively toward the back door.

4. The jury having rendered its verdict the defendant burst into tears of joy.

5. I knocked at the door I rang the doorbell and I finally peered in the window.

6. For Sara Franklin's appearance on the scene was a lifesaver.

7. In conclusion I want to thank all the friends who contributed to this party in my honor.

8. To you Marcia who made this unforgettable turnip casserole go my special thanks.

9. Furthermore I am grateful for the hours it must have taken Joan to prepare this memorable dessert of marshmallows chocolate chips and molasses topping.

10. "I am sure" Harriet added "that we will all sleep soundly after a dose or two of Alka-Seltzer."

11. Jack returned from his vacation exhausted and frustrated not rested and happy.

12. Even though we visited interesting spots in Rome we were frantic about Maria's continuing absence.

13. Our friend had last been seen talking with a dark-haired woman an Italian just before she disappeared.

14. Later we saw the woman near the Colosseum; however she professed to have no knowledge of our friend.

15. When we returned to the hotel Maria was there having merely asked the woman where to find some water and having missed the bus as a result.

16. Having to get up every morning at six, is a big problem for Billy.

17. Billy's roommates say, that the alarm clock has no effect on him.

18. He has trained himself to say in his sleep that his first class is not meeting that day.

19. Suzanne our cousin from Illinois is a big fan of the Chicago Cubs.

20. The bubbling sparkling fountain in our neighbors' garden is full of lovely colorful goldfish.

21. My green polyester raincoat matches my new plastic umbrella.

22. Since you have been away from home the town has changed a great deal.

23. You won't find Buster's hamburger stand on the corner of Tenth and Broad Streets any more; however there is a fried chicken place there now.

24. My dictionary lists fifteen meanings for the word *charge*.

25. Speaking quite loudly George complained that his coffee was cold and that his ice cream had melted.

26. Looking up he saw the restaurant proprietor stalking toward him; the man all three hundred pounds of him looked distinctly threatening.

27. George smiled weakly and said that he was only joking.

28. Matt said to forward all his mail to 199 Crescent Avenue Burlington North Carolina.

29. Helen's friends say that she is not being snobbish merely absent-minded when she fails to speak.

30. The apartment was dark and the only sound was the steady breathing of Lad my big collie.

Exercise 70 The Colon and the Dash

In the following sentences insert colons and dashes wherever they are needed or remove them if they are not needed. If a sentence is correctly punctuated, mark it **C**.

Example: The hiding place for the stolen emerald was a clever one () the bottom of a green glass vase.
∧

1. I'm trying my best to keep up with my regular assignments, but sometimes oh, well, you've had the same experience.

2. Those who contributed either work or money to our fund drive include Scott, Fred, Peggy, Liz, and Theo.

3. Marty gave us each a wonderful gift can you imagine? a pretty porcelain figurine.

4. All freshmen will be required to follow this rule do not start eating your lunch until all upperclassmen at your table have started.

5. Henry says that he is not interested in the money his father is a millionaire, you know and he will be glad to work without pay.

6. Ms. Halliday said, "The plane leaves Tampa at 5 25 P.M. on Wednesday."

7. Wayne's three medical colleagues Drs. Wright, Penfield, and Williams are all from the same state Alabama.

8. There is only one question I have for you, Frieda how did you keep the surprise party a surprise?

9. My irate letter to the IRS began as follows "Dear Sirs You have once again confused my name with my sister's."

10. The following chapters in your text will be covered on the midterm test One, Two, Three, Six, and Seven.

11. London is a lively city, and there is always wonderful entertainment, including oh, by the way, have you seen that amusing comedy *Noises Off*?

12. When I was four that's before I could swim I fell out of Father's fishing boat and into the lake.

13. The Italian foods I love are: spaghetti, fettuccine, ravioli, and lasagna.

14. The headwaiter was quite formal "Sir and Madam," he said, "I will escort you to your table."

15. In Georgia people are fond of boiled peanuts and yes, I said boiled! often take them in jars to eat at football games.

16. Boiled peanuts are a bit mushy; however, they have a delicious flavor, and oh, Mary, of course people take the shells off before eating them.

17. The quotation you are looking for, Mildred, is St. Luke 2 8.

18. Now, children, here is the spelling list for your next Tommy, will you stop that giggling!

19. The best book I have read this year is titled *Hamilton Peters Man of Destiny*.

20. My poor dog has had fleas this summer, and I am desperate for a oh my, not another folk remedy, please.

Exercise 71   Quotation Marks

In the following sentences insert quotation marks wherever they are needed. Remove those not needed and replace them with the proper marks of punctuation or mechanics where necessary. If a sentence is correctly punctuated, mark it **C**.

Example: You should read Poe's short story ˇThe Purloined Letter[;ˇ it is said to be the forerunner of today's mystery fiction.

1. A man with a new idea is a crank, wrote Mark Twain, until his idea comes true.

2. He said "that you and I could not use his cassette player," Sara.

3. What caused Lucille to say, Dolores, I no longer trust you?

4. Robert Frost's poem Mending Wall is frequently quoted.

5. David excitedly told us, Ellen has finally said, Yes.

6. Uncle Fred has a battered and ragged hat that he calls his old standby.

7. He says that there is one good thing about it: bad weather can never hurt it.

8. The children's book "Charlotte's Web" is among E. B. White's most beloved works.

9. That curving highway between Elberton and Anderson is known by the local people as Accident Alley.

10. Gary called, "Bring me a glass of water when you come upstairs, Don." "I am thirsty again."

11. Charles Lamb's humorous essay A Dissertation on Roast Pig was published in *London Magazine* in 1822.

12. At the close of the program the audience stood and sang America the Beautiful.

13. The final chapter in the novel was intriguingly titled *A Criminal at Bay.*

14. The Keats poem Ode to a Nightingale is in the book Dorothy gave me.

15. Are you sure that Myra said, "This is my last day at work?"

16. "I am really glad, Nat said, that Jimmy and Sharon are going to the rock concert with us."

17. Ruth Winslow says that she has never read *The Catcher in the Rye.*

18. I wonder who first called a psychiatrist a shrink.

19. Nell often tells George "that he is as slow as molasses in January."

20. Benny Goodman remained the King of Swing whenever he played his licorice stick.

Exercise 72   Review of Punctuation

In the following sentences insert all necessary punctuation marks; remove all unnecessary marks, replacing them with the proper ones wherever needed. If a sentence is correctly punctuated, mark it **C.**

Example: I have just read an article in *Home and Garden* called✓ Petunias for Pretty Patios.✓

1. Chuck please return my call this is an emergency!

2. Wear a red carnation so that I will know you at the airport, said Frances.

3. Will you please deliver the flowers that I ordered to my friend at the hospital.

4. Sara Teasdale's poem Barter contains the following lines Spend all you have for loveliness, / Buy it and never count the cost.

5. Mr. Rodney the owner of the furniture store said that the table should be delivered in about three weeks, however there is always the chance of a delay.

6. Mother asked for the fourth time Are you certain that there is no school tomorrow?

7. The lemonade was tart sweet and icy cold.

8. Whoever made this lemonade should patent it put it on the market and make a million dollars.

9. I tried on the feather hat I looked in the mirror and then I burst out laughing.

10. The word *osculatory* is classified by Fowler in *Modern English Usage* as a polysyllabic humor word.

11. Actually *osculatory* is simply a deliberately comic reference don't interrupt, Leo to kissing.

12. My friends Marian and Ned live in Fort Worth Texas where they both work for an aviation company.

13. Stop it at once cried Mrs. Langhorne I am surprised at you children and your pranks.

14. Dr. Montgomery is a surgeon his wife is a Ph.D.

249

15. Elizabeth Barrett Browning 1806–1861 was the wife of the poet Robert Browning and was a poet in her own right.

16. I'm not sure that I fully understand the Wall Street term bull market.

17. Montague Wilson said in his speech I am the fifth generation of my family to have lived in this wonderful community applause followed this statement.

18. Whenever you visit England winter or summer plan to take: an umbrella, a raincoat, and a warm sweater.

19. Foreign students from Austria, France, Holland, and Spain were arriving in the United States that day, many nervous at being away from their homes for the first time, but they were all eagerly awaiting the adventure ahead.

20. A biblical quotation that is known almost universally is First Corinthians 13 4.

21. While I was trying to get the baby to sleep Grace was washing the dishes and Frank was repairing the living room lamp Jackie however sat calmly watching television.

22. My three professors Dr. Henry, Dr. Abernathy, and Mr. Malone are all giving me tests on the same day.

23. I will get no sleep the night before but there is just one way to pass those tests study, study, study.

24. If one of those tests were not in calculus I might have a better oh, don't worry about it, Mother.

25. Outside the yard was a sparkling green after the rain.

26. The title of the Hemingway novel *For Whom the Bell Tolls* was taken from John Donne's famous line ". . . never send to know for whom the bell tolls; it tolls for thee."

Exercise 73 Review of Punctuation

In the following sentences insert all necessary punctuation marks; remove all incorrectly used marks, replacing them with the proper ones wherever needed. If a sentence is correctly punctuated, mark it **C**.

Example: Molly∧David∧and I went walking on the beach this morning⌃we lost track of time and were late for lunch.

1. To Pat Thomas was the typical male chauvinist.

2. To her surprise however he allowed her to pay for their lunch.

3. After all, said Thomas, she was the one who invited me.

4. I worked and worked and eventually concluded that there was no way I could make the old bicycle run again.

5. Being careful to release the clutch slowly I drove smoothly up the hill.

6. Being careful to release the clutch properly is an important factor in driving smoothly.

7. After following the directions in Figure A, place the two corresponding edges of fabric together see Figure B and baste loosely.

8. The morning having turned out to be overcast and dreary John and Margo postponed their hike to Toccoa Falls.

9. John said, "This is the kind of day for a roaring fire and a good book;" Margo, however, was unhappy about the change of plan.

10. Janie half crying reported, Father said, No one will be allowed to go skating unless this weather improves.

11. Coach Magill has nicknamed our star kicker The Big Toe from Alamo.

12. Mrs. Martindale said that she was aware of the unfair allocation of work among us boys.

13. I waited two months for the company to repair my watch then I wrote a letter to the Better Business Bureau.

14. The voice on the telephone said, Hi How are you doing today? I bet you can't guess who this is.

15. I replied that I didn't care who it was I had been taking a shower and had answered the phone dripping wet.

16. Well, said the voice this is Judy, with Adorable Photographers, and have I got a deal for oh, don't hang up yet.

17. In the new book *Personal Computers for the Kindergarten Crowd,* the first chapter is titled Eliminating the Study of Arithmetic.

18. Fran said to use cream of tartar as a thickener for the sauce not flour.

19. My husband's oldest brother Andrew McMillan lives in the Scottish Highlands.

20. Ray asked me Why did Michael say It's now or never.

21. Here are the steps in learning to sew 1 threading the needle, 2 knotting the thread, 3 holding the needle correctly, and 4 moving the needle through the fabric in even stitches.

22. Kathleen said, "I understand how you feel." "You should be quite happy about your good fortune."

23. Knowing that the stranger would probably return after dark Mary Lou put a heavy table and two chairs against the door as a barricade.

24. As I was dealing the slippery cards kept falling to the floor.

25. Alex my friend who lives in Helena Montana is planning to move to Florida on January 1 1987.

20

Mechanics: Capital Letters, Italics, the Apostrophe, the Hyphen

■ 20a Capital Letters

1. Capitalize the first word of a sentence, of a line of traditional poetry, and of a direct quotation:

All the students attended the meeting.

"Under the spreading chestnut tree / The village smithy stands."

He said, "She does not wish to see you."

2. Capitalize proper nouns, words used as proper nouns, and adjectives derived from proper nouns:

Great Britain, William, the Bible

President, Senator, Captain, University (when these are used with or substituted for the name of a particular president, person of high rank, or university), and similarly

Mother, Grandfather, Uncle (as in *We told Mother to go to bed, We bought Grandfather a bicycle,* and *We buried Uncle in Arlington Cemetery,* but not in *My mother is ill, His grandfather is eighty-two,* and *Our uncle was wounded at Gettysburg*)

British, Shakespearean, Scandinavian

3. Capitalize the names of days, months, and holidays:

Monday, February, Fourth of July, Ash Wednesday, Veterans Day

4. Capitalize the names of historical periods and events:

the Middle Ages, the French Revolution, the Battle of the Bulge, the Reformation

5. Capitalize the first word in the titles of books, chapters, essays, short stories, short poems, songs, and works of art. Capitalize also all other words in these titles except articles, prepositions, and conjunctions:

The Last of the Mohicans, "Without Benefit of Clergy," "Ode to the West Wind," "Only a Bird in a Gilded Cage," El Greco's *View of Toledo*

6. Capitalize names of the Deity, religions, and religious organizations:

Jehovah, God, the Redeemer, Buddhism, Church of England, Society of Jesus, Order of St. Francis.

7. Capitalize the names of governing bodies, political parties, governmental agencies, and civic and social organizations:

The House of Commons, the Senate, the Democratic Party, the Internal Revenue Service, the Chamber of Commerce, Daughters of the American Revolution

8. Capitalize the points of the compass when they refer to a specific region but not when they indicate direction:

He lived in the East all his life.

They traveled west for about a hundred miles and then turned south.

9. Capitalize the names of studies only if they are derived from proper nouns or are the names of specific courses of instruction:

He was studying physics, chemistry, and German.

He failed Mathematics 101 and Human Biology 1.

10. Capitalize personifications:

O wild West Wind, thou breath of Autumn's being.

Daughters of Time, the hypocritic Days.

Be with me, Beauty, for the fire is dying.

■ 20b Italics

1. Italicize words that you wish to emphasize. (In manuscript indicate italics by underlining.)

Do you mean to say that she ate them *all*?

He could hardly have been *the* Robert Frost.

Note: Use this device sparingly. Frequent use of italics for emphasis is a sign of an immature style.

2. Italicize numbers, letters, and words referred to as such:

He made his 7 and his 9 very much alike.

She has never yet learned to pronounce *statistics*.

In his handwriting he uses the old-fashioned *s*.

3. Italicize the names of books, magazines, and newspapers. (Smaller units of books, such as chapters, stories, essays, and poems, are usually set in quotation marks.)

A Tale of Two Cities, the *Atlantic Monthly*, the Atlanta *Journal*

Note: In the names of newspapers or magazines it is not always necessary to italicize the definite article or the name of a city.

4. Italicize the names of ships, trains, and airplanes:

the *Queen Elizabeth*, the *Twentieth-Century Limited*, the *Spirit of St. Louis*

5. Italicize foreign words and phrases in an English context:

The *coup d'état* led to his becoming emperor.

6. Italicize the titles of paintings, statues, and other works of art:

Gainsborough's *Blue Boy*, Rodin's *The Thinker*

■ 20c The Apostrophe

1. Use the apostrophe and *s* to form the possessive case of singular nouns:

the boar's head, Mary's lamb, the boss's orders

Note: Proper names ending in *s* may form the possessive by adding *'s* if the resulting word is not unpleasant or difficult to sound:

Keats's poems, Charles's work, *but* Ulysses' return

2. Use an apostrophe without *s* to form the possessive of plural nouns ending in *s*:

Soldiers' quarters, boys' clothes

3. Use an apostrophe and *s* to form the possessive of plural nouns not ending in *s*:

Men's coats, children's shoes, the alumni's contributions

4. The possessive of words indicating time is formed like the possessive of other nouns:

A week's delay, a day's journey, *but* a two days' visit

5. The apostrophe is frequently omitted in the names of organizations and institutions:

The Farmers Hardware Company, Boys High School, State Teachers College

6. In forming the possessives of compounds, use the apostrophe according to the meaning and the logic of the construction:

Beaumont and Fletcher's plays [Plays written by Beaumont and Fletcher jointly.]

Smith's and Jones's children [The children of Smith and the children of Jones.]

John and Mary's house [The house belonging to John and Mary.]

Somebody else's business [The business of somebody else.]

7. Use an apostrophe to indicate the omission of letters in contractions and of digits in numerals:

Isn't, don't, 'tis

Martha's been sunbathing.

the Class of '23

Note: Be sure that the apostrophe is placed at the exact point where the letter or digit is omitted. Do not write *is'nt, do'nt.*

8. Use an apostrophe and *s* to indicate the plural of letters, numerals, signs, and words used as such:

Dot your *i*'s and cross your *t*'s.

His telephone number contains four *8*'s.

In your next theme omit the *&*'s.

He uses too many *so*'s.

■ 20d The Hyphen

In English, compounds are made in three ways:

(1) by writing the words solid (*bedroom, watchmaker, starlight*),

(2) by writing them separately (*ice cream, motion picture, mountain lion*), or

(3) by separating the words with a hyphen (*name-caller, ne'er-do-well, finger-paint*).

The resulting confusion, like so much confusion in English, lies in the fact that the language is constantly changing. A compound may begin its career as two words; then it may move on to the form with a hyphen; and finally it may end as a solid formation — its destiny accomplished, as it were. So we have *bedroom* (written solid) but *dining room* (two words). We have the noun *bluepoint* to refer to an oyster, but we use the two words *blue point* to describe a Siamese cat. A decision may be *far-reaching,* but a forecaster is *farseeing.* The only solution to this confusing problem is to consult a dictionary. But this authority is not always satisfactory because many compounds are made for the occasion and are not in the dictionary — and dictionaries may disagree. Furthermore, a compound with a hyphen may be correct in one part of a sentence and incorrect in another, or it may be correct as a noun and incorrect as a verb. The stylebook of one publisher says, "If you take hyphens seriously, you will surely go mad." Nevertheless, there is a sort of logic in the use of the hyphen, as well as a kind of common sense; furthermore, one can learn some of the pitfalls to avoid.

Consider the following sentences:

He is a great admirer of Henry Kissinger, the ex-Republican Secretary of State. [Is Mr. Kissinger no longer a Republican? The phrase should read *the former Republican Secretary of State.*]

The parents enjoyed their children's recreation of the first Thanksgiving. [In this sentence *re-creation* is the appropriate word, and the hyphen distinguishes it from *recreation.*]

I would think that your sixteen year old brother could scramble an egg. [In this sentence *sixteen, year,* and *old* form a compound modifier and should be hyphenated. The phrase should read *your sixteen-year-old brother.*]

He introduced me to his uncle, an old car enthusiast. [Is his uncle old? Or is his uncle interested in old cars? The phrase is clarified with a hyphen: *an old-car enthusiast.*]

Did you hear the reporter's interview with the singing whale authority? [Did the reporter interview a whale authority who sings or an authority on singing whales? Appropriate hyphenation clears up the confusion; the phrase should read *with the singing-whale authority.*]

The following rules indicate common practice and are fairly reliable:

1. Compound numerals (*twenty-one* through *ninety-nine*) are always written with a hyphen:

twenty-six, forty-eight, fifty-two

2. Fractions are written with a hyphen if they are adjectival:

His speech was one-third fact and two-thirds demagoguery.

But   Three fourths of the apples are rotten.

3. Compounds with *self* are written with a hyphen:

self-styled, self-taught, self-centered

Note the exceptions *selfsame, selfhood, selfless.*

4. The hyphen is used in certain expressions of family relationship:

great-grandfather, great-aunt

5. Most compounds beginning with *ex, pre,* and *pro* are written with a hyphen:

ex-president, pre-Christian, pro-British

6. The hyphen is commonly used with compounds with prepositional phrases:

mother-in-law, stick-in-the-mud, heart-to-heart

7. One of the commonest uses of hyphens is to form compound modifiers for nouns and pronouns:

An eight-year-old child, a well-done steak, a blue-green sea

Note: Such compounds are hyphenated when they immediately precede the word they modify, but frequently they are not hyphenated when they are used predicatively:

His well-spoken words pleased the audience [*but* His words were well spoken].

She made a number of off-the-record comments [*but* Her comments were made off the record].

8. Hyphens are used in coined or occasional compounds:

She gave him a kind of you-ought-to-know-better look.

Her bird-on-the-nest hat was sensational.

9. The hyphen is used in compound nouns that name the same person in two different capacities:

Author-publisher, musician-statesman, tycoon-playboy

10. The hyphen is frequently used to avoid confusion between words:

Re-claim [to distinguish from *reclaim*]

Re-cover [to distinguish from *recover*]

11. Hyphens are used to avoid clumsy spellings:

Bull-like, semi-independent, ante-election, pre-empt

Note: *Cooperate* and *coordinate* are common enough to be accepted.

12. The hyphen is used at the end of a line of writing to indicate the division of a word continued on the next line. The division must always come at the end of a syllable. Do not divide words of one syllable:

PROPER DIVISIONS: con-tin-ued, in-di-cate, au-di-ence

IMPROPER DIVISIONS: wo-rd, laugh-ed, comp-ound

Note: If you are uncertain about the division of a word, consult your dictionary.

■ 20e Numbers

1. Numbers that can be expressed in one or two words should be written out: five girls; seventeen giraffes; twenty-five books; four hundred tickets; ten thousand people.

2. Numbers of more than two words should be written as numerals: 9,425; 650; 700,000.

3. Numbers that start a sentence should be written out, even though they would ordinarily be written as numerals: *Four hundred and forty* dollars is a good price for that cashmere coat.

Exercise 74 Capitals

In the following sentences change the small letters to capital letters wherever necessary and vice versa. If a sentence is correct as it stands, mark it **C**.

Example: I hear that the $\overset{H}{\cancel{H}}$endersons plan to drive to $\overset{C}{\cancel{c}}$alifornia by the

southern route.

1. Have you read Richard Lockridge's mystery novel *Death In A Sunny Place*?

2. Sam said, "why won't you go with me to the hockey game?"

3. Gerald made delicious peach ice cream for our labor day picnic.

4. Last Summer our family had a reunion at Hilton Head island, off the south

   carolina coast.

5. When I called uncle Tommy last saturday, he was just getting ready to go fishing.

6. Grandfather has been a member of the democratic party all his life; grandmother,

   however, switches frequently from one party to another.

7. Mark has a difficult schedule this Semester; he is taking French, Trigonometry,

   and Ancient History.

8. After living in the south for eighteen years, Hugh found the cold Winters of Min-

   nesota hard to endure.

9. Mrs. Birdwell is a member of the Daughters Of The American Revolution, and

   both of her Sisters are members also.

10. James is upset because he made a *D* in psychology 302.

11. As we drove West, the setting Sun was on the horizon, almost blinding in its

    brilliance.

12. Recently reelected for a fourth term, senator Smith is an advocate of arms control.

13. Have you ever read Keats's "Ode On A Grecian Urn"?

14. In the last two lines of the poem Keats makes the urn itself seem to speak:

    "Beauty is truth, truth beauty, — that is all / ye know on earth, and all ye

    need to know."

15. Rembrandt's famous painting *Man With A Gilt Helmet* is in a museum in west

    Berlin.

Exercise 75 Italics

In the following sentences underline all the words that should be italicized and remove italics that are incorrectly used, replacing them with other marks if necessary. If a sentence is correct as it stands, mark it **C**.

Example: When we were in Paris, we saw da Vinci's famous painting La Gioconda, more frequently called Mona Lisa.

1. I have read several novels of John Galsworthy; the one I like best is The Man of Property.

2. Several noted American authors, including Herman Melville, Henry James, and Mark Twain, published their fiction in serial form in Harper's Monthly Magazine.

3. That word never often returns to haunt those of us who are dogmatic.

4. One of the funniest short stories I have ever read is Eudora Welty's "Why I Live at the P.O."

5. The initials R.I.P. stand for the Latin prayer requiescat in pace, meaning "may he rest in peace."

6. Our political science teacher insists that we stay au courant on national politics.

7. Did you know that the French luxury liner Liberté was originally a German ship named Europa?

8. I can still hardly believe that Frank ate six — yes, I said six — hamburgers at the party last night.

9. I read in the Atlanta Journal yesterday that AMTRAK plans to reactivate the old " Silver Meteor," to run along the Atlantic coast.

10. Laurie has learned to spell Mississippi, as well as the names of the other Southern states.

11. She says that some of her schoolmates say "crooked letter" for each s in the word.

12. Cruising the Greek Isles aboard the Golden Odyssey is my idea of a wonderful vacation.

13. Looking at the huge French menu before me, I decided that gigot rôti, petits pois, and champignons would be a fine choice.

14. Rosemary was interested in the desserts; she couldn't decide between framboises chantilly and crème brulée.

15. Ivan's address is easy to remember; it has two 5's followed by two 4's.

16. The botanical name of the jack-in-the-pulpit is Arisaema triphyllum.

17. After reading an informative article in *Southern Accents*, I am planning to plant some dahlias in my garden next year.

18. Thad says that he always feels a thrill when everyone stands and sings the *Star-Spangled Banner*.

19. What is the title of that lovely, haunting song from the Broadway show Cats?

20. A music critic who writes for the *New York Times* said that this year's production of Aida should top all previous performances of the opera.

21. Well, I do think that Marge's reply to Harry's comment was a ridiculous non sequitur.

Exercise 76 The Apostrophe

In the following sentences underline all words that should have apostrophes and all those that have apostrophes incorrectly used; then write the word(s) correctly in the space at the right. If a sentence is correct, mark it **C.**

Example: Be careful when you talk with Carol; we
underline{wouldnt} want to hurt her feelings.   _____*wouldn't*_____

1. The Kennedy's are moving to New Orleans, where Mrs.
   Kennedy lived for many years before her marriage.   _____

2. One of Keats's best-known poems is his "Ode to Autumn."   _____

3. A golden-crested heron has built it's nest very near our fishing dock on the river.   _____

4. Four year's study in Paris has turned Gretchen into a marvelous cook.   _____

5. Whats the answer to the terrible problem of water pollution?   _____

6. Of course, most people agree that the large industries' responsibility cannot be minimized.   _____

7. Agnes story about the accident was greatly exaggerated.   _____

8. Martha denied that the dirty dish left on the table was her's.   _____

9. Its been a long time since we four have been on a vacation
   together.   _____

10. Nell's and Gary's new station wagon is a bright yellow, with
    wood-grain trim.   _____

11. Whose turn is it to take the clothes to the launderette?   _____

12. There wo'nt be time between planes for you to call your
    friend in Tucson, Linda.   _____

13. A weeks supply of chocolate ice cream lasts just three days
    in the Olivers household.   _____

14. Mrs. Oliver says that her two sons appetite for chocolate
    comes from their fathers side of the family.   _____

15. Mr. Oliver's response to his wife's accusation is that he won
    her heart with a five-pound Whitmans Sampler.   _____

16. The number of *fantastics* and *terrifics* in Mrs. Williams _____
    speech reflected a somewhat limited vocabulary. _____

17. The Class of 80 had a large attendance for Alumni Day; this
    class's school spirit has always been wonderful. _____

18. The women's exercise class meets at nine oclock on Friday's. _____

19. Katherine asked, "Is'nt this the place to register for the door
    prizes?" _____

20. Bucks been trying for half an hour to get Bob on the phone. _____

Exercise 77 The Hyphen

In the sentences below, underline the incorrect compounds and write the correct forms at the right. If a sentence is correct, mark it **C.** Some sentences contain more than one error.

Example: Ed used <u>six foot</u> planks for the shelves
in his bookcase.   *six-foot*

1. Alicia had that "if you knew what I know" expression as we crowded around her with questions.   _____

2. Meg was wearing her lavender blue sweater, and her mother of pearl necklace looked beautiful with it.   _____

3. When I was in New York last week, I saw ex-Democratic President Jimmy Carter in the hotel lobby.   _____

4. My grandmother's only sister, Great aunt Mabel, will be ninety five on her next birthday.   _____

5. Some of the so called art in that exhibition could almost have been done by a four year old child.   _____

6. Mr. Roberts, teacher coach at Lincoln High School, spends every afternoon on the practice field and every evening in the library.   _____

7. Joe's hand me down tuxedo doesn't fit very well.   _____

8. It was frustrating to retrace the twenty mile stretch that we had covered after making a wrong turn.   _____

9. Marty's world weary attitude is amusing; she is actually rather childlike.   _____

10. Fleming implied in his remarks that indifference to football is downright unAmerican.   _____

11. I doubt that Henry is going to be happy with that well done steak; I heard him ask for a rare one.   _____

12. Louisa is a self taught typist, a fact that is apparent to all who receive letters from her.   _____

13. The man's bulllike physique made him an awesome opponent in the wrestling ring.   _____

14. My well meaning statement was taken to suggest
    that I consider Jake a ne'er do well.   _____

15. The Virginia Kentucky game was about to begin,
    and the filled to capacity stadium was noisy with
    cheering fans.   _____

16. My employer, Mr. Fairchild, is an English print
    collector.   _____

17. Jim is a would be author who never seems despon-
    dent over his ever growing stack of rejection slips.   _____

18. Felicia describes her hard to handle three year old
    as a high spirited little angel.   _____

19. Oh, what I would give for a two week vacation at
    St. Tropez!   _____

20. The celllike room was dark and airless, with a low
    ceiling and mildew covered walls.   _____

Exercise 78 Review of Mechanics

Underline the errors in the following sentences and then write the correct forms in the spaces at the right. If a sentence is correct, mark it **C**.

Example: Edwin and I sailed <u>South</u> toward St.
Thomas, a lovely tropical island in the   *south*
Caribbean <u>sea</u>.   *Sea*

1. Thats a far fetched story, Quincy, but I am inclined
   to believe that your's is a true account of the
   incident.   _____

2. Do you mean that Brad is actually enjoying Differ-
   ential Calculus?   _____

3. I hear that Bobs proposing to Helen was a great
   surprise to Anita, who's hopes were high for herself.   _____

4. Matt said, "you're not holding the racquet correctly, uncle George."   _____

5. I am enclosing forty dollars $40.00 as payment in
   full for the knife sharpener that you advertised.   _____

6. My copy of *Architectural Digest* has disappeared
   from the coffee table, where I left it with this weeks
   Sunday *Times*.   _____

7. "Well," said Sally, "we all know that *tempus fugit*
   when were having fun."   _____

8. Remember these important safety instructions when
   using this lamp: 1 be sure that the polarized plug
   fits properly into the outlet, 2 never use an exten-
   sion cord unless the plug can be fully inserted, and
   3 never attempt to clean the lamp with anything
   moist until it has been disconnected.   _____

9. The Franklins and the Martins jointly owned vacation house is high up on Fort Mountain.   _____

10. Glenn, have you ever read The Last of the Mohi-
    cans?   _____

11. My math professor says that he almost decided to
    study Economics.

    _____

12. I think that the word you are trying to remember is
    inestimable.

    _____

13. That long drawn out meeting of the entertainment
    committee resulted in a bitter quarrel between the
    chairman and the treasurer.

    _____

14. Mrs. Denson took offense when Mr. Thompson re-
    ferred to her husband Thompson's former business
    associate as "Whats his name."

    _____

15. John, Caroline, Don, and I attended Carmen when
    it was brought to Memphis by the metropolitan
    opera company.

    _____

16. Last Spring we spent a weekend on the outer
    banks, a group of islands on the North Carolina
    coast.

    _____

17. The final t is silent in the French pronunciation of
    the word cabaret.

    _____

18. The Browns think that their's is by far the prettiest
    cat in the neighborhood, but I have never thought
    that the persian is a beautiful animal.

    _____

19. I prefer the tawny beige coat and the sky blue eyes
    of the elegant siamese cat.

    _____

20. My Father's favorite cat, however, is a cat named
    midnight, with a shiny black coat and wicked look-
    ing yellow green eyes.

    _____

21

Use of the Dictionary

A convenient and valuable source of linguistic information is a standard dictionary. It is easy to use, and, if used intelligently, very informative. Many people do not realize that a dictionary contains important facts far beyond simple definitions and guides to pronunciation and spelling. One of the best investments that you can make is the purchase of a standard collegiate dictionary. Your frequent use of a good dictionary, besides being a necessary step toward the development of an effective vocabulary, is essential for understanding the material you encounter daily. In any college course, in the newspapers, and in regular communication with others, you will read and hear unfamiliar words. Your desire to learn the meaning, spelling, and pronunciation of a new word should lead you to a dictionary providing this information along with other features such as the derivation of the word and its level of usage. It may also discuss the word's synonyms and frequently an antonym to illuminate still further its precise shade of meaning.

The best dictionaries have taken years of preparation by hundreds of workers directed by the finest scholars of the time. Unabridged dictionaries are comprehensive in their explanations and descriptions of words, containing thousands more entries than the more commonly used desk dictionary. In the United States perhaps the best-known unabridged dictionary is *Webster's Third New International Dictionary of the English Language*, often called simply *Webster's Third*. It was published by the G. & C. Merriam Company of Springfield, Massachusetts, in 1961; there have been several subsequent printings and supplements. This work, though it is too bulky to be used as a casual desk dictionary (and for most purposes unnecessary), may be found in a college library.

Any one of several extremely reliable collegiate dictionaries is the best choice for you. Severely abridged paperback editions of these dictionaries are a poor substitute, as they do not contain the detailed information that you may find necessary for specialized assignments in your college courses. Most language authorities recommend the latest editions of the following standard college dictionaries: *Webster's New Collegiate Dictionary*, published by G. & C. Merriam Co., Springfield, Massachusetts; *Webster's New World Dictionary of the American Language*, Simon and Schuster, New York; *The American Heritage Dictionary of the English Language*, The American Heritage Publishing Co., Inc., and Houghton Mifflin Co., Boston; *The Random House Dictionary of the English Language*, Random House, New York; *Funk and Wagnall's Standard Collegiate Dictionary*, Harcourt, Brace and World, Inc., New York.

Select one of these dictionaries and buy it as soon as you get to college; then follow the list of suggestions given below in order to familiarize yourself with the dictionary and the ways in which you can get the maximum use from this very handy and easy-to-use reference work.

1. Read all the introductory material in the front of the dictionary because this explains what information the book has to offer. If some of it seems too scholarly for you to understand, read on, and at least find out what it is mainly concerned with and what you can expect to find in its entries.

2. Study carefully the key to pronunciation, and check it with words that you know so that you will be sure of understanding it. A need for guidance in pronunciation is one of the most common reasons for consulting a dictionary.

3. Refer often to the table of abbreviations, which is most likely to be found inside the front cover of your dictionary. To save space, dictionaries necessarily use many abbreviations, and these are explained in the table. Become familiar with these abbreviations so that no piece of information escapes your notice.

4. Examine the appendixes to learn what information is given in them. Some dictionaries list biographical and geographic information in their appendixes; others list them in the main entries in the book. Other information often found in the appendixes of a dictionary includes tables of interpretations of various specialized symbols, like those connected with mathematics, chemistry, music, chess, medicine, and pharmacy; a directory of colleges and universities; a table of weights and measures; a dictionary of English given names, and so on.

One of the most important things a dictionary can tell you is the *level of usage* of a given term. The English language, ever-changing and full of colorful informality, functions on many levels. Young people may use the expression *laid back* to describe a person who has a relaxed, uncomplicated approach to life. Politicians and reporters use the term *bottom line* to mean the end result of something. An educated adult may in conversation refer to *lots of trouble*. And an editor of a magazine may write of the *dichotomy between work and leisure classes* or, in a book review, of an *involuted search for self*. Each of these expressions is in a sense proper in its own context. Judgment of a term as "good English" is usually determined by the level on which it is used. The magazine editor would not in a formal article use the term *laid back*; The youth of today would hardly think or write using terms like *dichotomy*. Your dictionary will tell you whether the use of a word in a particular sense is slang, informal (colloquial), dialectal, archaic, obsolete, or none of these, i.e., Standard English.

Slang is the term used to describe the spontaneous, vivid, and sometimes racy inventions used frequently in the speech and writings of groups like teenagers, gangsters, popular musicians, soldiers, and sports writers — not that these groups necessarily have anything else in common. The life of a slang expression is usually short, but sometimes, if it is striking enough and colorful enough, it may gain universal usage and become at least an informal part of the national vocabulary.

The term *informal* or *colloquial* is applied to words or expressions that are acceptable in the speech of the educated but not in formal writing. It is all right to say, "He's going to have *lots of trouble* explaining his whereabouts on the night of June third," but it is not Standard English to write this statement formally.

Dialect, another usage label, means that a word or expression is common to the speech of a particular group or geographical region. *Archaic* means that the word or term is rarely used today, except in certain contexts like church ritual, but that it may be found fairly frequently in early writings. *Obsolete* means that the term is no longer used but may be found in early writings. In addition, as a part of its usage discussion, a dictionary will inform you if a word or term is commonly considered obscene, vulgar, or profane.

To see how a dictionary presents its information, consider now the following entry from *The Random House Dictionary of the English Language:**

> **bur·den**[1] (bûr′dən), *n.* **1.** that which is carried; load: *a horse's burden of rider and pack.* **2.** that which is borne with difficulty; obligation or trouble: *the burden of leadership.* **3.** *Naut.* **a.** the weight of a ship's cargo. **b.** the carrying capacity of a ship: *a ship of a hundred-tons burden.* **4.** *Mining.* the earth or rock to be moved by a charge of explosives. **5.** *Accounting.* overhead (def. 6). —*v.t.* **6.** to load heavily. **7.** to load oppressively; trouble. [ME, var. of *burthen,* OE *byrthen;* akin to G *Bürde,* Goth *baurthei;* see BEAR[1]] —**bur′den·er,** *n.* —**bur′den·less,** *adj.*
> —**Syn. 1.** See **load. 2.** weight, encumbrance, impediment.

Here we are given the correct spelling of the word *burden* and its proper division into syllables. The small numeral[1] after the entry word indicates that this is the first of two or more words with the same spelling but differing radically in meaning and derivation and therefore listed separately. Next, the proper pronunciation is given. It becomes clear immediately that you need to learn the significance of the signs, called diacritical marks, that indicate pronunciation. In this entry the first five numbered definitions are preceded by *n* (for *noun*) and the last two by *v.t.* (for *verb, transitive*). After 3, *Naut.* (*Nautical*) means that the definitions given under 3 are special technical senses of the word as used in shipping. The same interpretation is true of definitions 4 and 5. The information

*Reproduced by permission from *The Random House Dictionary of the English Language,* The Unabridged Edition. Copyright © 1983 by Random House, Inc.

in brackets gives the derivation or origin of the word. It tells that *burden* is a variant form of the older word *burthen,* which is derived from the Old English form *byrthen,* and that the word is linguistically akin to the word *bear* as described in the first *bear* entry elsewhere in the dictionary. Finally we learn that the synonyms of *burden*[1] are discussed under the entry *load.* The second entry, *burden*[2], is arranged on the same principles.

Consider now the following entry from *Webster's New World Dictionary of the American Language:**

> **drunk** (druŋk) [ME. *dronke < drunken:* see DRUNKEN] *pp. & archaic pt. of* DRINK —*adj.* [*usually used in the predicate*] **1.** overcome by alcoholic liquor to the point of losing control over one's faculties; intoxicated   **2.** overcome by any powerful emotion [*drunk* with joy] **3.** [Colloq.] *same as* DRUNKEN (sense 2) —*n.* [Slang] **1.** a drunken person **2.** a drinking spree
> *SYN.*—**drunk** is the simple, direct word, usually used in the predicate, for one who is overcome by alcoholic liquor [he is *drunk*]; **drunken,** usually used attributively, is equivalent to **drunk** but sometimes implies habitual, intemperate drinking of liquor [a *drunken* bum]; **intoxicated** and **inebriated** are euphemisms, the former often expressing slight drunkenness and the latter, a state of drunken exhilaration; there are many euphemistic and slang terms in English expressing varying degrees of drunkenness: e.g., **tipsy** (slight), **tight** (moderate, but without great loss of muscular coordination), **blind** (great), **blotto** (to the point of unconsciousness), etc. —*ANT.* **sober**

Here we learn that the adjective *drunk,* with the specific meanings that follow, is the past participle and was formerly a past tense of the verb *to drink.* Two definitions are given: the first of these is the common one; the second is often used figuratively. The discussion of synonyms gives us the fine shades of distinction among a group of words that mean essentially the same thing. In addition, one antonym, or word of opposite meaning, is given. The final part of the entry, defining *drunk* as a noun, explains that when the word is used as a noun, meaning a person in a drunken condition or a period of heavy drinking, the word is slang.

The kind of knowledge that a good dictionary can give you far exceeds what has been discussed here. Most good dictionaries, for instance, pay special attention to biography and geography. One can learn when Beethoven died and the name of the capital of Peru. One can find the height of Mount Everest and the approximate number of islands in the Philippines. Literature, mythology, and particularly science are well covered in the modern dictionary. Finally, special appendixes sometimes include such miscellaneous information as the meanings of common Christian names, foreign words and phrases, abbreviations, and the symbols used in the preparation of copy for the printer and in proofreading. Some books even contain a dictionary of rhymes. The following exercises illustrate the variety of information one may obtain from a good dictionary.

Exercise 79 Word Origins

After each of the following words indicate in the first column at the right the first systematically recorded language from which the word is derived, and in the second column the meaning of the source word.

	Language	**Meaning**
Example: girdle	*Old English*	*to encircle, enclose*
1. cell		
2. fool		
3. shape		
4. cemetery		
5. skewer		
6. catamaran		
7. kudzu		
8. boss		
9. chocolate		
10. silhouette		
11. pajama(s)		
12. chimney		
13. mandate		
14. kosher		
15. crazy		
16. martial		
17. athlete		
18. innocent		
19. mile		
20. chipmunk		
21. peach		
22. octopus		
23. chintz		

Word	Language	Meaning
24. music	_____	_____
25. platform	_____	_____

Exercise 80 British and American Usage

The following words illustrate the differences between British and American usage. Write the equivalents of these British terms:

Example: lorry _____ *truck* _____

 1. biscuit _____

 2. bonnet _____

 3. bounder _____

 4. bowler _____

 5. chemist _____

 6. corn (n.) _____

 7. draper _____

 8. dustman _____

 9. fell (n.) _____

10. football _____

11. gaol _____

12. geyser _____

13. ironmonger _____

14. lift (n.) _____

15. pasty (n.) _____

16. petrol _____

17. pillarbox _____

18. post (v.) _____

19. pub _____

20. public school _____

21. queue (n.) _____

22. rates _____

23. removal _____

24. roundabout (n.) _____

25. runners _____

26. sieve (v.) _____

27. spanner _____

28. sultanas _____

29. sweet (n.) _____

30. tin (n.) _____

31. tipping (n.) _____

32. torch _____

33. trolley _____

34. underground (n.), tube _____

35. verge _____

Name _____   Score _____

Exercise 81 Plurals

Write the plural form of each of the following nouns:

Example: spy _____ *spies* _____

1. thief _____
2. monkey _____
3. wife _____
4. roof _____
5. commander-in-chief _____
6. piano _____
7. spoonful _____
8. deer _____
9. tooth _____
10. thesis _____
11. alumnus _____
12. loaf _____
13. democracy _____
14. chairman _____
15. medium _____
16. ruby _____
17. octopus _____
18. echo _____
19. brother-in-law _____
20. alibi _____
21. lady _____
22. cello _____
23. sheep _____
24. witch _____
25. nucleus _____

26. supply _____

27. hero _____

28. ratio _____

29. potato _____

30. scarf _____

31. lens _____

32. trolley _____

33. half _____

34. shrimp _____

35. journey _____

Exercise 82 Levels of Usage

After each of the following sentences indicate the level of usage of the italicized words or expressions, using these abbreviations:

A for archaic,   **I** for informal or colloquial,
D for dialectic,   **S** for slang.

Note: *Most standard collegiate dictionaries agree in the classification of these words and expressions. Other dictionaries may differ in their classifications (or show none at all), so use a reliable collegiate dictionary whenever you need information about the level of usage of an expression.*

Dictionary used for this exercise: _____

Example: You must be *kidding* about your plans to spend the
summer in Tahiti, Marge.   _*I*_

1. Dot said, "What is so *almighty* wonderful about Frank's blond hair and blue eyes?"   _____

2. My father, who toured France last year, says that the ill and the *halt* make frequent pilgrimages to the shrine at Lourdes.   _____

3. That *chick* who went with Dan to the prom is from Anchorage, Alaska.   _____

4. I wish that my mother would *baby* me as much as Sophie's mother babies her.   _____

5. Ten of us went together to the Beach Boys' concert, and we had a *barrel of fun*.   _____

6. All of the bridesmaids looked beautiful; they were *bedight* with flowered wreaths for their hair.   _____

7. I told Woody that it was *cheap* of him to let Tim pick up the check for their dinner.   _____

8. Don said that he had never seen one woman with so much luggage in all his *born days*.   _____

9. Those little toy animals that glow in the dark are a *hot* item with the toddler set.   _____

10. I confess that I had not realized what a *jerk* Sam could be until he *pulled* his latest trick.   _____

11. Mona and Doc went fishing today and came home with a whole *slew* of flounders.   _____

12. The woman said, "*Howdy!* Have you come up the mountain from Franklin?"   _____

13. When the boys saw Mr. Flanders coming toward them holding a piece of the broken window, they knew that the *jig was up*.   _____

14. Louisa looked simply *smashing* in her emerald-green satin dress as she walked into the ballroom.   _____

15. Some *hoods* went through the parking lot last night and slashed the tires on most of the cars there.   _____

16. Mary Lou went blackberry picking this morning, and her *poke* was full of berries by nine o'clock.   _____

17. At the antique show we saw a lovely porcelain *charger* that the dealer said is at least two hundred years old.   _____

18. Harriet, I must say that you look like a *hick* in that old straw hat and those faded jeans.   _____

19. Surely you're not going to Fran's party in that *tacky get-up.*   _____

20. *Quoth* the raven to the poet, "Nevermore."   _____

21. If I should fail Chemistry 102, heaven *forfend*, I will have to go to summer school.   _____

22. Sheriff Andy Taylor told his deputy once again, "Barney, you are *something else*; do you know that?"   _____

23. "*Forsooth*," said the judge to the defendant, "this sentence pains me more than it does you."   _____

24. "How did I know," whined the prisoner, "that my so-called *buddies* would *double-cross* me?"   _____

25. "My mama *fetched me up* to be an honest, law-abiding citizen, your honor; I was *framed.*"   _____

Exercise 83   General Information

Refer to your dictionary for the information you will need to fill in the blanks below.

Example: Constellation in which the star Arcturus
is seen: *Boötes*

1. Derivation of the Airedale dog's name: _____

2. Name of the Roman goddess with whom the Greek
   goddess Artemis is often identified: _____

3. Number of items in a baker's dozen: _____

4. Location of the Canary Islands: _____

5. Name of the Shakespearean play in which the
   ruined fortress of Dunsinane appears: _____

6. Date of the completion of the Erie Canal: _____

7. Profession to which the term *Fourth Estate* refers: _____

8. Equivalent in U.S. gallons of the imperial gallon: _____

9. Birth and death years of the English novelist Jane
   Austen: _____

10. Legendary English king with whom the sword Ex-
    calibur is associated: _____

11. Another name for the African gnu: _____

12. Year in which Missouri was admitted to the United
    States: _____

13. Number of years between periodic appearances of
    Halley's comet: _____

14. City in which the barcarole was traditionally sung
    by boatmen: _____

15. Approximate length of the Malay Peninsula: _____

16. Religion founded by the Arabian prophet
    Mohammed: _____

17. Type of verse written by Ogden Nash: _____

18. Organization for which the acronym NATO is used: _____

19. Sport in which the Marquess of Queensberry rules
    are used: _____

20. Country of which Prague is the capital city: _____

Exercise 84 Borrowed Foreign Expressions

The following words and expressions occur frequently in our everyday speech and writing. They have been borrowed in their original forms from languages other than English and have in most instances become integral parts of our language. After consulting your dictionary, write the meaning of each expression and the language from which it has been borrowed.

Example: smorgasbord *appetizers such as cheese, fish, meats, or salads served buffet style (Swedish)*

1. arpeggio _____

2. rapport _____

3. hallelujah _____

4. fiord _____

5. dour _____

6. ghetto _____

7. troika _____

8. coleslaw _____

9. croissant _____

10. pretzel _____

11. papoose _____

12. in camera _____

_____

13. tortilla _____

_____

14. chic _____

_____

15. polka _____

_____

16. wok _____

_____

17. décolleté _____

_____

18. hibachi _____

_____

19. batik _____

_____

20. balalaika _____

_____

22

Diction

Diction is one's choice of words in the expression of ideas. Because one speaks and writes on various levels of usage, the same expression may be appropriate to one level but not to another. The diction, for instance, of formal writing seems overprecise in informal conversation, and the acceptable diction of everyday speech seems out of place in serious, formal composition. But on all levels of speech and writing, faulty diction appears — in wordiness, in trite expressions, and in faulty idiom.

■ 22a Wordiness

Wordiness is the use of too many words — more words, that is, than are necessary to express an idea correctly and clearly. Many sentences written by college students may be greatly improved by reducing the number of words. The following kind of sentence is common in student themes:

> WORDY: There is a man in our neighborhood, and he has written three novels.

> BETTER: A man in our neighborhood has written three novels.

> A neighbor of ours has written three novels.

What is called **excessive predication** is responsible for a common type of wordiness. Usually this fault results from the too frequent use of *and* and *but*. It may usually be remedied by proper subordination:

> WORDY: The test was hard, and the students were resentful, and their instructor was irritated.

> BETTER: Because the students resented the hard test, their instructor was irritated.

Another kind of wordiness originates in the desire to impress but ends in pretentious nonsense. It is the language of those persons who refer to bad weather as the "inclemency of the elements," who speak of "blessed events" and "passing away" instead of birth and death. Following are further examples of this kind of wordiness:

Our horse Hap has gone to the big round-up in the sky.

Our horse Hap has died.

Due to the fact that he was enamored of Angela, Thomas comported himself in such a way as to appear ridiculous.

Because he was in love with Angela, Thomas behaved foolishly.

I regret extremely the necessity of your departure.

I am sorry you must go.

Sometimes, of course, expressions like these are used facetiously. But do not make a habit of such usage.

Jargon is also a kind of wordiness, popular among people of specialized occupations. It has now spread to much everyday writing and speaking, probably because it is believed to make its users sound and appear knowledgeable. It is the jargon of government officials, social workers, educators on all levels, and others. Its basic principles seem to be these: Never use one word where two or more will do the work. Never use a concrete expression if it is possible to use an abstract one. Never be plain if you can be fancy. The clear sign of this kind of writing and speaking is the repeated use of such phrases as *frame of reference, in terms of, point in time,* and compounds formed with the suffix *-wise.* The writers of this new jargon never simply look at the budget; they "consider the status budget-wise." They don't study crime among the young; they "examine social conditions in terms of juvenile delinquency." They "critique," they "utilize," they "expedite," and they "finalize." They speak of the "culturally deprived," the "classroom learning situation," "meaningful experiences," "togetherness," and "lifestyle." All these expressions reflect a desire to be a part of the "in-group" (another example of this jargon) by picking up catchwords that seem to show a certain sophistication; what they really show is a failure to use precise language and a lack of judgment.

Redundancy, or unnecessary repetition, is another common type of wordiness, due to carelessness or ignorance of the meanings of certain words. Note the following examples of redundancy:

Repeat that again, please. [Why *again*?]

His solution was equally as good as hers. [Why *equally*?]

The consensus of opinion of the group was that Mrs. Jacobs will make a good mayor. [Use either *consensus of the group* or *the opinion of the group.*]

This location is more preferable to that one. [The word *preferable* means "more desirable"; therefore, the word *more* is unnecessary. The sentence should read *This location is preferable to that one.*]

The union continues to remain at odds with factory management. [*Continues* and *remain* mean essentially the same thing. Say, *The union continues at odds with factory management* or *The union remains at odds with factory management.*]

It was a dog large in size and brown in color. [*It was a large brown dog.*]

Mrs. Frost rarely ever wears her fur coat. [*Mrs. Frost rarely wears her fur coat.*]

■ 22b Vagueness

A general impression of vague thinking is given by the too frequent use of abstract words instead of concrete words. Note especially the vagueness of such common words as *asset, factor, phase, case, nature, character, line,* and *field.* All these have basic meanings and should be used cautiously in any other sense. The following examples show that the best way to treat these words is to get rid of them:

In cases where a person receives a ticket for speeding, he must pay a fine of fifty dollars. [*In cases where* can be replaced with the single word *if.*]

Industry and intelligence are important assets in business success. [Omit *assets* and the sense remains the same.]

The course is of a very difficult nature. [*The course is very difficult.*]

Jerry was aware of the fact that he was risking his savings. [*Jerry was aware that he was risking his savings.*]

Whenever you are tempted to use such words, stop and ask yourself just what you are trying to say. Then find the exact words to say it, cutting out all the "deadwood."

■ 22c Triteness

Trite means worn. Certain phrases have been used so often that they have lost their original freshness. Oratory, sermons, newspaper headlines and captions, and pretentious writing in general are frequently marred by such diction. Expressions of this kind are often called **clichés.** The following list is merely illustrative; you can probably think of numerous ones to add to these:

upset the applecart	proud possessor
an ace up his sleeve	nipped in the bud
dull thud	few and far between
one fell swoop	on pins and needles
up on Cloud Nine	make one's blood boil
grim reaper	eat one's heart out
last but not least	having a ball
face the music	as luck would have it
as straight as a die	quick as a wink
bitter end	gung ho

Avoid also quotation of trite phrases from literature and proverbs. Expressions like the following have already served their purpose:

a lean and hungry look	the best laid plans of mice and men
a sadder but wiser man	where angels fear to tread
a rolling stone	love never faileth
those who live in glass houses	to be or not to be

■ 22d Euphemisms

Euphemisms are expressions used to avoid the outright statement of disagreeable ideas or to give dignity to something essentially lowly or undignified. The Victorians were notoriously euphemistic: they called their legs "limbs," and instead of the accurate and descriptive terms *sweat* and *spit,* they substituted the vague but more delicate words "perspire" and "expectorate." Unfortunately, the Victorians were not the last to use euphemisms. While we cannot admire or condone some of today's obscenely explicit language, there is little justification for the fuzzy-minded delicacy of euphemisms. There is a decided difference between choosing an expression that offers a tactful, rather than hurtful, connotation and choosing an expression that is deliberately misleading. Pregnancy is euphemistically referred to as "expecting"; a garbage collector is a "sanitation engineer"; a janitor is a "superintendent," etc. *Death,* of course, has numerous euphemistic substitutes such as "passing on," "going to his reward," and many others.

Again, it should be emphasized that the laudable wish to spare the feelings of others is not to be confused with the sort of prudery or false sense of gentility that most often produces euphemisms. Unless your use of a euphemism is inspired by the necessity to soften a blow or to avoid offensiveness, use the more factual term. Ordinarily, avoid euphemisms — or change the subject.

■ 22e Idiom

Construction characteristic of a language is called **idiom.** The established usage of a language, the special way in which a thing is said or a phrase is formed, must be observed if writing is to be properly idiomatic. In English the normal sentence pattern has the subject first, then the verb, and then the direct object. In French, if the direct object is a pronoun, it usually (except in the imperative) precedes the verb. In English an adjective that directly modifies a noun usually precedes it. In French the adjective usually follows the noun. In English we say, "It is hot." The French say, "It makes hot." Such differences make learning a foreign language difficult.

Another meaning of the word *idiom* is somewhat contrary to this one. The word is also used for all those expressions that seem to defy logical grammatical practice, expressions that cannot be translated literally into another language.

"Many is the day" and "You had better" are good examples. Fortunately, idioms of this sort cause little trouble to native speakers.

In English, as in most modern European languages, one of the greatest difficulties lies in the idiomatic use of prepositions after certain nouns, adjectives, and verbs. Oddly enough, one agrees *with* a person but *to* a proposal, and several persons may agree *upon* a plan. One may have a desire *for* something but be desirous *of* it. One is angry *at* or *about* an act but *with* a person. These uses of prepositions may seem strange and perverse, but they are part of the idiomatic structure of English and must be learned. Good dictionaries frequently indicate correct usage in questions of this kind. Do not look up the preposition but rather the word with which it is used. The definition of this word will usually indicate the correct preposition to use with it.

■ 22f Connotation

In selecting words that will express their thoughts accurately, careful writers pay attention to the **connotations** of certain expressions. *Connotation* is the associative meaning, or what the word suggests beyond its literal definition.

Through popular usage certain terms convey favorable or unfavorable impressions beyond their literal meanings; they frequently have emotional or evaluative qualities that are not part of their straightforward definitions. Careless use of a word with strong connotations may cause faulty communication of your ideas. On the other hand, skillful use of connotation can greatly enrich your ability to communicate accurately. For example, you would not refer to a public figure whom you admire and respect as a "politician," a term that suggests such qualities as insincerity and conniving for personal gain. The word *childish* is inappropriate when you mean "childlike." The adjective *thin* suggests something scanty or somehow not full enough (especially when describing a person's figure); but *slim* and *slender,* two words close to *thin* in literal meaning, imply grace and good proportion.

Again, your dictionary can provide these shades of meaning that will keep you from writing something far different from your intention and will help you develop a vocabulary you can use accurately.

■ 22g Slang

Slang is, as you know, one of the usage labels given in a dictionary to define extremely informal language, frequently earthy but often vividly expressive. It usually has no true equivalent in Standard English and has the advantage of being forceful and dynamic. Although many slang terms, because of these qualities, eventually become acceptable as colloquial English, many more remain current for only a year or two; then, like all overused expressions, they gradually lose their force. Old slang expressions are constantly being abandoned, while new ones are constantly coming into use. There is no need to list slang expressions here, as they so quickly become dated. Be aware, however, that they are easily recognizable and that you must avoid them in all but the most informal written contexts.

Glossary of Faulty Diction

The following glossary should help you rid your speech and writing of many errors. The term **colloquial** means that an expression is characteristic of everyday speech. **Dialectal** means that an expression is peculiar to a particular place or class.

Note: Remember that colloquialisms, the language we use in our everyday conversations with friends and associates, are perfectly acceptable in informal writing and speech. The purpose of this Glossary of Faulty Diction is to point out expressions that should be avoided in formal writing of any kind.

Above.   Avoid the use of *above* as a modifier in such phrases as *the* **above** *reference, the* **above** *names.* An exception to this rule is that the word is proper in legal documents.

Accept, Except.   *To accept* is *to receive; to except* is *to make an exception of, to omit. Except* (as a preposition) means *with the exception of.*

Accidently.   There is no such word. The correct form is *accidentally,* based on the adjective *accidental.*

A.D.   This is an abbreviation of *Anno Domini* (in the year of our Lord). Strictly considered, it should be used only with a date: *A.D. 1492.* But it has recently come to mean *of the Christian era,* and expressions like *the fifth century A.D.* have become common. Here logic has bowed to usage.

Administrate.   There is no such word. The verb is *administer;* the noun formed from it is *administration.*

Adverse, Averse.   *Adverse* means *unfavorable (The weatherman forecast* **adverse** *conditions for the yacht race). Averse* means *opposed to (Mother was* **averse** *to our plans for ice skating at midnight).*

Affect, Effect.   In common usage *affect* is a verb meaning *to influence, to have an effect upon* or *to like to have or use (He* **affects** *a gold-headed cane)* or *to pretend (She* **affects** *helplessness). Effect* is both verb and noun. *To effect* is *to produce, to bring about.* The noun *effect* is a *result, a consequence.*

Aggravate.   Colloquial when used to mean *provoke* or *irritate. Aggravate* means to make *worse (The rainy weather* **aggravated** *his rheumatism).*

Agree to, Agree with, Agree upon or **on.**   One agrees *to* a proposal, *with* a person, and *upon* or *on* a settlement (*We* **agreed to** *his suggestion that we go, The boy did not* **agree with** *his father, the two factions could not* **agree upon** *a settlement*).

Ain't.   This form is occasionally defended as a contraction of *am not,* but even those who defend it do not use it in writing.

Alibi.   Colloquial for *excuse.* In formal usage *alibi* has legal significance only and means a confirmation of one's absence from the scene of a crime at the time the crime was committed.

All ready, Already.   *All ready* means simply that all are ready (*The players were all ready*). *Already* means *previously* or *before now* (*He has already gone*).

All together, Altogether.   *All together* means all of a number taken or considered together (*She invited them all together*). *Altogether* means *entirely, completely* (*He was altogether wrong*).

Allusion, Illusion.   An *allusion* is a casual or indirect reference to something, usually without naming the thing itself (*The quotation in her speech was an allusion to Shakespeare's Macbeth*). An *illusion* is a false or unreal impression of reality (*After his unkind treatment of the puppy Mildred lost her illusions about Arthur*).

Alright.   This is not an acceptable alternate spelling for the words *all right*.

Alumnus, Alumna.   *Alumnus* is masculine and has the plural *alumni*. *Alumna* is feminine and has the plural *alumnae*.

Among, Between.   The common practice is to use *between* with two persons or objects (*between a rock and a hard place*) and *among* with more than two (*The crew quarreled among themselves*). Exception: *The plane traveled between New York, Chicago, and Miami*. Here *among* would be absurd.

Anyone, Any one.   *Anyone*, the indefinite pronoun, is one word. *Any one*, meaning any single person or any single thing, should be written as two words (*Any one of your friends will be glad to help you*).

Any place, No place.   Dialectal corruptions of *anywhere* and *nowhere*.

Apt, Liable, Likely.   *Apt* means *suitable, appropriate, tending to,* or *inclined to* (*an apt phrase, a man apt to succeed*). *Liable* means *exposed to something undesirable* (*liable to be injured, liable for damages*). *Likely* means *credible, probable, probably* (*He had a likely excuse*). It can also overlap to some extent with *apt* in its sense of probability (*It is likely — or apt — to rain today*).

As far as.   This expression is frequently misused when it is not followed by words that would complete a clause (*As far as her ability she is perfectly able to do the work*). This expression should always function as a subordinating conjunction, introducing both a subject and a verb (*As far as her ability is concerned, she is perfectly able to do the work*).

Asset.   In its essential meaning this word is used in law and accounting (*His assets exceeded his liabilities*). But it seems to have established itself in the meaning of *something useful or desirable*. When used in this sense, it is frequently redundant.

Attend, Tend.   *Attend* means *to be present at*. When meaning *to take care of*, it is followed by *to* (*He attends to his own business*). *Tend* without a preposition also means *to take care of* (*He tends his own garden*). *Tend to* means *to have a tendency to* (*She tends to become nervous when her children are noisy*).

Author, Host, Chair, Position.   These nouns and many others like them are frequently misused as verbs (*She has authored three best sellers, The Joneses plan to host a party for their friends, The woman who chairs the committee is a lawyer, Please position the chairs around the table*). In these four sentences there are perfectly adequate verbs that should be used: *written, give, is chairman of,* and *place*.

Awful, Awfully.   Either of these is colloquial when used to mean *very*.

Awhile, A while.   *Awhile* is used as an adverb (*They stayed **awhile** at their friend's house*). When used after the preposition *for*, *while* is a noun, the object of the preposition (*I thought for **a while** that you were going to miss the plane*). The adverb is written as one word; the object of the preposition and its article are written as two.

Bad, Badly.   *Bad* is an adjective, *badly* an adverb. Say *I feel **bad,*** not *I feel **badly,*** if you mean *I am ill* or *I am sorry*.

Balance.   Except in accounting, the use of *balance* for *difference, remainder, the rest* is colloquial.

Being as.   Dialectal for *since* or *because*.

Beside, Besides.   *Beside* is a preposition meaning *by the side of* (*Along came a spider and sat down **beside** her*). *Besides* is a preposition meaning *except* (*He had nothing **besides** his good name*) and an adverb meaning *in addition, moreover* (*He received a medal and fifty dollars **besides***).

Blame on.   Correct idiom calls for the use of *to blame* with *for*, not *on*. (*They **blamed** the driver **for** the accident*, not *They **blamed** the accident **on** the driver*.) *Blame on* is colloquial.

Boyfriend, Girlfriend.   These two terms are colloquial, meaning *a favored male or female friend, a sweetheart*. If no other term seems appropriate, write them as two words: *boy friend, girl friend*.

Burst, Bursted, Bust.   The principal parts of the verb *burst* are *burst, burst,* and *burst*. The use of *bursted* or *busted* for the past tense is incorrect. *Bust* is either sculpture or a part of the human body. Used for *failure* or as a verb for *burst* or *break*, it is slang.

But what.   Use *that* or *but that* instead of *but what* (*They had no doubt **that** help would come*).

Calvary, Cavalry.   Mistakes here are chiefly a matter of spelling, but it is important to be aware of the difference: *Calvary* is the name of the hill where Jesus was crucified; *cavalry* refers to troops trained to fight on horseback, or more recently in armored vehicles.

Cannot.   This word is the negative form of *can*. It is written as one word.

Cannot help but.   This is a mixed construction. *Cannot help* and *cannot but* are separate expressions, either of which is correct (*He **cannot but** attempt it,* or *He **cannot help** attempting it*).

Capital, Capitol.   *Capital* is a city; *capitol* is a building. *Capital* is also an adjective, usually meaning *chief, excellent*.

Case.   This is a vague and unnecessary word in many of its common uses today. Avoid *case* and seek the exact word.

Chairperson.   Use the terms *chairman* and *chairwoman* in preference to *chairperson*, which should be used only if it is an official title in an organization or if you are quoting directly someone who has used the term.

Chaise lounge.   The second word in this term is *longue*, not *lounge*. It is a French expression meaning "long chair," and the word *longue* is pronounced the same as the English *long*. Many people simply misread the similar spelling and think that the word is our English word *lounge*.

Cite, Site.   Cite means "to quote," or "to summon officially to appear in court"

(*Thomas* **cited** *Einstein as his authority, George was* **cited** *by the police for drunken driving*). *Site* is the position or area on which anything is, has been, or will be located (*We visited the* **site** *where our new home will be built*).

Claim.   Do not use simply to mean *say*. In the correct use of *claim* some disputed right is involved (*He* **claims** *to be the heir of a very wealthy man*).

Complement, Compliment.   In its usual sense *complement* means *something that completes* (*Her navy blue shoes and bag were a* **complement** *for her gray suit*). A *compliment* is an expression of courtesy or praise (*My* **compliments** *to the chef*).

Connotate.   There is no such verb as *connotate*; the verb is *connote*, and its noun form is *connotation*.

Considerable.   This word is an adjective meaning *worthy of consideration, important* (*The idea is at least* **considerable**). When used to denote a great deal or a great many, *considerable* is colloquial or informal.

Contact.   Colloquial and sometimes vague when used for *see, meet, communicate with*, as in *I must* **contact** *my agent*.

Continual, Continuous.   *Continual* means *repeated often* (*The interruptions were* **continual**). *Continuous* means *going on without interruption* (*For two days the pain was* **continuous**).

Convince, Persuade.   Do not use *convince* for *persuade* as in *I* **convinced** *him to wash the dishes. Convince* means *to overcome doubt* (*I* **convinced** *him of the soundness of my plan*). *Persuade* means *to win over by argument or entreaty* (*I* **persuaded** *him to wash the dishes*).

Couple.   This word, followed by *of*, is informal for *two* or *a few*.

Credible, Creditable.   *Credible* means *believable* (*His evidence was not* **credible**). *Creditable* means *deserving esteem or admiration* (*The acting of the male lead was a* **creditable** *performance*).

Critique.   This word is a noun, not a verb; it means a critical review or comment dealing with an artistic work. The correct verb is *evaluate*.

Cupfuls, Cupsful.   The plural of cupful is *cupfuls*, not *cupsful*.

Data.   *Data* is the plural of *datum, something given or known*. It usually refers to a body of facts or figures. It normally takes a plural verb (*These* **data** *are important*). At times, however, *data* may be considered a collective noun and used with a singular verb.

Definitely.   This is frequently used to mean *very* or *quite*. A trite expression, it should be avoided for this reason as well as for its lack of accuracy.

Different than.   Most good writers use *different from*, not *different than*.

Disinterested.   Often confused with *uninterested. Disinterested* means *unbiased, impartial; uninterested* means *lacking interest in*.

Don't.   A contraction of *do not*. Do not write *he, she*, or *it don't*.

Drapes.   Incorrect when used as a noun to mean *curtains. Drape* is the verb; *draperies* is the correct noun form.

Due to.   Do not use *due to* for *because of* as in **Due to** *a lengthy illness, he left college. Due to* is correctly used after a noun or linking verb (*His failure,* **due to** *laziness, was not surprising. The accident was* **due to** *carelessness*).

Dyeing, Dying. *Dyeing* refers to the coloring of materials with dye. Do not omit the *e*, which would confuse the word with *dying*, meaning *expiring*.

Emigrant, Immigrant. A person who moves from one place to another is both an *emigrant* and an *immigrant*, but he emigrates *from* one place and immigrates *to* the other.

Enthuse, Enthused. These words are colloquial and always unacceptable in writing.

Equally as. Do not use these two words together; omit either *equally* or *as*. Do not write *Water is **equally as** necessary as air*; write *Water is **as** necessary as air* or *Water and air are **equally** necessary.*

Etc. An abbreviation of Latin *et* (*and*) and *cetera* (*other things*). It should not be preceded by *and*, nor should it be used as a catch-all expression to avoid a clear and exact ending of an idea or a sentence.

Everyday, Every day. When written as one word (*everyday*), this expression is an adjective (*Mother's **everyday** china is ironstone*). When used adverbially to indicate how often something happens, it is written as two words (***Every day** at noon I eat an apple and drink a glass of milk*).

Exam. A colloquial abbreviation for *examination*. Compare *gym, dorm, lab,* and *prof.*

Expect. This word means *to look forward to* or *foresee*. Do not use it to mean *suspect* or *suppose.*

Fact that. This is an example of wordiness, usually amounting to redundancy. Most sentences can omit the phrase *the fact that* without changing the sense of what is said (***The fact that** he wanted a new bicycle was the reason why he stole the money* may be effectively reduced to *He stole the money because he wanted a new bicycle*). Whenever you are tempted to use this expression, try rewording the sentence without it; you will have a more concise and a clearer statement.

Farther, Further. The two words are often confused. *Farther* means *at or to a more distant point in space or time; further* means *to a greater extent, in addition*. One says *It is **farther** to Minneapolis from Chicago than from here*, but *We will talk **further** about this tomorrow.*

Faze. Colloquial for *to disturb* or *to agitate*. Most commonly used in the negative (*Mother's angry looks didn't **faze** Jimmy*).

Feel. *Feel* means to perceive through the physical senses or through the emotions. This word should not be used as a careless equivalent of *think* or *believe*, both of which refer to mental activity.

Fellow. Colloquial when used to mean a *person.*

Fewer, Less. Use *fewer* to refer to a number, *less* to refer to amount (*Where there are **fewer** persons, there is **less** noise*).

Fine. Colloquial when used as a term of general approval.

Fix. *Fix* is a verb, meaning *to make firm or stable*. Used as a noun meaning *a bad condition*, it is colloquial.

Flaunt, Flout. *Flaunt* means *to exhibit ostentatiously, to show off* (*She **flaunted** her new mink coat before her friends*). *Flout* means to show *contempt for, to scorn* (*Margaret often **flouts** the rules of good sportsmanship*).

Forego, Forgo. *Forego* means to *precede* or *go before* (*The **foregoing** data were* *gathered two years ago. Forgo* means *to give up, relinquish* (*I am afraid I must* **forgo** *the pleasure of meeting your friends today*).

Formally, Formerly. *Formally* means *in a formal manner* (*He was* **formally** *initiated into his fraternity last night*). *Formerly* means *at a former time* (*They* **formerly** *lived in Ohio*).

Gentleman, Lady. Do not use these words as synonyms for *man* and *woman.*

Got. This is a correct past participle of the verb *to get* (*He had* **got** *three traffic tickets in two days*). *Gotten* is an alternative past participle of *to get.*

Guess. Colloquial when used for *suppose* or *believe.*

Guy. Slang when used for *boy* or *man.*

Hanged, Hung. *Hanged* is the correct past tense or past participle of *hang* when capital punishment is meant (*The cattle rustlers were* **hanged** *at daybreak*). *Hung* is the past tense and past participle in every other sense of the term (*We* **hung** *popcorn and cranberries on the Christmas tree*).

Hardly, Scarcely. Do not use with a negative. *I* **can't hardly** *see it* borders on the illiterate. Write *I* **can hardly** *see it* or (if you cannot see it at all) *I* **can't** *see it.*

Healthful, Healthy. Places are *healthful* if persons may be *healthy* living in them.

Hopefully. This word means *in a hopeful manner* (*She* **hopefully** *began getting ready for her blind date*). Do not use this modifier to mean *it is hoped* or *let us hope* (**Hopefully**, *the new rail system for Atlanta will be completed within five years*).

If, Whether. In careful writing do not use *if* for *whether. Let me know* **if** *you are coming* does not mean exactly the same thing as *Let me know* **whether** *you are coming.* The latter leaves no doubt that a reply is expected.

Imply, Infer. *Imply* means *to suggest, to express indirectly. Infer* means *to conclude,* as on the basis of suggestion or implication. A writer *implies* to a reader; a reader *infers* from a writer.

Incidently. There is no such word. The correct form is *incidentally,* based on the adjective *incidental.*

Into, In to. *Into* is a preposition meaning *toward the inside* and is followed by an object of the preposition. Do not use the one-word form of this expression when the object of the preposition is the object of *to* only and *in* is an adverbial modifier. Say *He went* **into** *the building* but *The men handed their application forms* **in to** *the personnel manager.*

Irregardless. No such word exists. *Regardless* is the correct word.

Its, It's. The form *its* is possessive (*Every dog has* **its** *day*). *It's* is a contraction of *it is* (**It's** *a pity she's a bore*).

It's me. Formal English requires *It is I. It's* **me** is informal or colloquial, perfectly acceptable in conversation but not proper for written English. Compare the French idiom *C'est moi.*

Kid. Used to mean a child or young person, *kid* is slang.

Kind, Sort. These are singular forms and should be modified accordingly (*this kind, that sort*). *Kinds* and *sorts* are plural, and they, of course, have plural modifiers.

Kind of, Sort of. Do not use these to mean *rather* as in *He was* **kind of** (or **sort of**) *lazy.*

Last, Latest.   *Last* implies that there will be no more. *Latest* does not prevent the possibility of another appearance later. The proper sense of both is seen in the sentence *After seeing his **latest** play, we hope that it is his **last**.*

Lend, Loan.   The use of *loan* as a verb is incorrect. *Loan* is a noun. The distinction between the two words may be seen in the sentence *If you will **lend** me ten dollars until Friday, I will appreciate the **loan**.*

Like, As.   Confusion in the use of these two words results from using *like* as a conjunction. The preposition *like* should be followed by an object (*He ran **like** an antelope*). The conjunction *as* is followed by a clause (*He did **as** he wished, He talked **as** though he were crazy*). The incorrect use of *as* as a preposition is a kind of reaction against the use of *like* as a conjunction. Consider the sentence: *Many species of oaks, **as** the red oak, the white oak, the water oak, are found in the Southeast.* Here the correct word is *like*, not *as*.

Literally.   The word means *faithfully, to the letter, letter for letter, exactly.* Do not use in the sense of *completely*, or *in effect*. A sentence may be copied *literally*; but one never, except under extraordinary circumstances, **literally** *devours a book.* Frequently, the word *virtually*, meaning *in effect or essence, though not in fact,* is the correct word.

Lot, Lots.   Colloquial or informal when used to mean *many* or *much.*

Mad.   The essential meaning of *mad* is *insane.* When used to mean *angry*, it is informal.

May Be, Maybe.   *May be* is a verb phrase (*It **may be** that you are right*). *Maybe* used as an adverb means *perhaps* (***Maybe** you are right*).

Mean.   Used for disagreeable (*He has a **mean** disposition, He is **mean** to me*), the word is informal or colloquial.

Media.   *Media* is the plural of *medium, a means, agency,* or *instrumentality.* It is often incorrectly used in the plural as though it were singular, as in *The **media** is playing an important role in political races this year.*

Midnight, Noon.   Neither of these words needs the word *twelve* before it. They themselves refer to specific times, so *twelve* is redundant.

Most.   Do not use for *almost.* **Almost** *all of them are here* or **Most** *of them are here* is correct. **Most all** *of them are here* is incorrect.

Muchly.   There is no such word as *muchly.* *Much* is both adjective and adverb (***Much** water has flowed over the dam. Thank you very **much***).

Mutual.   The use of *mutual* for *common* is usually avoided by careful writers. **Common** *knowledge,* **common** *property,* **common** *dislikes* are things shared by two or more persons. **Mutual** *admiration* means *admiration of each for the other.*

Myself.   Colloquial when used as a substitute for *I* or *me*, as in *He and **myself** were there.* It is correctly used intensively (*I **myself** will do it*) and reflexively (*I blame only **myself***).

Nauseated, Nauseous.   These two words are frequently confused. *Nauseated* means "feeling a sickness at the stomach; a sensation of impending vomiting" (*I was **nauseated** because of having eaten my lunch too fast*). *Nauseous* means "sickening, disgusting; loathsome" (*The **nauseous** odor of the gas was affecting everyone in the building*).

Nice.   *Nice* is a catch-all word that has lost its force because it has no clearcut, specific meaning as a modifier. When writing in praise of something, select an adjective that conveys more specific information than *nice* does.

Of. Unnecessary after such prepositions as *off, inside, outside* (not *He fell **off of** the cliff* but *He fell **off** the cliff*).

On account of. Do not use as a conjunction; the phrase should be followed by an object of the preposition *of* (***on account of** his illness*). *He was absent **on account of** he was sick* is incorrect.

Oral, Verbal, Written. Use *oral* to refer to spoken words (*An **oral** examination is sometimes nerve-wracking for a student*); use *verbal* to contrast a communication in words to some other kind of communication (*His scowl told me more than any **verbal** message could*); use *written* when referring to anything put on paper.

Orientate. There is no such word. The verb is *orient*, meaning *to cause to become familiar with or adjusted to facts or a situation* (*He **oriented** himself by finding the North Star*). The noun is *orientation*.

Over with. The *with* is unnecessary in such expressions as *The game was **over with** by five o'clock*.

Party. Colloquial when used to mean *a person*. Properly used in legal documents (***party** of the first part*).

Peeve. Either as a verb or noun, *peeve* is informal diction.

Personally. This word is often redundant and is a hackneyed, sometimes irritating expression, as in ***Personally,** I think you are making a big mistake*.

Plan on. Omit *on*. In standard practice idiom calls for an infinitive or a direct object after *plan*. *They **planned** to go* or *They **planned** a reception* are both correct usage.

Plenty. This word is a noun, not an adverb. Do not write *He was **plenty** worried*.

Pore, Pour. *Pore*, meaning *to meditate* or *to study intently and with steady application*, is a verb used with the preposition *over* (*She **pored over** her chemistry assignment for several hours*). It should not be confused with *pour*, meaning *to set a liquid flowing or falling* (*They **poured** the tea into fragile china cups*).

Principal, Principle. *Principal* is both adjective and noun (***principal** parts, **principal** of the school, **principal** and interest*). *Principle* is a noun only (***principles** of philosophy, a man of **principle***).

Pupil, Student. Schoolchildren in the elementary grades are called *pupils*; in grades nine through twelve *student* or *pupil* is correct; for college the term must always be *student*.

Quote, Quotation. *Quote* is a verb and should not be used as a noun, as in *The **quote** you gave is from Shakespeare, not the Bible*. *Quotation* is the noun.

Real. Do not use for *really*. *Real* is an adjective; *really* is an adverb (*The **real** gems are **really** beautiful*).

Reason is because. This is not idiomatic English. The subject-linking verb construction calls for a predicate nominative, but *because* is a subordinating conjunction that introduces an adverbial clause. Write *The **reason** I was late **is that** I had an accident*, not *The **reason** I was late **is because** I had an accident*.

Respectfully, Respectively. *Respectfully* means *with respect*, as in *The young used to act **respectfully** toward their elders*. *Respectively* is a word seldom needed; it means *in the order designated,* as in *The men and women took their seats on the right and left* **respectively.**

Reverend. This word, like *Honorable,* is not a noun, but an honorific adjective. It is not a title like *doctor* or *president.* It is properly used preceding *Mr.* or the given name or initials, as in *the* **Reverend** *Mr. Gilbreath, the* **Reverend** *Earl Gilbreath, the* **Reverend** *J. E. Gilbreath.* To use the word as a title as in **Reverend,** *will you lead us in prayer?* or *Is there a* **Reverend** *in the house?* is incorrect. **Reverend** *Gilbreath* instead of *the* **Reverend** *Mr. Gilbreath* is almost as bad.

Right. In the sense of *very* or *extremely, right* is colloquial or dialectal. Do not write (or say) *I'm* **right** *glad to know you.*

Same. The word is an adjective, not a pronoun. Do not use it as in *We received your order and will give* **same** *immediate attention.* Substitute *it* for *same.*

Savings. This word is frequently misused in the plural when the singular is the correct form. It is particularly puzzling that many people use this plural with a singular article, as in *The 10 percent discount gives you a* **savings** *of nine dollars. A saving* is the proper usage here. Another common error occurs with *Daylight* **Saving** *Time;* the right form again is *Saving,* not *Savings.*

Shape. In formal writing do not use *shape* for *condition* as in *He played badly because he was in poor* **shape.** In this sense *shape* is informal.

Should of, would of. Do not use these terms for *should have, would have.*

Situation. This is another catch-all term, frequently used redundantly, as in *It was a fourth down* **situation.** Fourth down *is* a situation, so the word itself is repetitious. This vague term can usually be omitted or replaced with a more specific word.

So. Avoid the use of *so* for *very,* as in *Thank you* **so** *much. So* used as an adverb means *thus* or *like this.*

Some. Do not use for *somewhat,* as in *She is* **some** *better after her illness.*

Species. This word is both singular and plural. One may speak of *one species* or *three species.* The word usually refers to a kind of plant or animal.

Sprightly, Spritely. *Sprightly* means *animated, vivacious, lively.* There is no such word as *spritely,* but many people use this term, probably because it suggests the word *sprite,* an *elf* or *fairy.* Do not write *Her* **spritely** *conversation was fascinating.*

Stationary, Stationery. *Stationary* means *fixed, not moving.* Remember that *stationery,* which is paper for writing letters, is sold by a *stationer.*

Statue, Stature, Statute. A *statue* is a piece of sculpture. *Stature* is bodily height, often used figuratively to mean *level of achievement, status,* or *importance.* A *statute* is a law or regulation.

Strata. This is the plural of the Latin *stratum.* One speaks of *a stratum* of rock but of *several strata.*

Super, Fantastic, Incredible. When used to describe something exciting or marvelous, these overworked words actually add little to our everyday conversation because they have lost their original force. At any rate, they must never be a part of written formal English, as they are simply slang, and trite slang at that.

Suppose, Supposed. Many people incorrectly use the first form *suppose* before an infinitive when the second form *supposed* is needed, as in *Am I **suppose** to meet you at five o'clock?* The past participle *supposed* must go along with the auxiliary verb *am* to form the passive voice. This error almost certainly arises from an inability to hear the final *d* when it precedes the *t* in the *to* of the infinitive. The correct form is *Am I **supposed** to meet you at five o'clock?*

Sure, Surely. Do not use the adjective *sure* for the adverb *surely*. *I am **sure** that you are right* and *I am **surely** glad to be here* are correct.

Trustee, Trusty. The word *trustee* means *a person elected or appointed to direct funds or policy* for a person or an institution, as in *Mr. Higginbotham is a **trustee** on the bank's board of directors.* A *trusty*, on the other hand, is a prisoner granted special privileges because he is believed trustworthy, as in *Although he was a **trusty**, Harris escaped from prison early today.*

Too. *Too* means *in addition*, or *excessively*. It is incorrect to use the word to mean *very* or *very much*, as in *I was not **too** impressed with her latest book* or *I'm afraid I don't know him **too** well.*

Try and. Use *try to*, not *try and*, in such expressions as *Try **to** get here on time* (not *Try **and** get here on time*).

Type. Colloquial in expressions like *this **type** book;* write *this **type of** book.*

Undoubtably, Undoubtedly. There is no such word as *undoubtably*. The correct word is *undoubtedly*.

Unique. If referring to something as the only one of its kind, you may correctly use *unique*. (*The Grand Canyon is a **unique** geological formation.*) The word does not mean *rare, strange*, or *remarkable*, and there are no degrees of *uniqueness*; to say that something is *the **most unique** thing one has ever seen* is faulty diction.

Use (Used) to could. Do not use for *once could* or *used to be able to*.

Very. Do not use as a modifier of a past participle, as in ***very** broken*. English idiom calls for ***badly** broken* or ***very badly** broken*.

Wait for, Wait on. *To wait for* means *to look forward to, to expect* (*For two hours I have **waited for** you*). *To wait on* means *to serve* (*The butler and two maids **waited on** the guests at dinner*).

Want in, Want off, Want out. These forms are dialectal. Do not use them for *want to come in, want to get off, want to get out*.

Way. Colloquial when used for *away* as in ***Way** down upon the Swanee River*.

Ways. Colloquial when used for *way* as in *a long **ways** to go*.

Whose, Who's. The possessive form is *whose* (***Whose** book is this?*). *Who's* is a contraction of *who is* (***Who's** at the door?*). The use of *whose* as a neuter possessive is confirmed by the history of the word and the practice of good writers. *The house **whose** roof is leaking* is more natural and less clumsy than *the house the roof **of which** is leaking*.

Your, You're. The possessive form is *your* (*Tell me **your** name*). *You're* is a contraction of *you are*.

Exercise 85 Diction

Rewrite the following sentences, reducing wordiness. Be careful that your reduction does not lead to a series of short, choppy sentences, sometimes referred to as "primer style."

Example: Salary-wise, my job is not of the type that I have always considered that a good job should be, but nevertheless, in my opinion, one sometimes has to make occasional sacrifices in order to use the talents that he has.

My job does not pay a good salary, but I am willing to sacrifice money for the chance to use my talents.

1. When we saw the boat coming into view up the river, it was moving at a fast rate of speed, and I believe that the person who was operating the boat must have been an inexperienced novice in my opinion.

2. The bulletin board notice stressed the importance of the strong necessity for student assistance applications to be turned in promptly to the office which handles student affairs and which needs all necessary information to be available at the proper time.

3. The police are convinced of the certainty that the fatal slaying took place last night at nine o'clock in the evening, and that the perpetrator was a female person who appeared to be acquainted with her victim whom she apparently knew.

4. I think that Betsy's hair, which is red, is equally as beautiful as Jane's hair, which is black, and as a matter of personal taste, I like both redheads and brunettes.

5. Honestly, I am telling the truth when I say that Harvey is a universally well-liked, popular person who will never go back on his friends or be disloyal.

6. When they were ready to leave, our departing guests who had been visiting us suddenly came to the conclusion that they had decided to stay one more week.

7. My brother says that he wants to return back to his old boyhood haunts in the Adirondacks where he used to spend a great deal of time as a child.

8. Sarah is an attractive girl whom everyone is drawn to, and she is a very unique person in her personality.

9. The fact of the matter is that, given the opportunity to display her talent and creativity, Martha would be able to demonstrate that she is an artist second to none in her ability to produce top-quality work.

10. Jenny's new beret, which is a beautiful royal blue color, was brought to her from Paris, France, by her grandmother, and the beret is lovely on Jenny because of her red-gold colored hair.

Exercise 86 | Diction

Rewrite the following sentences, reducing wordiness. Be careful that your reduction does not lead to a series of short, choppy declarative sentences, sometimes called "primer style."

Example: Pete found that he had been erroneously misinformed by the airport information service, which told him that Gloria's plane would be arriving at 8 P.M. that night.

The airport information service had misinformed Pete in saying that Gloria's plane would arrive at 8 P.M.

1. Henry and I went to ask Virginia to go to a movie with us, and the movie was an old one, and Virginia decided that she did not want to see it again, so Henry and I went without her.

2. In terms of finalizing our plans for building a new house which will be our future residence, John and I are considering the possibility of perhaps building a home made of red brick combined with white frame.

3. In the conversation that Terry and Steve had with each other they agreed that they were in accord in connection with their views concerning national politics.

4. In circumstances where a child is the only child, it is often the case that the parents will be indulgent with the child and let him have his way.

5. Mother gave Lil the chance of making a choice between chocolate ripple ice cream and strawberry ice cream, and she made the selection of chocolate ripple.

6. Our latest project that we are working on is making a den for Father out of the room downstairs in the basement, and we have been carpeting the floor and putting new wallpaper on the walls to improve the looks of the place.

7. There is no new development at this point in time concerning the argument between Marilyn and Don, and I am in doubt as to whether they will ever solve their differences from the standpoint of future friendship.

8. It was a truly meaningful experience that I had when I attended the lecture that Mr. Rowse gave on the subject of Shakespeare and his sonnets.

9. In examining the overall picture of college students and their lifestyle, it is found that many students nowadays are interested in the traditional way of life, and they have rejected the old rebellious attitudes of a decade ago and are no longer concerned with them.

10. Considering the fact that Evelyn is a native of England, it is interesting to note that she utilizes many terms of American slang more often than do her friends who are citizens of the United States.

Exercise 87 Diction

The following sentences contain one or more trite expressions or euphemisms. Underline the trite and euphemistic phrases, and for each one write either **T** or **E** in the space at the right.

Example: Tom <u>got up with the chickens</u> to have breakfast, and
he really <u>ate like a horse</u>.   *T, T*

1. Last night I had a terrible tummy ache, which was probably the
   result of eating too much lasagna.   _____

2. In the final analysis, it appears that Jack is determined to please his
   peer group, and I suppose that this attitude is par for the course.   _____

3. Old Mr. Tatum passed away last Thursday, and he will be sorely
   missed by all who knew him.   _____

4. It certainly stands to reason that Americans in all walks of life should
   be willing to make the supreme sacrifice for their country.   _____

5. Terry, Charlotte, Meg, and, last but not least, Steve are to be con-
   gratulated on their good fortune as proud possessors of Good Citi-
   zenship awards.   _____

6. I have worked like a dog to make my term paper fill the bill, and
   you better believe that I'm expecting a good grade.   _____

7. Gary is now driving a previously owned Chrysler, and I hope that
   he hasn't bought a pig in a poke.   _____

8. Although he is in his golden years, Dr. Newton plays eighteen holes
   of golf a day and is as fresh as a daisy when he's finished.   _____

9. Sam blames inadequate cash flow for his financial embarrassment,
   but he says that all things considered, his future looks bright.   _____

10. I do believe that Sam is a smart cookie and that with a little intestinal
    fortitude he can save the day.   _____

11. We were doomed to disappointment when we went on our annual
    outing; it rained cats and dogs, and we were all soaked to the skin.   _____

12. After we got back home, though, we had a ball, playing games and
    dancing, just as happy as larks.   _____

13. Rip Rossiter, the professional football player, has been told to turn in
    his playbook, so he is feeling down on the world.   _____

14. The two factions have concluded that to interface would be helpful in solving the dispute, and their leaders are hoping for a meeting of minds. _____

15. Phyllis has outdone herself again with that delicious pound cake; she is really one in a million. _____

16. When I had the accident, Harry was a tower of strength, calling the doctor, keeping the crowd away, and standing by me when the chips were down. _____

17. It looks as though Grandfather has defeated the grim reaper once again; he is recovering nicely from his heart attack and will leave the hospital for the senior citizens' home tomorrow. _____

18. It's like a breath of fresh air to be with Ginny; she is more fun than a barrel of monkeys. _____

19. I told Pete that he is as crazy as a loon to try that steep climb up Brasstown Bald mountain, but he is stubborn as a mule when he wants to do something. _____

20. Quick as a flash, Pete told me that I was just a gloomy Gus and that I ought to be horsewhipped for being such a wet blanket. _____

Exercise 88 Diction

The following sentences contain unidiomatic uses of prepositions. Underline each preposition that is incorrectly used and write the correct form at the right.

Example: Mamie and Susan are angry <u>at</u> Jo for going
home without them.   _____*with*_____

1. Walter came running in the library and said that the gym
   was on fire.   _____

2. There is an argument going on between those five cheer-
   leaders about the way to form a human pyramid.   _____

3. Our whole family enjoys listening at "A Prairie Home Companion" every Saturday.   _____

4. Mrs. Greer said, "I will agree with your proposal to fine
   parking violators if you will assign me a free parking space
   besides the City Hall."   _____

5. Sid's plans for what he will be doing the summer after
   graduation are quite different than his father's.   _____

6. Beside wanting to go to Marineland, I also want to see
   Epcot while we are in Florida.   _____

7. I tried to get off of the boat, but it was rocking so badly that
   I couldn't keep my balance.   _____

8. Morris is terrible with doing anything mechanical; he is
   better in writing and playing the piano.   _____

9. Unfortunately, Horner's bunt went right in the pitcher's
   glove.   _____

10. The foreign diplomat boarded on the plane as soon as its
    doors opened.   _____

11. I was standing there waiting on June to finish her letter
    when the strangest thing of the world happened.   _____

12. The slice of delicious coconut cake fell off my plate and on
    the floor.   _____

13. Of all my travels I have never seen any other mountains
    quite on a par to the Swiss Alps.   _____

14. I am sure you know that I am devoted and care a great deal for Aunt Amelia. _____

15. Several out of the alumni objected against the idea of waiting to May for our class reunion. _____

Exercise 89 Diction

The following exercises (89–92) are based on the Glossary of Faulty Diction in Chapter 22. Underline all errors, colloquialisms (informal expressions), and slang and write the correct or preferred forms at the right.

Example: This damp weather has had a terrible <u>affect</u> on

my sinuses.   _____*effect*_____

1. Mr. Lomax says that he is going fishing tomorrow irregard-less of the weather.   _____

2. Are you really planning on going to that air-conditioned res-taurant without a sweater?   _____

3. Pat was in such a hurry to get to the wedding on time that she literally swallowed her dinner whole.   _____

4. I was sort of disappointed that Mary and Sue didn't invite me to go skating with them.   _____

5. Betty asked Frances to critique the essay that she had writ-ten for Philosophy 321.   _____

6. Barry said that he couldn't hardly get up early enough to deliver Doug's papers for him.   _____

7. I wish you would except my apology, Marilyn; I hate for there to be trouble among us.   _____

8. Being as Larry is ill, he is apt to miss the game tonight.   _____

9. I feel that the less calories there are in a dessert, the less I will enjoy it.   _____

10. Ruth's dying her hair that brilliant shade of red is aggravat-ing to her mother.   _____

11. Please don't blame your injured foot on Ray; he stepped on it accidently, you know.   _____

12. Are you inferring that Ray is clumsy and stupid?   _____

13. That guy who was using profanity at the basketball game is definitely no gentleman.   _____

14. Donna was enthused over the fact that she had been asked to host a party for the board of directors.   _____

15. Undoubtably you will be impressed with Reverend Jones's sermon; he is a man of high principal.   _____

Exercise 90 Diction

Underline all errors, colloquialisms, and slang expressions in the following sentences and write the correct or preferred forms at the right.

Example: Hilda Sharpe has been elected chairperson of a committee that will in-   *chairman*
vestigate ways to improve the library.   ___*chairwoman*___

1. Bob claims that he was studying his French last
   night, so my seeing him at the bowling alley
   must have been an optical allusion.   _____

2. It don't make any difference to me if Luther does
   or does not decide to go swimming with us.   _____

3. Ralph turned his test paper into the professor
   and then had the sinking feeling that he had got
   one quote confused with another.   _____

4. After he had spent half the night pouring over
   that Shakespeare play, he was peeved with himself for making that sort of error.   _____

5. "I should of reread my paper before turning it
   in," said Ralph, "but hopefully I won't fail."   _____

6. Marty was trying to convince her father to lend
   her his car, but he seemed totally disinterested
   in her pleas.   _____

7. I am planning on getting Mr. Martin to loan me
   his typewriter until mine can be repaired.   _____

8. Are you suppose to bring the salad for our cov-
   ered-dish supper, Louise?   _____

9. The reason that I did not wait for you, Luke, is
   because Dick and myself were late for choir
   practice.   _____

10. It was real late, and Dick was muchly concerned
    that Mr. Anderson would be mad at us if we
    weren't on time for practice.   _____

11. The party who backed into my station wagon in the parking lot could not have helped but know that he had done lots of damage.   _____

12. Alice was awfully quiet when Mother kept asking about what had happened to the last slice of chocolate pie.   _____

13. Mrs. Samson chaired the meeting with great poise; afterward, everyone complemented her on her tact during the argument situation.   _____

14. Last night I stayed up until twelve midnight on account of I was reading a whodunit that I just couldn't put down.   _____

15. Many Europeans, as the French for instance, are amazed that most Americans speak only English.   _____

Exercise 91 Diction

Underline all errors, colloquialisms, and trite expressions; then write the correct or preferred form at the right.

Example: I was <u>right</u> upset when my dog
knocked the postman off his feet. _____ *quite* _____

1. If you will loan me your pen, I will return it at
the end of this period. _____

2. It is against my father's principals for me to borrow ahead on my allowance. _____

3. Meg was feeling nauseous, so she went outside
to get some fresh air. _____

4. When I was a kid, lots of my friends liked to go
to the movies on Saturday afternoon. _____

5. There was always a serial, with Indians and set-
tlers battling each other, until the calvary arrived
to save the day. _____

6. My friend Richard is very into scuba diving; he
can't hardly wait until spring holidays and the
chance to go to St. Thomas. _____

7. I think that less than twenty people showed for
the meeting Dr. Means chaired last night. _____

8. Shirley felt badly that her roommate was
aggravated with her. _____

9. Mr. Franklin messengered the important papers
to me, and they arrived before my plane took
off. _____

10. Hopefully, Dianne, your next move will take you
and your family to a healthy climate. _____

11. Many people feel that the new tax laws will
impact unfavorably upon them. _____

12. Judson spent the morning laying around the house when he was suppose to be cutting firewood.   _____

13. A man of his statue is certain to be in the highest strata of government.   _____

14. Its a mystery to me how that rabbit got out of it's pen last night.   _____

15. I have never seen a more disinterested group of participants than those at the so-called pep rally last night.   _____

16. Everyday Frederick swims forty laps, and you can bet your bottom dollar that he will lose weight by Christmas.   _____

17. I only wanted one quart of milk, Josephine, and you have brought enough to sink a battleship.   _____

18. Emily was anxious to get to the church on time, but Lois and Mary Louise delayed her by arguing among themselves about which car to take.   _____

19. Martha Sue says that it don't matter a whole lot whether I use two cupsful of sugar or three in my caramel icing.   _____

20. The fact that you have flaunted the college's rules of good conduct has created averse attitudes in many of your fellow classmates.   _____

Exercise 92 Diction

Underline all errors and colloquialisms; then write the correct or preferred forms at the right.

Example: Frances said that she was not <u>adverse</u> to being the nominee for president of the skiing club. _____*averse*_____

1. At exactly twelve midnight the posse hung the cattle rustler. _____

2. I hope that Lionel will let us know if he is going with us to New Orleans. _____

3. We have tried to convince him to go for at least a couple of weeks, but he seems not to be really enthused. _____

4. The fellow should be more decisive; I cannot help but think that Lionel is wishy-washy. _____

5. Dorry's favorite episode in *Gone with the Wind* is Scarlett's making herself a dress out of the parlor drapes. _____

6. As the story goes, Scarlett looked all together lovely in the green velvet dress and received many complements. _____

7. My great-grandfather was an alumni of Emory University and was graduated there at age sixteen. _____

8. Incidently, I heard Mrs. Rawlings tell Mr. Bishop that she will not agree with his proposal to plant gingko trees along Prince Avenue. _____

9. Standing there in the dark, I tried to orientate myself, but I nearly screamed when a twig accidently brushed across my face. _____

10. It is awful hard to except the idea that Marcia and I will be going to different schools next year. _____

11. It will take awhile to get use to my new sur-
roundings, but I suppose everything will turn
out alright.   _____

12. Martin claims that he can swim a mile under water; his continuous boasting is definitely hard to
take.   _____

13. We decided to forego the dubious pleasure of an
evening with Rudy; that gentleman's crude manners make him a person to be avoided.   _____

14. Andrew, Milton, and myself poured over the entertainment section of the paper, trying to select
a good movie.   _____

15. Anyone of the shows would have been satisfactory as far as their quality, but those guys are
hard to please.   _____

16. I don't know but what this data is inaccurate; I
must examine them farther.   _____

17. The word *home* connotates warmth, affection,
and welcome; I personally think that it is a beautiful word.   _____

18. Marge's spritely letter, written on lavender
stationary, was most entertaining.   _____

19. Whose going to administrate the scholarship
fund, now that the woman who formally did so
has retired?   _____

20. Heavy red mud was clinging to his shoes, due to
the downpour of the night before, but the fact
that he was ruining the carpet didn't seem to
faze him.   _____

23

Building a Vocabulary

As you know from your own experience, one of your greatest needs for success-ful composition is to improve your vocabulary. One of the best ways to build a vocabulary, of course, is always to look up in a dictionary the meanings of unfamiliar words that you hear or read. This chapter on vocabulary will provide you with a minimal body of information concerning word formation and the derivations of various words comprising the English language. For a more inten-sified study of all aspects of this fascinating subject, including ways to strengthen your own vocabulary, consult and use frequently a book devoted exclusively to this purpose.

Learning the derivation of a word will fix in your mind the meaning and spelling of that word. Because the largest part of our English vocabulary comes from three main sources — the Old English, the Greek, and the Latin languages — a knowledge of commonly used prefixes, roots, and suffixes from these languages will prove useful.

A *prefix* is a short element — a syllable or syllables — that comes before the main part of the word, which is the *root*. A *suffix* is added to the end of the word. Thus the word *hypodermic* has *hypo-*, meaning "under," as its *prefix*; *derm*, mean-ing "skin," as its *root*; and *-ic*, meaning "having to do with," as its *suffix*. You see that the *prefix* and the *suffix* of a word modify the meaning of the *root*. The word *hypodermic*, then, when used as an adjective, means "having to do with some-thing under the skin."

There are actually more words of classical origin, that is, Greek and Latin, than of Old English in our language; however, we use Old English words much more frequently in every sentence that we write or speak. For instance, the Old English prefixes *un-* (not) and *for-* (from) are found in many of our words, such as *unfair* and *forbid*. The Old English root-word *hlaf* (loaf) gives us the word *lord*, a lord being a loafkeeper or warden (*hlaf-weard*). The root-word *god* (God) gives us *goodbye*, a contraction of *God be with ye*. Old English suffixes such as *-ish* (having the qualities of) and *-ly* (like) are seen in many words such as *foolish* and *courtly*.

If you combine the Greek root *tele*, meaning "at a distance," with *graph* (writing), *phone* (sound), *scope* (seeing), *pathy* (feeling), you have *telegraph* (writing at a distance), *telephone* (sound at a distance), *telescope* (seeing at a distance), *telepathy* (feeling at a distance).

The Latin root *duc* is seen in such words as *adduce, aqueduct, conduce, conduct, induce, produce, reduce, seduce, conductor, ducal,* and *ductile*. If you know that *duc* means "to lead," and if you know the meanings of the prefixes and suffixes combined with it, you can make out the meanings of most of these words.

Each prefix, root, and suffix that you learn may lead to a knowledge of many new words or give a clearer understanding of many you already know. Therefore, a list of some of the most common prefixes, roots, and suffixes is given below. Look up others in your dictionary, or, as suggested earlier, get a good vocabulary textbook and use it often.

■ 23a Prefixes

Prefixes Showing Number or Amount

BI– (*bis–*) two	(*bi*)annual, (*bis*)sextile
CENT– (*centi–*) hundred	(*cent*)enarian, (*centi*)pede
DEC– (*deca–*) ten	(*dec*)ade, (*Deca*)logue
HEMI– half	(*hemi*)sphere, (*hemi*)stich
MILLI– (*mille–*) thousand	(*milli*)on, (*mille*)nnium
MULTI– many, much	(*multi*)form, (*multi*)graph
MON– (*mono–*) one	(*mono*)gyny, (*mono*)tone
OCTA– (*octo–*) eight	(*octa*)ve, (*octo*)pus
PAN– all	(*pan*)acea, (*pan*)demonium, (*pan*)orama
PENTA– five	(*penta*)gon, (*Penta*)teuch
POLY– much, many	(*poly*)glot, (*poly*)chrome
PROT– (*proto–*) first	(*prot*)agonist, (*proto*)type
SEMI– half	(*semi*)circle, (*semi*)final
TRI– three	(*tri*)angle, (*tri*)ad
UNI– one	(*uni*)fy, (*uni*)cameral

Prefixes Showing Relationship in Place and Time

AB– (*a–, abs–*) from, away from	(*a*)vert, (*ab*)sent, (*abs*)tract
AD– (*ac–, af–, al–, ag–, an–, ap–, ar–, as–, at–*) to, at	(*ad*)mit, (*ac*)cede, (*af*)fect, (*al*)lude, (*ag*)gregate, (*an*)nounce, (*ap*)pear, (*ar*)rive, (*as*)sume, (*at*)tain
AMB– (*ambi–*) around, both	(*ambi*)dextrous, (*ambi*)guous
ANTE– (*ant–*) before	(*ante*)cedent, (*ante*)date
ANTI– (*ant–*) against	(*anti*)thesis, (*ant*)agonist
CATA– away, against, down	(*cata*)clysm, (*cata*)strophe
CIRCUM– around, about	(*circum*)scribe, (*circum*)stance
CON– (*com–, col–, cor–*) with, together, at the same time	(*con*)tract, (*com*)pete, (*col*)league, (*cor*)relate

CONTRA– (*counter–*) opposite, against   (*contra*)dict, (*counter*)mand
DE– from, away from, down   (*de*)pend, (*de*)form, (*de*)tract
DIA– through, across   (*dia*)gram, (*dia*)meter
DIS– (*di, dif–*) off, away from   (*dis*)tract, (*di*)verge, (*dif*)fuse
EN– (*em–, in–*) in, into   (*en*)counter, (*em*)brace, (*in*)duct
EPI– on, over, among, outside   (*epi*)dermis, (*epi*)demic
EX– (*e–, ec–, ef–*) out of, from   (*ex*)pel, (*e*)lect, (*ec*)centric, (*ef*)face
EXTRA– (*extro–*) outside, beyond   (*extra*)mural, (*extro*)vert
HYPO– under   (*hypo*)dermic, (*hypo*)crite
INTER– among, between, within   (*inter*)fere, (*inter*)rupt
INTRO– (*intra–*) within   (*intro*)spection, (*intra*)mural
OB– (*oc–, of–, op–*) against, to, before, toward   (*ob*)ject, (*oc*)casion, (*of*)fer, (*op*)press
PER– through, by   (*per*)ceiver, (*per*)ennial
PERI– around, about   (*peri*)meter, (*peri*)odical
POST– after   (*post*)script, (*post*)erity
PRE– before   (*pre*)cedent, (*pre*)decessor
PRO– before in time or position   (*pro*)logue, (*pro*)bate
RETRO– back, backward   (*retro*)gress, (*retro*)spect
SE– aside, apart   (*se*)clude, (*se*)duce
SUB– (*suc–, suf–, sug–, sum–, sup–, sus–*) under, below   (*sub*)scribe, (*suc*)cumb, (*suf*)fer, (*sug*)gest, (*sum*)mon, (*sup*)pose, (*sus*)pect
SUPER– (*sur–*) above, over   (*super*)sede, (*super*)b, (*sur*)pass
TRANS– (*tra–, traf–, tres–*) across   (*trans*)port, (*tra*)vesty, (*traf*)fic, (*tres*)pass
ULTRA– beyond   (*ultra*)marine, (*ultra*)modern

Prefixes Showing Negation

A– (*an–*) without   (*an*)onymous, (*a*)theist
IN– (*ig–, im–, il–, ir–*) not   (*in*)accurate, (*ig*)nore, (*im*)pair, (*il*)legal, (*ir*)responsible
NON– not   (*non*)essential, (*non*)entity
UN– not   (*un*)tidy, (*un*)happy

■ 23b Greek Roots

ARCH	chief, rule	(*arch*)bishop an(*archy*), mon(*archy*)
AUTO	self	(*auto*)graph, (*auto*)mobile, (*auto*)matic
BIO	life	(*bio*)logy, (*bio*)graphy, (*bio*)chemistry
CAU(S)T	burn	(*caust*)ic, holo(*caust*), (*caut*)erize
CHRON(O)	time	(*chron*)icle, (*chron*)ic, (*chrono*)logy
COSM(O)	order, arrangement	(*cosm*)os, (*cosm*)ic, (*cosmo*)graphy
CRIT	judge, discern	(*crit*)ic, (*crit*)erion
DEM(O)	people	(*demo*)crat, (*demo*)cracy, (*dem*)agogue
DERM	skin	epi(*dermis*), (*derm*)a, pachy(*derm*), (*derm*)ophobe
DYN(A)(M)	power	(*dynam*)ic, (*dynam*)o, (*dyn*)asty
GRAPH	write	auto(*graph*), (*graph*)ic, geo(*graphy*)
HIPPO	horse	(*hippo*)potamus, (*hippo*)drome
HYDR(O)	water	(*hydr*)ant, (*hydr*)a, (*hydro*)gen
LOG(Y), LOGUE	saying, science	(*log*)ic, bio(*logy*), eu(*logy*), dia(*logue*)

MET(E)R	measure	thermo(*meter*), speedo(*meter*), (*metr*)ic
MICRO	small	(*micro*)be, (*micro*)scope, (*micro*)cosm
MOR(O)	fool	(*moro*)n, sopho(*more*)
NYM	name	ano(*nym*)ous, pseudo(*nym*)
PATH	experience, suffer	a(*path*)y, sym(*path*)y, (*path*)os
PED	child	(*ped*)agogue, (*ped*)ant, (*ped*)iatrician
PHIL	love	(*phil*)anthropy, (*phil*)osophy, (*phil*)ander
PHON(O)	sound	(*phono*)graph, (*phon*)etic, (*phono*)gram
PSYCH(O)	mind, soul	(*psycho*)logy, (*psych*)ic, (*Psych*)e
SOPH	wisdom	philo(*sopher*), (*soph*)ist, (*soph*)istication
THEO	God	(*theo*)logy, (*theo*)sophy, (*theo*)cratic
THERM	heat	(*therm*)ostat, (*therm*)ometer, (*therm*)os

■ 23c Latin Roots

AM	love	(*am*)ity, (*am*)orist, (*am*)orous
ANIM	breath, soul, spirit	(*anim*)al, (*anim*)ate, un(*anim*)ous
AQU(A)	water	(*aqu*)educt, (*aqua*)tic, (*aqua*)rium
AUD	hear	(*aud*)itor, (*aud*)ience, (*aud*)itorium
CAPIT	head	(*capit*)al, (*capit*)ate, (*capit*)alize
CAP(T), CEP(T), CIP(T)	take	(*cap*)tive, pre(*cept*), pre(*cip*)itate
CED, CESS	go, yield	ante(*ced*)ent, con(*cede*), ex(*cess*)ive
CENT	hundred	(*cent*)ury, (*cent*)urion, per(*cent*)age
CER(N), CRI(M,T), CRE(M,T)	separate, judge, choose	dis(*cern*), (*crim*)inal, dis(*crete*)
CRED	believe, trust	(*cred*)it, in(*cred*)ible, (*cred*)ulity
CLAR	clear, bright	(*clar*)ity, (*clar*)ify, de(*clar*)ation
CORD	heart	dis(*cord*), con(*cord*), (*cord*)ial
CORP(OR)	body, substance	(*corpor*)al, (*corp*)se, (*corp*)ulent
DOM(IN)	tame, subdue	(*domin*)ant, (*domin*)ate, (*domin*)ion
DON	give	(*don*)or, (*don*)ate
DORM	sleep	(*dorm*)ant, (*dorm*)itory, (*dorm*)ient
DUC	lead	con(*duc*)t, (*duc*)tile, aque(*duc*)t
FER	bear	in(fer)ence, (*fer*)tile, re(*fer*)
FORT	strong	(*fort*)ress, (*fort*)e, (*fort*)itude
FRAG, FRING, FRACT	break	(*frag*)ile, in(*fring*)e, (*fract*)ure
GEN	beget, origin	en(*gen*)der, con(*gen*)ital, (*gen*)eration
JAC(T), JEC(T)	cast	e(*jac*)ulate, pro(*ject*), e(*ject*)
LATE	carry	col(*late*), vacil(*late*), re(*late*)
MI(SS,T)	send	dis(*miss*), (*miss*)ionary, re(*mit*)
NOMIN, NOMEN	name	(*nomin*)ate, (*nomen*)clature
NOV	new	(*nov*)el, (*nov*)ice, in(*nov*)ation
PED	foot	(*ped*)al, centi(*pede*), (*ped*)estrian
PLEN, PLET	full	(*plen*)ty, (*plen*)itude, re(*plete*)
PORT	bear	(*port*)er, de(*port*), im(*port*)ance
POTENT	able, powerful	(*potent*), (*potent*)ial, (*potent*)ate
SECT	cut	dis(*sect*), in(*sect*), (*sect*)ion

■ 23d Suffixes

Noun Suffixes

1. *Suffixes Denoting an Agent*

–ANT (*–ent*) one who, that which	ten(*ant*), ag(*ent*)
–AR (*–er*) one who	schol(*ar*), farm(*er*)
–ARD (*–art*) one who (often deprecative)	cow(*ard*), bragg(*art*)
–EER one who	privat(*eer*), auction(*eer*)
–ESS a woman who	waitr(*ess*), seamstr(*ess*)
–IER (*–yer*) one who	cash(*ier*), law(*yer*)
–IST one who	novel(*ist*), Commun(*ist*)
–OR one who, that which	act(*or*), tract(*or*)
–STER one who, that which	young(*ster*), road(*ster*)

2. *Suffix Denoting the Receiver of an Action*

–EE one who is the object of some action	appoint(*ee*), divorc(*ee*)

3. *Suffixes Denoting Smallness or Diminutiveness*

–CULE (*–cle*)	mole(*cule*), ventri(*cle*)
–ETTE	din(*ette*), cigar(*ette*)
–LET	ring(*let*), brace(*let*)
–LING	duck(*ling*), prince(*ling*)

4. *Suffixes Denoting Place*

–ARY indicating location or repository	diction(*ary*), api(*ary*)
–ERY place or establishment	bak(*ery*), nunn(*ery*)
–ORY (*–arium, –orium*) place for, concerned with	dormit(*ory*), audit(*orium*)

5. *Suffixes Denoting Act, State, Quality, or Condition*

–ACY denoting quality, state	accur(*acy*), delic(*acy*)
–AL pertaining to action	refus(*al*), deni(*al*)
–ANCE (*–ancy*) denoting action or state	brilli(*ance*), buoy(*ancy*)
–ATION denoting result	migr(*ation*), el(*ation*)
–DOM denoting a general condition	wis(*dom*), bore(*dom*)
–ENCE (*–ency*) state, quality of	abstin(*ence*), consist(*ency*)
–ERY denoting quality, action	fool(*ery*), prud(*ery*)
–HOOD state, quality	knight(*hood*), false(*hood*)
–ICE condition or quality	serv(*ice*), just(*ice*)
–ION (*–sion*) state or condition	un(*ion*), ten(*sion*)
–ISM denoting action, state, or condition	bapt(*ism*), plagiar(*ism*)
–ITY (*–ety*) action, state, or condition	joll(*ity*), gai(*ety*)
–MENT action or state resulting from	punish(*ment*), frag(*ment*)
–NESS quality, state of	good(*ness*), prepared(*ness*)
–OR denoting action, state, or quality	hon(*or*), lab(*or*)

–TH pertaining to condition, state, or action	warm(*th*), steal(*th*)
–URE denoting action, result, or instrument	legislat(*ure*), pleas(*ure*)

Adjective Suffixes

–ABLE (*–ible*, *–ile*) capable of being	lov(*able*), ed(*ible*), contract(*ile*)
–AC relating to, like	elegi(*ac*), cardi(*ac*)
–ACIOUS inclined to	pugn(*acious*), aud(*acious*)
–AL pertaining to	radic(*al*), cordi(*al*)
–AN pertaining to	sylv(*an*), urb(*an*)
–ANT (*–ent*) inclined to	pleas(*ant*), converg(*ent*)
–AR pertaining to	sol(*ar*), regul(*ar*)
–ARY pertaining to	contr(*ary*), revolution(*ary*)
–ATIVE inclined to	demonstr(*ative*), talk(*ative*)
–FUL full of	joy(*ful*), pain(*ful*)
–IC (*–ical*) pertaining to	volcan(*ic*), angel(*ical*)
–ISH like, relating to, being	devil(*ish*), boy(*ish*)
–IVE inclined to, having the nature of	elus(*ive*), nat(*ive*)
–LESS without, unable to be	piti(*less*), resist(*less*)
–OSE full of	bellic(*ose*), mor(*ose*)
–OUS full of	pi(*ous*), fam(*ous*)
–ULENT (*–olent*) full of	fraud(*ulent*), vi(*olent*)

Verb Suffixes

The following verb suffixes usually mean "to make" (to become, to increase, etc.).

–ATE	toler(*ate*), vener(*ate*)
–EN	madd(*en*), wid(*en*)
–FY	magni(*fy*), beauti(*fy*)
–IZE (*–ise*)	colon(*ize*), exerc(*ise*)

Name _____   Score _____

| | **Exercise 93** | Word Analysis: Prefixes |

Break the following English words into their parts, and give the literal meaning of each part as derived from the source. Consult the lists of prefixes and roots given on previous pages. Use your dictionary if you find a part not given in these lists. Be able to use each word in a sentence.

Word	Prefix (and literal meaning)	Root (and literal meaning)	Meaning of Whole Word
dismiss	*dis-, apart, away from*	*-mittere, to send*	*to send away; to cause or allow to leave*
1. antecedent			
2. antidote			
3. catapult			
4. circuit			
5. counterfeit			
6. contemporary			
7. descend			
8. diagonal			

323

Word	Prefix (and literal meaning)	Root (and literal meaning)	Meaning of Whole Word
9. disobey	_____	_____	_____
	_____	_____	_____
10. embroider	_____	_____	_____
	_____	_____	_____
11. epigram	_____	_____	_____
	_____	_____	_____
12. excel	_____	_____	_____
	_____	_____	_____
13. extraordinary	_____	_____	_____
	_____	_____	_____
14. hyperbole	_____	_____	_____
	_____	_____	_____
15. hypnotism	_____	_____	_____
	_____	_____	_____
16. hypotenuse	_____	_____	_____
	_____	_____	_____
17. introvert	_____	_____	_____
	_____	_____	_____
18. multiply	_____	_____	_____
	_____	_____	_____
19. observe	_____	_____	_____
	_____	_____	_____

Word	Prefix (and literal meaning)	Root (and literal meaning)	Meaning of Whole Word
20. octagon	_____	_____	_____
	_____	_____	_____
21. permanent	_____	_____	_____
	_____	_____	_____
22. peripheral	_____	_____	_____
	_____	_____	_____
23. polysyllabic	_____	_____	_____
	_____	_____	_____
24. postpone	_____	_____	_____
	_____	_____	_____
25. prepare	_____	_____	_____
	_____	_____	_____
26. suburb	_____	_____	_____
	_____	_____	_____
27. superficial	_____	_____	_____
	_____	_____	_____
28. transition	_____	_____	_____
	_____	_____	_____
29. triceps	_____	_____	_____
	_____	_____	_____
30. uniform	_____	_____	_____
	_____	_____	_____

Name _____   Score _____

Exercise 94   Word Analysis: Suffixes

Break the following English words into their parts, and give the literal meaning of each part as derived from its source. Consult the lists of suffixes and roots given on previous pages. Use your dictionary if you find a part not given in the lists. Be able to use each word in a sentence.

Word	Root (and literal meaning)	Suffix (and literal meaning)	Meaning of Whole Word
dentist	*dent-, tooth*	*-ist, one who*	*one whose profession is the care of teeth*
1. alteration			
2. audible			
3. boyish			
4. braggart			
5. capture			
6. coronation			
7. creative			
8. cowardice			

Word	Root (and literal meaning)	Suffix (and literal meaning)	Meaning of Whole Word
9. granary	_____	_____	_____
	_____	_____	_____
10. hireling	_____	_____	_____
	_____	_____	_____
11. laboratory	_____	_____	_____
	_____	_____	_____
12. logical	_____	_____	_____
	_____	_____	_____
13. lovable	_____	_____	_____
	_____	_____	_____
14. martyrdom	_____	_____	_____
	_____	_____	_____
15. migrant	_____	_____	_____
	_____	_____	_____
16. mindful	_____	_____	_____
	_____	_____	_____
17. monument	_____	_____	_____
	_____	_____	_____
18. nominee	_____	_____	_____
	_____	_____	_____
19. ordinary	_____	_____	_____
	_____	_____	_____

Word	Root (and literal meaning)	Suffix (and literal meaning)	Meaning of Whole Word
20. piglet	_____	_____	_____
	_____	_____	_____
21. pioneer	_____	_____	_____
	_____	_____	_____
22. pitiless	_____	_____	_____
	_____	_____	_____
23. purify	_____	_____	_____
	_____	_____	_____
24. speaker	_____	_____	_____
	_____	_____	_____
25. stupor	_____	_____	_____
	_____	_____	_____
26. terror	_____	_____	_____
	_____	_____	_____
27. verbose	_____	_____	_____
	_____	_____	_____
28. visitor	_____	_____	_____
	_____	_____	_____
29. vivacious	_____	_____	_____
	_____	_____	_____
30. wealth	_____	_____	_____
	_____	_____	_____

Name _____   Score _____

Exercise 95   Word Analysis: Roots

For each root listed below write the meaning and at least three words containing the root. Do not use the same word with two roots. If the root given is not listed on the previous pages, look it up in your dictionary, which is also the best source for finding the words you need. Remember that some words containing these roots will have prefixes.

Root	Meaning	Words Containing Root
clam	*cry out*	*clamor, exclamation, claim*
1. ager		
2. ambulare		
3. cycle (kyklos)		
4. facere		
5. facies		
6. genus		
7. gratia		
8. hydro (hydor)		
9. nomen		
10. ordo		
11. pes (pedes, pl.)		
12. port		
13. privare		
14. quaerere		
15. regulare		
16. schisma		
17. schola		
18. valuer		
19. videre		
20. vivere		

Name _____   Score _____

Exercise 96 **Vocabulary: Prefixes and Suffixes**

A. Underline the prefix in each of the following words, give its meaning, and use the word in a sentence so as to show the meaning of the prefix.

Word	Meaning of Prefix	Sentence
*con*vention	*together*	*The annual convention of the Trial Lawyers' Association will be in Memphis in May.*
1. antithesis		
2. contradict		
3. demoralize		
4. disgusted		
5. endorse		
6. extend		
7. intercede		
8. permeate		
9. tricycle		
10. undeserved		

333

B. In the following list of words underline each suffix, give its meaning, and use the word in a sentence.

Word	Meaning of Suffix	Sentence
verify	to make, become, increase	Max will verify the accuracy of these data.
1. adviser		
2. cemetery		
3. corpulent		
4. courteous		
5. defendant		
6. impulsive		
7. lunacy		
8. magnificence		
9. merciless		
10. motherhood		

Exercise 97   Vocabulary: Greek and Latin Roots

A. Use the derivatives of *auto,* meaning "self," necessary to complete the following statements. (In this and the following exercises, remember that these roots may be found in words containing prefixes.)

1. The writing of one's own biography is _____.

2. A dictator, or absolute ruler, is sometimes known as an _____.

3. In manufacturing there is a system called _____, in which some processes of production are performed or controlled by self-operating machines or devices.

4. The word _____ refers to a person or animal acting in an automatic or mechanical way.

5. An examination of a dead body, in order to "see with one's own eyes" the cause of the death, is known as an _____.

B. Use the derivatives of *placere,* meaning "to please," necessary to complete the following statements.

1. A _____ is a statement in defense or justification.

2. A polite social or humorous remark is a _____.

3. To _____ is to fail to please or to be annoying or disagreeable to someone.

4. The act or quality of giving pleasure is described as _____.

5. Enjoyment, delight, or satisfaction is a feeling of _____.

C. Use the derivatives of *signum,* "a mark or token," necessary to complete the following sentences.

1. A _____ is something that indicates a fact or quality or communicates information.

2. A gesture or action that conveys a command, direction, or warning is called a _____.

3. A _____ event, fact, or statement is one that is full of meaning or consequence.

335

4. A seal, especially one used in marking documents as official, is also known as a

   _____.

5. A person's name, written by himself, is his _____.

D. Use the derivatives of *verbum*, meaning "word," to complete the following sentences.

1. The _____, a word that expresses action, existence, or occurrence,

   is a necessary element of a complete sentence.

2. To use words in the communication of meaning is to _____.

3. To quote _____ is to repeat a statement word for word.

4. An excess of words beyond those needed for concise expression is defined as

   _____.

5. When one's expression is long-winded or too full of words, it is _____.

24

Spelling

Spelling is an important aspect of written communication. Instructors seldom have the opportunity, however, to spend adequate classroom time on the subject. The responsibility for the mastery of spelling, therefore, rests almost solely on the individual student.

Here are a few practical suggestions on how to approach the problem of spelling:

1. Always use the dictionary when you are in doubt about the spelling of a word.

2. If there is a rule applicable to the type of words that you misspell, learn that rule.

3. Employ any "tricks" that might assist you in remembering the spelling of particular words giving you trouble. If, for example, you confuse the meaning and hence the spelling of *statue* and *stature*, remember that the longer word refers to bodily "longness." Certain troublesome words can be spelled correctly if you will remember their prefixes (as in *dis/appoint*) or their suffixes (as in *cool/ly*). Also, it might help you to remember that there are only three *-ceed* words: *exceed, proceed,* and *succeed.*

4. Keep a list of the words that you misspell. In writing down these words, observe their syllabication and any peculiarities of construction. Try to "see" — that is, to have a mental picture of — these words.

5. Practice the correct pronunciation of troublesome words. Misspelling is often the result of mispronunciation.

Of the many rules governing spelling, four are particularly useful since they are widely applicable. Study these four rules carefully.

■ 24a Final e

Drop the final *e* before a suffix begnning with a vowel (*-ing, -ous,* etc.) but retain the final *e* before a suffix beginning with a consonant (*-ment, -ly,* etc.):

Final *e* dropped: come + ing = coming
                      fame + ous = famous
                      love + able = lovable
                      guide + ance = guidance

Final *e* retained: move + ment = movement
                      fate + ful = fateful
                      sole + ly = solely

Exceptions: Acknowledge, acknowledgment; abridge, abridgment; judge, judgment; dye, dyeing; singe, singeing; hoe, hoeing; mile, mileage; due, duly; awe, awful; whole, wholly. The final **e** is retained after **c** or **g** when the suffix begins with **a** or **o**: peace, peaceable; courage, courageous.

■ 24b Final Consonant

Double a final consonant before a suffix beginning with a vowel if (1) the word is of one syllable or is accented on the last syllable and (2) the final consonant is preceded by a single vowel:

Word of one syllable: stop + ed = stopped

Word in which the accent falls on the last syllable: occur + ence = occurrence

Word in which the accent does not fall on the last syllable: differ + ence = difference

■ 24c *ei* and *ie*

When **ei** and **ie** have the long **ee** sound (as in *keep*), use **i** before **e** except after **c**. (The word *lice* will aid you in remembering this rule; **i** follows **l** and all other consonants except **c**, while **e** follows **c**.)

ie	*ei* (after *c*)
chief	ceiling
field	receive
niece	deceive
siege	conceit

Exceptions *(grouped to form a sentence):*   Neither financier seized either species of weird leisure.

■ 24d Final *y*

In words ending in *y* preceded by a consonant, change the *y* to *i* before any suffix except one beginning with *i.*

Suffix beginning with a letter other than *i*:

fly + es = flies
ally + es = allies
easy + ly = easily
mercy + ful = merciful
study + ous = studious

Suffix beginning with *i*:

fly + ing = flying
study + ing = studying

■ 24e Spelling List

The following list is made up of approximately 480 frequently misspelled words. Since these are commonly used words, you should learn to spell all of them after you have mastered the words on your individual list.

absence	appreciate	camouflage
academic	appropriate	candidate
accept	arctic	captain
accessible	argument	carburetor
accidentally	arithmetic	carriage
accommodate	around	category
accumulate	arrangement	cavalry
accustomed	ascend	ceiling
acknowledge	assassin	cemetery
acknowledgment	association	certain
acquaintance	athletics	changeable
acquire	attendance	characteristic
across	attractive	chauffeur
address	audience	choose
adolescent	autumn	chosen
advantage	auxiliary	clothes
aggravate	awkward	colloquial
allege	bankruptcy	colonel
all right	barbarous	column
altogether	becoming	coming
always	beginning	commission
amateur	believe	committee
among	beneficial	comparative
amount	benefited	compel
analysis	brilliant	compelled
angel	Britain	competent
anonymous	broccoli	competition
anxiety	buoyant	complement
any more	bureau	completely
apology	business	compliment
apparatus	cafeteria	compulsory
apparent	caffeine	confident
appearance	calendar	congratulate

connoisseur
conqueror
conscience
conscientious
conscious
contemptible
continuous
controversy
convenient
coolly
council
counsel
courteous
criticism
curiosity
curriculum
dealt
deceit
decide
defendant
definite
dependent
descend
descent
describe
description
desert
desirable
despair
desperate
dessert
dictionary
dietitian (dietician)
difference
dilapidated
dining
diphtheria
disappear
disappoint
disastrous
discipline
discussion
disease
dissatisfied
dissipate
distribute
divine
division
dormitories
drudgery

dual
duchess
duel
dyeing
dying
ecstasy
efficiency
eighth
eligible
eliminate
embarrassed
eminent
emphasize
enthusiastic
environment
equipped
equivalent
erroneous
especially
exaggerate
excellent
except
exercise
exhaust
exhilaration
existence
exorbitant
expel
expelled
experience
explanation
extraordinary
familiar
fascinate
February
finally
financial
financier
flier
foregoing
forehead
foreign
foreword
forfeit
forgo
formally
formerly
forth
forty
fourth

fraternity
friend
fulfill
fundamental
furniture
futile
gauge
generally
genius
government
grammar
granddaughter
grandeur
grievance
guarantee
guerrilla
handkerchief
harass
having
height
hindrance
hitchhike
hoping
humorous
hygiene
hypocrisy
illusion
imaginary
imitation
immediately
incidentally
independence
indispensable
inevitable
infinite
influential
ingenious
innocence
instance
instant
integrity
intellectual
intelligence
intentionally
interested
irrelevant
irresistible
its
it's
judgment

kindergarten
knowledge
laboratory
led
legitimate
leisure
library
likable
literature
livelihood
loose
lose
lovable
magazine
maintain
maintenance
maneuver
manual
manufacture
marriage
mathematics
meant
medicine
mediocre
miniature
mirror
mischievous
misspell
momentous
monotonous
morale
mortgage
murmur
muscle
mysterious
naive
naturally
necessary
nevertheless
nickel
niece
ninety
ninth
noticeable
notoriety
nowadays
nucleus
obedience
obstacle
occasion

occasionally
occurrence
o'clock
off
omission
omitted
operate
opinion
opportunity
optimism
organization
original
outrageous
overrun
paid
pamphlet
parallel
paralysis
paralyzed
parliament
particularly
partner
passed
past
pastime
perform
permanent
permissible
perseverance
persistent
personal
personnel
perspiration
persuade
physically
physician
picnicking
piece
pleasant
pneumonia
politician
politics
politicking
possession
possible
practically
precede
precedence
preference
preferred

prejudice
preparation
prevalent
principal
principle
privilege
probably
procedure
proceed
professor
prominent
pronunciation
propaganda
psychology
publicly
purchase
pursue
quantity
quarter
questionnaire
quiet
quite
quiz
quizzes
realize
really
recognize
recommend
referred
region
reign
rein
relevant
religious
remembrance
repetition
representative
resistance
respectfully
respectively
restaurant
rhetoric
rheumatism
rhythm
ridiculous
sacrifice
sacrilegious
salable
salary
sandwich

schedule
science
scissors
secretary
seize
sense
sentence
separate
sergeant
severely
sheriff
shining
shriek
siege
significant
silhouette
similar
sincerely
skiing
sophomore
source
speak
specimen
speech
stationary
stationery
statue
stature
statute

strength
strenuous
stretch
studying
superintendent
supersede
surprise
susceptible
syllable
symmetry
temperament
temperature
tendency
their
thorough
too
tournament
tragedy
transferred
tremendous
truly
Tuesday
twelfth
tying
tyranny
unanimous
undoubtedly
universally
unnecessary

until
unusual
usable
using
usually
vaccine
vacuum
valuable
vegetable
vengeance
vigilance
vigorous
village
villain
waive
wave
weather
Wednesday
weird
whether
wholly
who's
whose
wield
women
writing
written
yacht
yield

Exercise 98   Spelling

A. Combine the specified suffix with each of the following words and write the correct form in the space provided.

Example: approve + al   _____*approval*_____

1. acknowledge + ment   _____

2. associate + tion   _____

3. begin + ing   _____

4. category + ize   _____

5. change + able   _____

6. compel + ed   _____

7. disaster + ous   _____

8. fly + er   _____

9. inevitable + ly   _____

10. maintain + ance   _____

11. mischief + ous   _____

12. necessary + ly   _____

13. nine + th   _____

14. notice + able   _____

15. occur + ence   _____

16. permit + able   _____

17. persevere + ance   _____

18. personal + ly   _____

19. perspire + ation   _____

20. precede + ence   _____

21. prefer + ed   _____

22. proceed + ure   _____

23. pronounce + ation   _____

24. public + ly   _____

25. quiz + ed   _____

26. remember + ance   _____

27. sale + able   _____

28. ski + ing   _____

29. true + ly   _____

30. twelve + th   _____

B. Supply either *ei* or *ie* in each of the following words. Then write the correct form in the space provided.

Example: fr_*ie*_nd   _*friend*_

1. w__rd   _____   11. dec__t   _____

2. gr__ve   _____   12. handkerch__f   _____

3. cash__r   _____   13. hyg__ne   _____

4. sl__gh   _____   14. misch__f   _____

5. forf__t   _____   15. n__ce   _____

6. ach__vement   _____   16. r__gn   _____

7. fr__ght   _____   17. y__ld   _____

8. pr__st   _____   18. th__r   _____

9. h__r   _____   19. spec__s   _____

10. bel__ve   _____   20. f__ld   _____

Exercise 99 Spelling

If there is a misspelled word in any line of five words given below, underline it and write it correctly in the space at the right. If all five words are correctly spelled, write **C** in the blank.

Example: *harass, pursue, knowlege, nowadays, genius*   *knowledge*

1. excellent, diptheria, remembrance, strength, women   _____

2. secretary, accessable, courteous, tyranny, probably   _____

3. chosen, curiosity, discussion, alledge, dining   _____

4. definite, confident, especially, believe, defendent   _____

5. exhileration, controversy, descend, speech, shriek   _____

6. necessary, obedience, propaganda, occassionally, morale   _____

7. extrordinary, lovable, flier, omitted, overrun   _____

8. quanity, prejudice, government, manual, medicine   _____

9. privilege, tremendous, persistent, pamphlet, naive   _____

10. gauge, Febuary, livelihood, obstacle, truly   _____

11. yacht, weird, sergeant, fullfil, vacuum   _____

12. vigilance, valueable, source, quizzed, prevalent   _____

13. scissors, guerrilla, incidently, parallel, hoping   _____

14. perform, original, sacrifice, mispell, ridiculous   _____

15. opinion, piece, yeild, rhythm, villain   _____

16. pneumonia, strenuous, guarantee, preceed, o'clock   _____

17. mirror, particularly, momentous, irrevalent, forgo   _____

18. humorous, grammer, mediocre, hindrance, meant   _____

19. partner, unanimous, hypocricy, tendency, village   _____

20. undoubtedly, prominent, silouette, usable, surprise   _____

Exercise 100 Spelling

Underline any word which is misspelled. Then write it correctly at the right. If a sentence contains no misspelled word, write **C** in the blank.

Example: Chester says that <u>mathmatics</u> is his worst
subject.   *mathematics*

1. Tony, I think you will have to forego the basketball game
   tonight; I need your help with this laundry.   _____

2. Mr. Bainbridge began his talk by saying that it was a
   priviledge for him to speak to such an extraordinary
   group of students.   _____

3. Jack is a loveable person; it's a shame that he is somewhat irresponsible.   _____

4. Hugh was dissapointed that it was not convenient for
   Marian to meet him for lunch.   _____

5. The private detective recieved an anonymous letter telling
   him where to find the stolen jewels.   _____

6. Please don't dessert me now; I need help in learning to
   operate this computer.   _____

7. Frederick, I know that its not easy to get out of bed on
   these cold mornings.   _____

8. We believe the young woman to be thoroughly competant
   and think that you will find her conscientious as well. _____

9. Irma cooly took her seat among the dignitaries; one
   would have thought from her demeanor that she might
   be a duchess.   _____

10. Andy's old car, a 1971 model, is dilapadated and uncom-
    fortable, but it continues to get him back and forth to
    work.   _____

11. We could not believe that the formally beautiful, luxuri-
    ous hotel was now so mediocre.   _____

12. The plaintiff's attorney objected that the testimony of
    the defense witness was wholly irrevelant.   _____

13. For lunch we had tuna fish sanwiches, sliced tomatoes, and undoubtedly the best cheesecake that I have ever eaten.   _____

14. Frank used the vaccuum cleaner, wielded the dust mop, polished the brass andirons, and generally made himself useful.   _____

15. We don't go up to the lake anymore; our canoe has a leak in it, and the water is too muddy for swimming.   _____

16. Yes, Jane and Ken are also disatisfied with conditions at the lake; they think that we should form a grievance committee.   _____

17. The tomato aspic that I made for supper turned out disasterously, so I suppose I must acknowledge that I am not the world's best cook.   _____

18. Those little boys have been harassing the neighbors with their practical jokes; I've never seen such mischievious children.   _____

19. Rachel can be naive on occasion, but we all concede that her charm is irresistable.   _____

20. The palace at Versailles is incredibly luxurious; many have tried to imitate its grandure, but no one has achieved it.   _____

21. We had just arrived at the restaraunt when we saw David and Bonnie coming in, so we enthusiastically invited them to join us.   _____

22. Ruth tried to camouflage her disappointment, but it was obvious that her roommate's hypocricy was hard to swallow.   _____

23. Mrs. Landers told us that her grandaughter will study in Paris next year; she is especially interested in fashion design.   _____

24. The principal of Jefferson High School announced publically yesterday that he will seek the nomination for U.S. Representative from our district.   _____

25. He thinks that he will enjoy politicking, and he believes that he can fullfil the needs and desires of the constituents.   _____

Paragraph Tests   Paragraph Test 1

Each of the following paragraphs contains twenty errors in grammar, punctuation, mechanics, diction, or spelling. Mark each error that you find with a check mark (√) as close to the error as possible or bracket any groups of words that need correction. Then, with these marks as guides, rewrite the paragraphs, eliminating all errors. If you find and correct all errors, your score for the paragraph will be *100*. Any error that you fail to correct counts off five points. If, in rewriting a paragraph, you eliminate existing errors but make others, each of these will count off five points.

Last Saturday Peter Tom and I spent the day at Lake Sequoyah. When the boys decided to look for some fishing gear I sat lazily on the dock watching a lone swimmer. The woman in the lake that was swimming slowly sank beneath the water and I cried out to my friends that someone was drownding. Peter and Tom ran, swiftly, to the shore and dove in, swimming franticly toward the spot where the woman disappeared. Peter dove repeatedly under the surface and so did Tom, but they could find no sign of the woman. In the meantime someone had called the fire departments rescue squad and I soon heard the whooping sound of the approaching vehicle. Professional divers went quickly into action, but every one of them were coming up empty-handed. Because I cannot swim I was still watching from the dock when suddenly I saw a woman walk out of the lake onto the opposite shore, about a mile from the dock. She had obviously been swimming under water, probably coming up for air ocassionally but all the time moving farther and farther from the spot where the search was taking place. When the woman realized what had been going on, she was at a loss to understand the excitement that she herself had created, and naturally I felt pretty foolish. If I was to do things over again, I would not jump to hasty conclusions.

Paragraph Test 2

My little red sports car has an unusual history. I bought it from a used-car dealer who told me that it had first belonged to a race driver. He had used it as a personal car but he got a larger one, when his family started growing and would not hold all the children. Next, the car was owned by a mysterious woman who had disappeared from town just after a murder occurred it was thought that the woman was implicated, but this was never proved. When I got the car it needed a new, front bumper and a fresh, paint job. I had had it only one week when it was stolen. It was found six weeks after it was stolen by two off-duty policemen. In the car, when I recovered it, was a childs doll, a german camera, a wallet, and a five-thousand dollar Swiss watch. The wallet contained almost a thousand dollars in fifty dollar bills, but no identification. Another packet of bills were found in a secret compartment under the driver's seat that contained about ten thousand dollars. I wish that my car could tell me about it's mysterious life and I hope that it will settle down now to a calmer existence.

Paragraph Test 3

One of the high points of our recent trip to England, was a visit to Churchill's Cabinet War Rooms in London. These are the underground offices, meeting rooms, and living quarters, used during World War II by Prime Minister Winston Churchill, his War Cabinet and his Chiefs of Staff, for daily conferences for sending classified communications and for eating and sleeping during Nazi air raids on the city. The underground passage, consisting of sixteen rooms, were located beneath the area between Churchill's official residence at No. Ten Downing Street and the Government Office Building. A secret entry from each of these buildings were built for the convenience of the individuals involved. Each of these rooms have been kept exactly like they were when in use, including Churchill's bedroom the map room and a community dining room shared by those, who were meeting there at meal times. It was an awful eerie feeling for we visitors to see the red telephones, the table set for a meal, and Winston Churchills own bedroom, with it's narrow bed and sparse furnishings. The story is told that Mr. Churchill did not like to sleep there, even during air raids, Mrs. Churchill, however, insisted that he go there on air raid nights. She would have his valet go down and see him safely into bed, but as soon as the man had left Churchill would return to his bed at No. Ten. Those days of World War II seem long ago until one sees the actual spot, where danger was a constant companion and where crucial decisions and vital secret messages were part of these leaders' everyday lives.

Paragraph Test 4

Our trip from Paris to London was hectic. The taxi that took us to the railway station left us on a traffic island in the middle of a busy thoroughfare. Paris drivers are daredevils and they seem to care no more for the safety of pedestrians than for their own. Ty and myself had five heavy bags to get across to the station and we could not find even a luggage trolley. Somehow we finally made it to our train and then on to Boulogne where we got on a hover-craft departing for Dover, England. These trips across the English Channel are called flights, but they are slow going, with loud engine noise and with passengers packed in like cattle. More trouble with the luggage at Dover. There were trolleys but they were useless due to the long flights of stairs both up and down that led to our train. When we finally arrived at Charing Cross Station in London Ty said, Hopefully I can take a long, hot shower when we get to the hotel. We did not realize, however; that we reached London just at rush hour. The traffic was terrible, so it was an hour before our hotel was reached. Once there, I decided to lay down before doing anything else, but just as I dropped off to sleep, a lady came to bring fresh towels. I couldn't hardly keep from screaming at her; realizing, however, that I was real tired, I restrained myself. After a good nights rest we found London to be a delightful city to visit.

Paragraph Test 5

Its January, and I am reminded daily of the cold wet weeks that lie ahead. It is at this time of year that mother calls to ask the invariable question "Do you want to go to the beach this summer"? I remember Browning's "warm sea-scented beach", but I also remember my own last Summer's visit. I don't know if I want to ever go to the beach again. In February or March we rented a cottage, sight unseen, at Broad Beach. When we walked into the cottage on a hot July afternoon, we found the number of rooms that had been promised, but each one seemed smaller than the one before. Neither the living room nor the dining room were large enough to accommodate all of us. Moreover, we couldn't hardly have been considered a completely homogeneous group, despite our kinship. My brother and his wife brought their two children — a three-month-old son and a busy four-year-old daughter. My sister arrived with her latest fancy, a young man who's most obvious talent was laying in the front-porch hammock. Then there was my Grandmother who wanted her coffee promptly at seven each morning, and her nap immediately after lunch. And I ca'nt forget my father, who delighted us with his stories but who was adverse to cleaning shrimp and washing dishes. Anyone can appreciate my problem. Shall I be sensible and refuse to go? Or shall I again entertain the hope that this summer at the beach will be all that Browning, the real estate agent and my family promises?

Paragraph Test 6

The highest court in the judicial system of the United States is the Supreme Court. Presently, 8 associate justices and a chief justice comprise the court. However this has not always been constant, for instance the Judiciary Act of 1789 only required that there be six justices, including the chief justice. Thus the number of justices are determined not by the Nations Constitution but by the Congress. The Constitution does grant the President the power to appoint the justices, "with the Advice and Consent of the Senate". Because the justices often reflect the political philosophy of the chief executive by who they are selected presidents generally welcome vacancies on the court. Should a vacancy not seem probable within his term the President may be tempted to enlarge the court. In his second term Franklin D. Roosevelt wanted to increase the number of justices from nine to fifteen in the hope that he could establish a majority that would loan their support to his' New Deal programs. He failed to gain the necessary backing in Congress, consequently the number of justices remains the same as they have been since 1869.

Paragraph Test 7

The beginning of winter term was just a few days off when a Senior convinced me to consider taking English 410, History of the English Language. I managed to register late, sort of hoping that the class would be full. It was full but then I met Dr. Burger in the hall. I told him that I was sorry that I must miss his stimulating lectures, he promptly responded that he would make an acception to his rule, and would see me in class at twelve noon the next day. Now we are several weeks into the term, and I must confess that I am enjoying it. I have discovered that the history of English can be traced back thousands of years to either a time before human beings wrote or before they wrote on materials that could withstand the elements. I am fascinated with the idea that English is related to a host of other languages, all the way from Hindi to Icelandic. I have also found that language is one of those forms of human behavior that displays "infinite variety". For example, their is British English and American English. Then these may be divided into regional and subregional dialects. On the one hand, Dr. Burger can determine what section of the United States or Canada a student comes from by the way they pronounce certain words. On the other hand, he points out that every student has an idiolect because your speech is in some way most unique. If Dr. Burger will explain the Great Vowel Shift clearly and if he will not require us to trace the ins and outs of the personal pronouns, I will be able to with a good conscious recommend this course to some friends I have who are sophmores.

Paragraph Test 8

During the Summer before our senior year Jan, my college roommate, and I spent several weeks with her sister on the East Side of Manhattan, who had recently bought an apartment. Right away we enjoyed the sense of independence and freedom that an apartment always offered students, therefore we decided to spend our last year at the university living in an apartment rather than in the dormitory. We called the housing office to get a list of available off campus housing. The list revealed that no apartments were available, a few rooms in the homes of professors was all that remained. When the housing office offered no help, we bought the Sunday "Post" to read the want ads, marking those that appeared promising. After Jan and myself had spent several days looking at apartments that were overpriced and poorly cared for, we faced the fact that apartment hunting was more of an ordeal than we had thought it would be. Having no success on our own we went by Galloway's and Galloway's, a real estate agency. We described our attempts to find an apartment to Mrs. Shepherd, a real knowledgeable agent who sympathized with our situation but whom explained that the citys rapid growth during the past five years had created a shortage of apartments that in turn had caused higher rents. In fact, some apartment rents had literally doubled within a year. Having heard what kind of apartment we wanted and how much we were able to pay, her suggestion was that we might reconsider spending our senior year in the dormitory. We were discovering that economic realities can change your mind. Reluctantly, we decided that perhaps one more year of dormitory life would'nt be as bad as we had once thought.

Test on Lessons 1–7

A. In each of the following sentences underline the subject once and the verb twice; then circle the complement (or complements). In the first column at the right tell whether the verb is transitive active **(TA)**, transitive passive **(TP)**, or intransitive **(I)**. In the second column tell whether the complement is a direct object **(DO)**, an indirect **(IO)**, a predicate nominative **(PN)**, a predicate **(PA)**, an objective complement **(OC)**, or a retained object **(RO)**. Note that not all sentences have complements.

1. We have known her family for years. _____ _____

2. Brenda is truly a fine person. _____ _____

3. In the morning can you type this report for me? _____ _____

4. Part of her strength comes from strong family ties. _____ _____

5. The research unit has prepared its report. _____ _____

6. While at the bookstore, please buy me Nesbit's
   Megatrends. _____ _____

7. Few understand the need for silence. _____ _____

8. Rice University offered Rufus a full four-year scholarship. _____ _____

9. Calvin's attire is not trendy but preppy. _____ _____

10. The underdevelopment of human resources is too costly
    to be acceptable. _____ _____

11. Do you have any questions at this time? _____ _____

12. The prospect of parenting is frightening to many people. _____ _____

B. What part of speech is each of the following underscored words?

1. <u>for</u> in the first sentence above _____

2. <u>truly</u> in the second sentence above _____

3. <u>this</u> in the third sentence above _____

4. <u>comes</u> in the fourth sentence above _____

5. <u>research</u> in the fifth sentence above _____

6. <u>While</u> in the sixth sentence above _____

7. <u>silence</u> in the seventh sentence above _____

8. <u>Rufus</u> in the eighth sentence above _____

9. <u>not</u> in the ninth sentence above _____

10. <u>costly</u> in the tenth sentence above _____

11. <u>any</u> in the eleventh sentence above _____

12. <u>people</u> in the twelfth sentence above _____

C. In each of the sentences below identify the *italicized* expression by writing one of the following numbers in the space at the right:

> **1** if it is a *prepositional phrase*,   **6** if it is an *absolute phrase*,
> **2** if it is a *participial phrase*,   **7** if it is a *noun clause*,
> **3** if it is a *gerund phrase*,   **8** if it is an *adjective clause*,
> **4** if it is an *infinitive phrase*,   **9** if it is an *adverbial clause*.
> **5** if it is an *appositive phrase*,

1. The Martins live in an uptown New York apartment, *overlooking the Hudson River.*   _____

2. I wonder *how I passed that physics test.*   _____

3. While attending the University of Toronto, I lived with a family *who owned a small farm.*   _____

4. *When Alberta visited London,* she was in awe of its history.   _____

5. Alan has not always enjoyed *reading poetry.*   _____

6. While in Charleston, if time permits, I plan *to attend the Spoleto Festival, USA.*   _____

7. Do you know what time Wanda's plane will arrive *at the airport?*   _____

8. *The play having ended,* we all gave the actors a standing ovation.   _____

9. Mark Van Doren, *a great teacher,* taught for many years *at Columbia University.*   _____

10. Thomas Merton, *a twentieth-century writer,* is perhaps best known for his autobiography.   _____

D. Underline the dependent clause (or clauses) in each of the following sentences. In the first column at the right tell whether the clause is a noun clause (**N**), an adjective clause (**Adj**), or an adverbial clause (**Adv**). In the second column tell how the noun clause is used (that is, whether it is a *subject, direct object,* etc.), or what the adjective or adverbial clause modifies.

1. Because Lisa's room gets the morning sun, it is the warmest room to dress in.   _____ _____

2. Mr. Belton telephoned that he would be late.   _____ _____

3. Natural Bridge, which is located in Virginia, is a breathtaking sight.   ———— ——————

4. While we were touring the Pennsylvania Dutch country, we saw an Amish barn raising.   ———— ——————

5. The worst thing that could have happened did happen.   ———— ——————

6. Hartwell Lake, which borders Georgia and South Carolina, is a manmade lake.   ———— ——————

7. I know that Linda will want to play golf with us.   ———— ——————

8. Herbert nearly fainted when I told him the price of the ticket.   ———— ——————

9. The truth is that the office will be closed that week.   ———— ——————

10. After shopping all day, Jane, who had not bought the first thing, was exhausted.   ———— ——————

E. In the following sentences insert all necessary commas and semicolons. Rewrite sentence fragments in such a way as to make complete sentences. If a sentence is correct, mark it **C.**

1. Dr. Gardner is a teacher at the local high school and he is also the author of several short stories.

2. Walter's habit of speaking without thinking about what he is saying.

3. After Don's little sister ate her piece of birthday cake she ran outside to play.

4. I think that the doctor gave Martha a placebo, she is such a hypochondriac.

5. Our family spent a week at the beach and three days in the mountains we were all exhausted when we arrived home.

6. A young woman wearing blue jeans.

7. Programs for next week's scheduled events will be available by Monday at the information table.

8. Alice Walker one of the leading black women writers will read from her novel *The Color Purple* at our annual meeting.

9. If the United States is to remain an effective competitor internationally three problems must be addressed: education, productivity, and research.

Test on Lessons 8–18

Correct all errors in the following sentences. Errors must be crossed out and corrections written above the sentence. A misplaced element may be underscored and its proper place in the sentence indicated by a caret (∧). In some cases the entire sentence will have to be rewritten. If a sentence is correct, write **C**.

1. The film is long, dreary, and the leading man is miscast.

2. Having been held up in traffic, people were already boarding the plane when I arrived at the gate.

3. I cannot believe that he has never sang the part of Lieutenant Pinkerton before.

4. Last month my plan was to have begun running every morning before breakfast.

5. I watched television until after midnight, which certainly did not help my performance in physics lab this morning.

6. Francine is as good if not better than any other poker player I know.

7. Eduardo sure has taken some good pictures of downtown San Francisco.

8. Appearing calmly, Marvin glanced through a magazine while he waited for the interviewer to call his name.

9. No one but he will ever persuade Paula to go spelunking.

10. I read an article in *Scientific American,* and it was about "smart cards" which contain microelectric chips, and they may replace conventional credit cards.

11. David is one of those people who reads every word in the newspaper every day.

12. If I was you, I would order the broiled flounder instead of the fried clams.

13. Jenny, I know that it was not him who called you.

14. Because the boys had already got the grill out and started the fire made it possible for us to have supper at seven.

15. At the back of the desk drawer I discovered a Christmas card from Dorothy, envelope of zinnia seeds, and small box of paper clips.

16. I left my binoculars at home, which made bird watching very difficult.

17. Terry Morrison is a good friend and whom I have known since kindergarten.

18. No one enjoys white-water canoeing more than her and Roger.

19. Spencer wishes that he was able to work at the planetarium this summer.

20. Surely you remember that two o'clock is when my favorite soap opera comes on Channel 5.

21. My brother thinks that W. C. Fields is funnier than any humorist he has ever heard or read.

22. Whom did you say played the lead in *Idiot's Delight*?

23. Now Wilma not only belongs to a book club but also a videocassette club.

24. The lights in the auditorium were lowered, which signaled the beginning of the performance.

25. I have read nearly all the books written by Barbara Pym.

26. While waiting for my train, the platform was crowded with skiers.

27. The reason the florist bought the van is because he can use it either to deliver flowers or to take his children to school.

28. The audience gasped when the detective discovered that his chief suspect had been hung from a rafter.

29. On the corner was a young woman whose hair was long, limp, and she was frail.

30. Stripping the land of trees, the construction crew began laying the foundation for the apartment complex.

31. To never taste a chili dog from the Varsity is to miss one of life's great pleasures.

32. Nina has not decided if she wants to take Russian history this term or next.

33. He put on his sweat suit, and he ran the two miles to the shopping center, and he bought a copy of *Barron's.*

34. Leslie's voice sounds real good since she began taking lessons from Madame Michel.

35. Neither Cindy nor I are able to fit into the costumes you ordered for us.

36. Did you notice that this morning almost felt like spring?

37. This recording of *West Side Story* is the best of the two.

38. I had just lain down my jacket and books when Clarence called to say that he had tickets to Road Atlanta.

39. The traffic on St. Lawrence Street is heavier than it is on any street in town.

40. Curtis has a badly twisted knee, and this will keep him from playing tennis this weekend.

41. When in the sixth grade, my teacher often read to us on Friday afternoons.

42. The evil queen commanded that the beautiful princess was banished from the kingdom.

43. To do well in French 103, an understanding of the vocabulary is essential.

44. Last night the basketball squad played its best game of the season.

45. The strata of ancient Egyptian society was discussed at the meeting of the Society for Historical Study.

46. Martha told Lucy that it was too hot for her to sunbathe on the roof.

47. At rush hour every man, woman, and child in the city seem to be trying to board the Metro.

48. Lacrosse may be rougher than any sport played in North America.

49. He has almost seen all the films in which Julie Christie appears.

50. The children ran quickly to explain to the principal that they were not responsible

    for Mr. Brock's broken window.

Test on Lessons 19–24

A. In the following sentences insert all necessary punctuation marks and correct all errors of punctuation and mechanics.

1. Oh Jackie will you bring me that book thats on the table at the top of the stairs.

2. Barry's and Louise's apartment is in a new subdivision called valley springs, the building has a washing machine and dryer in it's basement.

3. Our old basset hound said Frank is sleeping under the house.

4. Johns asking for another piece of cake means that theres not enough for Marie.

5. P.D. James novel "Death of an Expert Witness" was made into a mystery series for television.

6. Lets try to finish studying by eight oclock then we will have time to go over to Davids house for a while.

7. While Jerry, Marcus, and Pete were waiting for Alice, she was hurrying home, but she got there just after they had left.

8. Carl the captain of our debating team is a fine speaker and wait until I finish, Dora he is always well prepared.

9. In the novel The Hamlet William Faulkner describes Eula Varner in vivid terms p. 142.

10. Next fourth of July we are planning a celebration out at Kenny's lake house and we will invite about a hundred people.

11. Isn't it surprising that many well educated people cannot learn to pronounce the word nuclear?

12. Possibly one of the most popular of twentieth-century operas is Puccini's Madame Butterfly.

13. The Wilson's are moving to minneapolis in September, we plan to visit them there next Spring.

14. Alfred applied for a four year leave of absence; but the board granted him only two years.

15. Terry has failed Geometry again this Quarter; I am very much afraid that he will not graduate in the Class of 88.

B. After each of the following groups of words indicate the level of usage of the italicized word(s), using the following abbreviations: **A** for archaic, **D** for dialectal, **I** for informal (colloquial), and **S** for slang. Use your dictionary for this test.

1. Do you see *yon* mountain that is higher than all the rest?   _____

2. Macbeth said, "*Methought* I heard a voice cry, 'Sleep no more! Macbeth doth murder sleep!'"   _____

3. The old woman put her groceries into a *poke* and started the long walk home.   _____

4. At the Braves-Padres game last Sunday there was the biggest *rhubarb* that I've seen in a long time.   _____

5. I hear that Tom was badly *gypped* when he bought his new carpet.   _____

6. Don't worry, Jean; we have *lots* of time before the kickoff.   _____

7. That distinguished-looking man used to *jerk* sodas at our home-town drugstore.   _____

8. James sent us some *goobers* from his farm in Alabama, and they are delicious.   _____

9. Those boys that Dan *hangs out* with seem to be lazy and useless.   _____

10. Brad wants to be at the airport at least two hours before the plane takes off; he is such a *worrywart*.   _____

C. The following section of the test is based on the Glossary of Faulty Diction. Cross out all errors or colloquialisms and write the preferred forms above each sentence.

1. Stretched out on her chaise lounge, Gladys watched the gulls wheeling overhead.

2. I personally can hardly believe that we are finally on our way to Tahiti.

3. No one in the congregation recognized the quote that the Reverend Mr. Franklin gave this morning.

4. I noticed in today's paper that Jack Brown was sited for a traffic violation.

5. Surely between the three of us we have enough money to buy a dozen doughnuts.

6. My father was shocked to discover that his chief assistant is a woman lacking in principal.

7. You are apt to get a headache, Judy, if you skip lunch entirely.

8. Lewis wants to orientate his staff who will be working with the new computer.

9. You inferred to me that you would be leaving college after this year.

10. One thing can be said in favor of Larry: he tends to his own business.

11. Rod always forgets that Albany, not New York City, is the capitol of New York.

12. Hopefully, Doris, you will soon find out whether you got the scholarship.

13. Those guys that painted our house did an excellent job.

14. Dr. Miller critiqued Evelyn's thesis, and he suggested only minor

    corrections.

15. Sally, I am not at all enthused about your new shoes.

D. Give the meaning of each of the following prefixes or roots; then write two words containing each prefix or root.

1. *con-*   _____

    (1) _____   (2) _____

2. *chron(o)*   _____

    (1) _____   (2) _____

3. *cent-*   _____

    (1) _____   (2) _____

4. *bene-*   _____

    (1) _____   (2) _____

5. *aqua*   _____

    (1) _____   (2) _____

6. *cred*   _____

    (1) _____   (2) _____

7. *met(e)r*   _____

    (1) _____   (2) _____

8. *micro*   _____

    (1) _____   (2) _____

9. *scribe*   _____

    (1) _____   (2) _____

10. *homo*   _____

    (1) _____   (2) _____

E. If there is a misspelled word in any line of five words given below, write it correctly in the space at the right. If all five words are spelled correctly, write **C** in the space.

1. probably, scissors, strength, twelvth, weather   _____

2. skiing, Wednesday, weild, village, usable   _____

3. sophmore, syllable, possible, innocence, salary   _____

4. outrageous, professer, leisure, proceed, tragedy   _____

5. optimism, secertary, publicly, likable, mirror   _____

6. quizzes, mediocre, partner, pastime, led   _____

7. handkerchief, prominant, infinite, expel, height   _____

8. maintenance, pamphlet, nickle, gauge, familiar   _____

9. medicine, hypocrisy, genius, foreword, harrass   _____

10. compel, similar, category, sacreligious, descend   _____

11. defendent, emphasize, desirable, conscience, dealt   _____

12. restaurant, conquer, cavalry, arctic, assasin   _____

13. dispair, connoisseur, audience, clothes, angel   _____

14. broccoli, auxiliary, deceit, Britian, allege   _____

15. eminent, propaganda, unanimous, dining, minature   _____

Achievement Test

A. In the following sentences identify the part of speech of each *italicized* word by writing one of the following numbers in the space at the right:

1 if it is a *noun,*	**5** if it is an *adverb,*
2 if it is a *pronoun,*	**6** if it is a *preposition,*
3 if it is a *verb,*	**7** if it is a *conjunction,*
4 if it is an *adjective,*	**8** if it is an *interjection.*

1. Good conversation is an *art.* _____

2. *Beyond* that clump of trees is Mary Louise's house. _____

3. Every morning Dr. Kitteridge took the *same* route to his class. _____

4. *I* see the lake from my motel window. _____

5. Were you able to solve all the *problems?* _____

6. Our family *bought* a microcomputer for Christmas. _____

7. The study of a foreign language is *essential* for the educated person. _____

8. My brother and I are *already* planning to spend the summer touring Europe. _____

9. *Have* you *read* Ian Fleming's last book? _____

10. *For* over two centuries her family has farmed in Montana. _____

11. *Oh,* I really do think his scheme is ridiculous. _____

12. The *poet's* long-awaited book was well received by the critics. _____

13. Our report *is divided* into two sections. _____

14. A tour of the South Sea Islands is easily *and* quickly arranged. _____

15. *Unfortunately,* stereotypes serve only to strengthen biases. _____

16. Traditions are *important* to colleges and universities. _____

17. During fall term the college president has an *open* house each year for the students. _____

18. Did *you* leave the door open on purpose? _____

19. Dr. Richards has been actively involved *with* the children's clinic for many years. _____

20. While we study, Scott has gone to get *us* a pizza. _____

21. Lavinia cannot come, *but* she will send someone in her place. _____

22. Each of the *cakes* is cut into eight pieces.   _____

23. As you see, both the cat *and* its kittens are asleep.   _____

24. Were you in chemistry lab *yesterday*?   _____

25. *Most* of the students are on vacation this week.   _____

B. Each of the following sentences either contains an error of grammar or is correct. Indicate the error or the correctness by writing one of the following numbers in the space at the right:

      1 if the *case of the pronoun is incorrect,*
      2 if the *subject and the verb do not agree,*
      3 if a *pronoun and its antecedent do not agree,*
      4 if an *adjective* or *adverb is used incorrectly,*
      5 if the *sentence is correct.*

26. Whom did you say selected the menu for the banquet?   _____

27. Cabin Creek is near our farm.   _____

28. The annual meeting of the company's board of trustees were held in Houston, Texas.   _____

29. Each of us was anxious to receive their grades.   _____

30. Both sides of the road was hedged by rhododendron.   _____

31. He appears to be real nervous about the examination.   _____

32. According to the fire code there is too many people in this room.   _____

33. The committee requested that its members be on time.   _____

34. Which of her two latest novels do you think was best?   _____

35. Jane seldom does as good in philosophy as she does in calculus.   _____

36. All of us on the houseboat waved to whoever we saw on shore.   _____

37. My friend who owns a nursery says that we sure do need rain.   _____

38. Yesterday I felt so badly that I decided to go to the infirmary.   _____

39. The friendship that exists between he and my father has been a long one.   _____

40. Neither the chief mechanic nor his young assistant have been able to eliminate the knocking in my car's engine.   _____

41. The field hockey team has won its fourth straight game.   _____

42. Mr. Hellman received the data this morning and will share it with the staff tomorrow.   _____

43. On the top shelf in the hall closet was the checker board and the checkers. _____

44. The person who donated the money for the new gymnasium is thought to be her. _____

45. The weather is some better today than it was yesterday. _____

46. Either my brother or I are supposed to paint the deck furniture. _____

47. The two of us, Margie and me, plan to take the boat out in the sound this morning. _____

48. My next-door neighbor and long-time friend is moving to Lansing. _____

49. Alicia is one of those interior designers who encourages clients to make suggestions. _____

50. Tim feels real good about his chances of playing first-string guard. _____

C. Each of the following sentences either contains an error in sentence structure or is correct. Indicate the error or correctness by writing one of the following numbers in the space at the right:

      1 if the sentence contains a *dangling modifier,*
      2 if the sentence contains a *misplaced modifier,*
      3 if the sentence contains a *faulty reference of a pronoun,*
      4 if the sentence contains *faulty parallelism,*
      5 if the sentence is *correct.*

51. According to the gossip columnist the star's party was big, bright, and everyone had a marvelous time. _____

52. Even after closing the door, Jo's chatter kept me from concentrating on my economics. _____

53. We saw a film of John F. Kennedy's inauguration in Pearce Auditorium. _____

54. The three of us plan to find an apartment in Albany, settle in as quickly as possible, and begin work in July. _____

55. Ms. Vance is a home economist and who has recently begun a catering service. _____

56. Jack told his roommate that he needed a shave and a haircut. _____

57. While coming from Boston, the temperature dropped, and driving became treacherous. _____

58. Wally has called to ask me for a date long distance. _____

59. I had wanted to go to a movie, but this became impossible once Billie settled down for a visit. _____

60. To buy some clothes for spring, I either will have to give up lunch or ask for an advance on my allowance. _____

61. Judge Ramirez has the sensitivity to quickly perceive the basic issues of a dispute. _____

62. If one likes chocolate, you will not be able to resist Aunt Nan's chocolate charlotte. _____

63. Tourists always have and perhaps always will enjoy San Francisco's cable cars. _____

64. To afford this VCR, we will each have to pay a third of the price. _____

65. Mike called just as I was leaving home, which caused me to be late. _____

66. Taking a picnic lunch, our trip with the children will be quicker and more pleasant. _____

67. While learning fly-fishing, the line got tangled because I did not cast smoothly. _____

68. Dick, you should be ashamed; you almost ate the whole dish of fudge. _____

69. The poor dog came dragging in, covered with mud, briars, and he had a cut on one leg. _____

70. My brother called to tell me that he had a cold, and this was certainly bad news. _____

71. It is true, Logan, that I never have and never will like scrambled eggs. _____

72. Hugh asked George whether he could give him a lift to school on Friday. _____

73. Ed kept saying that he only wanted one slice of watermelon. _____

74. To study effectively, one must not allow distractions during the allotted study period. _____

75. When driving a golf ball, the head must be kept down. _____

D. Each of the following sentences contains an error in punctuation or mechanics, or is correct. Indicate the error or the correctness by writing one of the following numbers in the space at the right:

 1 if a *comma* has been omitted,
 2 if a *semicolon* has been omitted,
 3 if an *apostrophe* has been omitted,
 4 if *quotation marks* have been omitted,
 5 if the sentence is *correct*.

76. Jane who is her father's favorite child is somewhat spoiled. _____

77. We had been waiting in the cold rain by the bus stop fortunately, Harold came by in his car and picked us up. _____

78. Honestly, Melissa I had no idea that you were back in town.   _____

79. Glorias planning to make a tuna casserole for supper.   _____

80. My friend Mike is playing flute in the symphony tonight.   _____

81. I was surprised by your arrival I had not expected you back before tomorrow.   _____

82. Outside the yard looked barren and deserted in the cold January twilight.   _____

83. Hoping to see Dr. Lyons before the exam I waited outside his office for an hour.   _____

84. When are you leaving for Italy, Marcello? asked Sophia.   _____

85. Riding horseback well requires courage and perseverance.   _____

86. Riding horseback we went deep into the rain forest.   _____

87. Grants new address is 217 Princeton Way, York, Maine.   _____

88. I sat down at the typewriter with confidence then I stared at the blank paper for at least twenty minutes.   _____

89. To Jill Carter represented the voice of experience.   _____

90. I believe that this yellow raincoat is yours, Maggie.   _____

91. Joining in the singing was a loud bass voice that was off key I never found out whose it was.   _____

92. Being locked out of my house I tried frantically to force open a window.   _____

93. Its a point in your favor, Jenny, that you told the truth about your escapade.   _____

94. Whenever I read Shirley Jackson's short story The Lottery, I am struck again by its explosive ending.   _____

95. Mother's only sister Aunt Marie was a missionary for thirty years.   _____

96. On July 24, 1976 my family moved from Massachusetts to Kansas.   _____

97. That woman wearing the orange skirt and the red blouse lives next door to me.   _____

98. When you go to Florida in April I hope that you will bring me some Valencia oranges.   _____

99. I don't know how my new car got its fender dented I suppose someone backed into it in the parking lot.   _____

100. Have you ever heard Scottish pipers play that beautiful old hymn Amazing Grace?   _____

Glossary of Grammatical Terms

Absolute phrase.   A construction grammatically independent of the rest of the sentence. It is formed by use of a noun followed by a participle. It is not a subject and does not modify any word in the sentence.

> *The rain having ended,* we decided to walk home.

Abstract noun.   A noun that names a quality, condition, action, or idea; it cannot be perceived by one of the five physical senses.

> kindness   truth   courtesy   dishonesty

Active voice.   The form of a verb indicating that the subject of the sentence performs the action of the verb.

> The dog *ate* its supper.
>
> Mary *is going* to town.

Adjective.   A word that modifies, describes, limits, or adds to the meaning of a noun, pronoun, or any other substantive.

> *Your late* arrival caused trouble.
>
> Ellen is *beautiful.*

Adjective clause.   A dependent clause that modifies a noun, pronoun, or any other substantive.

> The girl *whom you met* is a flight attendant.
>
> The place *where I was born* is a thousand miles from here.

Adverb.   A word that modifies or adds to the meaning of a verb, adjective, or other adverb. It may also modify or qualify a phrase or clause, adding to the meaning of the whole idea expressed in the sentence.

> I finished the test *quickly.*
>
> Trent is *truly* worthy of this award.
>
> *Luckily,* we got to class on time.

Adverbial clause.   A dependent clause that functions exactly as if it were an adverb. It modifies verbs, adjectives, adverbs, or the whole idea expressed in the sentence's independent clause.

> *When I was a child,* I lived in Missouri.
>
> *After you have eaten lunch,* I will help you wash dishes.
>
> *Because you are tired,* I will drive home.
>
> Don't leave here *until you have finished your work.*

Ambiguous modifier.   A modifier carelessly placed between two sentence elements so that it may be taken to modify either element.

> The boy who had been walking *slowly* came into our driveway.

388

Ambiguous pronoun reference. Improper use of a pronoun that may grammatically refer to more than one word as its antecedent in a sentence.

> John told Fred that *he* should lose weight.

Antecedent. The substantive to which a pronoun refers and with which it must agree in person, number, and gender.

> *Peter* told Sue that *he* would be late for dinner.

Apostrophe. A mark of grammatical mechanics used to show possession, indicate omitted letters in contractions, or show plurals of letters or numerals.

> Ted's glove

> It's raining.

> Mind your *p*'s and *q*'s.

Appositive. A word or phrase that explains, identifies, or renames the word it follows and refers to.

> William Faulkner, author of "The Bear," was a native Mississippian.

Archaic words. Words that are out of date and no longer in general use.

> "*Oft* in the *stilly* night."

Articles. Three words, classified as adjectives, that appear before nouns or certain other substantives. *A* and *an* are indefinite articles; *the* is a definite article.

Auxiliary verbs. Verbs that help to form the various tenses of main verbs. The use of auxiliary verbs creates verb phrases and enables the writer to express time and time relationships much more precisely than by using simple present and past tenses. *Was, have,* and *will* are the auxiliary verbs in these examples:

> She *was going* with me.

> I *have finished* my work.

> Tom *will go* to New York.

Brackets. Marks of grammatical mechanics used to enclose any interpolation or insertion added to material being quoted.

> "Four score and seven years ago [Lincoln began] our forefathers brought forth on this continent. . . ."

Broad pronoun reference. Incorrect use of a pronoun to refer broadly to the whole idea of the preceding clause.

> She was late, **which** made me angry.

Capitalization. The use of capital letters for the first word of a sentence, a line of traditional poetry, or a direct quotation. Capitals are also used for the first letter of proper nouns, days of the week, months, holidays, and historical periods.

Case. The inflection of a noun or pronoun to show its relationship to another word or sentence element. Nouns change form only to show the possessive case. Pronouns have three forms to show case: nominative, objective, and possessive.

Clause. A group of words containing a subject and a verb. The two types of clause are independent and dependent. Dependent clauses cannot stand alone as completed thoughts; independent clauses express complete thoughts.

Cliché. An overused expression that has lost its original freshness.

dull thud	one fell swoop
bitter end	through thick and thin
having a ball	last but not least

Collective nouns. Those nouns that name groups of persons, places, or things functioning as units.

jury   team   class   club   herd

Colloquialism. Words or expressions (also referred to as informal diction) that are acceptable in the speech of the educated person but not in formal writing.

We have *lots* of apples on our trees this year.

Colon. The mark of punctuation that introduces a formal list or an explanation or amplification of a statement. Also used after the formal salutation in a letter, between hour and minute numerals of time, between chapter and verse of Bible references, and between titles and subtitles of books.

Comma. Punctuation mark used to indicate the smallest interruptions in thought or grammatical construction.

Comma splice. Incorrect use of a comma as punctuation between two independent clauses not joined by a coordinating conjunction. A stronger separation must be shown through use of a semicolon or a period.

I saw the plane landing, it was a 747 jet.

I saw the plane landing; it was a 747 jet.

Common noun. A noun that names a class of persons, places, things, or ideas.

woman	honesty
book	friendship
house	

Comparative degree. The inflection of an adjective or adverb that compares two things, persons, or actions.

Peggy's camera is *better* than yours.

Marcia felt the disappointment *more keenly* than Harry did.

Comparison. Indication of the extent to which one noun or verb has a particular quality in common with another noun or verb through use of the comparative degree of an adjective or adverb.

Complement. A word, phrase, or clause that completes the action of the verb and the sense of the sentence. It may be a direct object, an indirect object, a predicate adjective, a predicate noun, an objective complement, or a retained object.

Complex sentence. A sentence that contains one independent clause and one or more dependent clauses.

> I know what you are going to say.

Compound sentence. A sentence that contains at least two independent clauses and no dependent clause.

> I will ride with you, and Patsy will stay at home.

Compound-complex sentence. A sentence that contains at least two independent clauses and one or more dependent clauses.

> I was sorry that I could not attend the meeting, but my throat was sore.

Concrete noun. A noun that names a person, place, or thing that can be perceived by one of the five physical senses.

> desk   chocolate   aroma   shout   rain

Conjugation. The showing of all forms of a verb in all its tenses.

Conjunction. A word used to join words or groups of words. Coordinating conjunctions (like *and* and *but*) join sentence elements of equal rank. Subordinating conjunctions introduce subordinate, or dependent, elements, joining them to the main part of the sentence.

Conjunctive adverb. An adverb (sometimes called a transitional adverb) used to connect two independent clauses while modifying the sense of the sentence and showing the relationship between the two clauses.

> I had neglected to buy coffee yesterday; consequently, my breakfast today lacked a vital ingredient.

Connotation. The associative meaning of a word or expression; connotation goes beyond the literal dictionary definition.

Coordinate elements. Elements of equal rank within a sentence. They may be single words, phrases, or clauses, but they must have similar values as sentence parts.

Coordinating conjunction. A conjunction that joins two sentence elements of equal rank. The coordinating conjunctions are *and, but, or, nor, for, yet* in the sense of *but,* and *so* in the sense of *therefore.* The correlative conjunctions *either . . . or* and *neither . . . nor* are also coordinating conjunctions.

Correlative conjunctions. Coordinating conjunctions used in pairs, as shown in the entry on coordinating conjunctions.

> *either . . . or*   *neither . . . nor*
> *both . . . and*   *not only . . . but also*

Dangling modifier. A phrase or elliptical clause that does not modify any particular word in the sentence.

> *To be a good cook,* the kitchen must be conveniently arranged.

Dash. A mark of punctuation that indicates an abrupt shift or break in the thought of a sentence or sets off an informal or emphatic parenthesis. It is also used to set off an appositive or parenthetic element that is internally punctuated.

> I'm trying to be sympathetic, but — oh, Mack, you aren't even listening.

> The three of us — Jim, Susan, and Dot — are trying out for parts in the play.

Demonstrative adjective. An adjective that modifies a substantive by pointing it out.

> *this* picture   *these* glasses
> *that* woman   *those* apples

Demonstrative pronoun. A pronoun that points out persons, things, qualities, or ideas.

> *Those* are my friends.

> *These* are the problems.

> *That* is the question.

> My answer is *this.*

Dependent clause. A group of words that contains a subject and a verb but that cannot stand alone as a complete thought. It begins with a subordinating word. Dependent clauses function as grammatical units within a sentence; that is, as nouns, adjectives, and adverbs.

Dialectal words. Words whose usage is common to the speech of a particular group or geographical region.

> *branch* for creek

> *polecat* for skunk

> *poke* for sack or bag

Diction. One's style of writing or speaking in terms of word choice.

Direct object. A noun or other substantive that completes the verb and receives the action expressed in the verb.

> The child ate the *candy.*

> Carol hates *arithmetic.*

> Frank thought the *fine* excessive.

Elliptical clause or expression. A grammatically incomplete expression whose meaning is nevertheless clear; frequently a dependent clause from which subject and/or verb is omitted.

> *When a child,* I had a great many freckles.

Essential appositive. An appositive that positively identifies that which it re-names, most frequently by use of a proper noun. Essential appositives are not set off by commas.

> The actress *Katharine Hepburn* has had a long and distinguished career.

Essential clause (modifier). An adjective or adverbial clause that is necessary in a sentence because it identifies or points out a particular person or thing. An essential clause is not set off by commas.

> A child *who grows up in the country* learns a great deal about nature.

Euphemism. An expression used to avoid the outright statement of a dis-agreeable, delicate, or painful idea, or to give dignity to something essen-tially lowly or undignified.

> The Jacobs family had a *blessed event* at their house last week.
>
> Mr. Thompson's present *financial embarrassment* is said to be the result of *uneven cash flow*.
>
> Sally received a *pink slip* in her pay envelope last week.

Excessive predication. The use of too many independent clauses, strung to-gether with coordinating conjunctions. Proper subordination of less impor-tant ideas is the remedy for excessive predication.

> I went to a movie, and I ate two boxes of popcorn, and I later had a stomach ache.

Expletive. An idiomatic introductory word, used to begin a sentence when the subject is deferred to a later position.

> *There* are too many cooks in this kitchen.
>
> *It* has been raining since Monday.

Gerund. A verbal used as a noun. In its present tense it always ends in *-ing*. It may function as a sentence element in any way that a noun can.

> *Riding* a bicycle in the street can be risky.

Hyphen. A mechanical mark that is used in compound numbers and other compound words formed from phrases. It is also used at the end of a line to indicate the division of a word continued on the next line.

> *thirty-four*   *ex-governor*
> *sister-in-law*   *sixteen-year-old* boy

Idiom. The characteristic construction used to form sentences in a particular language; the pattern and sequence of words normal to that language.

Illogical comparison. Comparison, usually through careless writing, of two things that do not have a point of similarity. In "My car is newer than Mark," *car* and *Mark* have no point in common to be compared. A logical comparison would state:

> My car is newer than Mark's.

Indefinite pronouns.   Pronouns that do not point out a specific person, place, or thing, but only a general class. Many indefinite pronouns are concerned with indefinite quantity:

>   some   any   each   everyone   several

Independent clause.   A group of words containing a subject and verb and expressing a complete thought. It may stand alone as a simple sentence, or it may be combined with other independent clauses or with dependent clauses to form a compound or complex sentence.

Indirect object.   A word or words denoting the person or thing indirectly affected by the action of a transitive verb. It is the person or thing to which something is given or for which something is done. Words such as *give, offer, grant, lend* represent the idea of something done for the indirect object. The idea of taking something away can also have an indirect object, with the use of words like *deny, refuse,* and the like.

Infinitive.   A verbal consisting of the simple form of a verb preceded by *to,* and used as a noun, adjective, or adverb.

>   I want *to win.*
>
>   I have work *to do.*
>
>   You must leave now *to get* there on time.

Inflection.   A change in the form of a word to indicate a change in its meaning or use. Nouns show inflection only in plural and possessive forms. Some pronouns are inflected to show case, number, and gender. Verbs are inflected to show person, number, voice, and mood. Most adjectives are inflected to show comparative and superlative degrees.

Informal diction.   Words or expressions that are acceptable in the speech of the educated but not in formal writing. Also called colloquial diction.

Intensive pronouns.   Pronouns combined with *-self* or *-selves* and used in conjunction with nouns and simple pronouns for emphasis.

>   I *myself* will write the letter.
>
>   Frank did the work *himself.*

Interjection.   An exclamatory word thrown into a sentence or sometimes used alone. It is grammatically independent of the rest of the sentence.

>   *Oh,* why are you doing that?
>
>   *Goodness!* I am hot!

Interrogative pronoun.   A pronoun that is part of a sentence asking a question.

>   *What* is that noise?
>
>   *Which* of the cakes do you prefer?

Intransitive verb.   A verb whose action is not directed toward a receiver.

> Mike *walked* around the block.

> The river *is overflowing*.

> You *are* foolish.

Irregular verb.   A verb that forms its past tense not by adding -*d* or -*ed*, but by a change in the vowel of the root verb.

sing	sang	choose	chose
ride	rode	do	did
begin	began		

Italics.   A device of mechanics that uses a printing style sloping to the right in the manner of handwriting. Italics are used to emphasize a word or expression or to designate book, play, opera, magazine, newspaper, painting, sculpture, television show and ship titles. In typing or handwriting, italics are shown by underlining.

Jargon.   Vague, pretentious language so general in meaning that many words may be omitted without loss of the sense of a statement.

Levels of usage.   Divisions of usage within the categories of Standard and Substandard English. The following are usage labels usually applied by most dictionaries and grammarians: formal, informal, dialectal, slang, archaic, and obsolete.

Linking verb.   An intransitive verb that makes a statement not by expressing action but by indicating a state of being or a condition. It follows the subject and must be followed by a predicate noun or predicate adjective to complete the sense of the sentence. The verb *to be* in all its forms is the most common linking verb; however, any other verb that expresses a state of being and is followed by a noun identifying the subject or an adjective describing it is a linking verb. Some examples are *appear, become, look, seem, smell, sound, taste,* and *feel.*

Misplaced modifier.   A word or phrase that by its position in the sentence does not seem to modify the word it is intended to modify. A modifier should be as close as is logically possible to the word it modifies.

> The crystal chandelier brilliantly lit the huge banquet table that hung from the ceiling.

> *Correction:*

> The crystal chandelier that hung from the ceiling brilliantly lit the huge banquet table.

Mixed construction.   A shift in the original construction of a sentence, causing the sentence to be confused in its meaning and incorrect in its grammatical structure.

> Honesty *is when* someone is truthful in word and deed.

Modifier. A word, phrase, or other sentence element that describes, qualifies, or limits another element in the same sentence.

Mood. The form a verb may take to indicate whether it is used to make a statement, give a command, or express a condition contrary to fact. Moods of a verb are *indicative, imperative,* and *subjunctive.*

Nominative case. The case of a noun or pronoun that is the subject or the predicate noun of a sentence. Nouns in the nominative case are not inflected; personal pronouns have inflections for each of the three cases.

Nonessential appositive. An appositive that is not necessary in the identification of the word with which it is in apposition. It merely provides additional information as a method of renaming. Note that a nonessential appositive is set off by commas.

> P.D. James, *a mystery novelist,* is an Englishwoman.

Nonessential modifier. A modifier that is not necessary to the meaning of the sentence but simply provides additional description rather than identification. Nonessential modifiers are set off by commas.

> My father, *who is a lawyer,* often has to travel in connection with his practice.

Noun. The part of speech that names a person, place, thing, or idea.

Noun clause. A dependent clause that functions within the sentence as a noun.

> Tell me *what you want for breakfast.*

Number. Inflection of verbs, nouns, and pronouns indicating whether they are *singular* or *plural.*

tree	*trees*	he *loves*	they *love*
woman	*women*	*I*	*we*

Object. A sentence element that receives directly or indirectly the action of a verb, gerund, participle, or infinitive; or shows relationship as object of the preposition to some other element in the sentence.

Object of a preposition. The substantive that follows a preposition and shows a relationship between the object of the preposition and some other element in the sentence.

Objective case. The case of a noun or pronoun that receives the action of a verb, either directly or indirectly, or that refers to that receiver. The object of the preposition is also in the objective case.

Objective complement. A noun, pronoun, or adjective that completes the action of the verb and refers to the direct object.

> Henry VIII made Catherine of Aragon his *queen.*

> Todd considers Marilyn quite *intelligent.*

Parallelism.   The use of equal, or parallel, grammatical constructions within a sentence. Coordinate elements of equal rank should be expressed in parallel language.

> The girl was tall, slender, and beautiful.   (*Three adjectives are used.*)
>
> She is a woman who is conscientious and who is a splendid worker.   (*Two adjective clauses are used.*)

Parentheses.   A device of punctuation that encloses parenthetic information like brief explanation of a foregoing term or a figure repeated to ensure accuracy.

> Lincoln said (in the Gettysburg Address), "Four score and seven years ago. . . ."
>
> I am enclosing eight dollars ($8) to cover the cost of my order.

Parenthetical expressions.   Expressions that are not a part of the central statement of a sentence but are used as comments upon the statement. Parenthetical expressions are usually, but not always, enclosed by commas.

> He is, *as the saying goes,* a real football buff.
>
> What *do you suppose* can be done?

Participle.   A verb form that functions as an adjective while retaining some of the characteristics of a verb. It is called a *verbal.*

> *shining* light   *worn* coat   *known* danger.

Parts of speech.   The various elements that go to make up a sentence. There are eight parts of speech: noun, pronoun, adjective, verb, adverb, preposition, conjunction, and interjection.

Passive voice.   The inflection of a transitive verb showing that the subject of the sentence is the receiver of the verb's action.

> He *was taken* to jail.

Person.   The inflection of verbs and personal pronouns indicating the speaker (first person), the person spoken to (second person), or the person or thing spoken about (third person).

Personal pronouns.   Pronouns used in one of the three persons (*I; you; he, she, it*) and their plural forms as well.

Phrase.   A group of words generally without a subject and predicate, used as a single part of speech.

> *Living alone* has some advantages. (*gerund phrase, used as subject*)
>
> Marcia, *waving wildly,* tried to catch our attention. (*participial phrase, used to modify* **Marcia**)
>
> I want *to go to Paris.* (*infinitive phrase, used as direct object*)
>
> His cousin, *a computer specialist,* lives in Nevada. (*appositive phrase, in apposition with* **cousin**)
>
> We climbed *up the mountain.* (*prepositional phrase, used adverbially*)

Positive degree (of adjectives and adverbs).   The regular form of an adjective or an adverb.

Possessive case.   The inflection of a noun or pronoun, showing possession.

> *Janet's* last name is Rogers.
>
> *My* friend has moved away.
>
> The cat has lost *its* tongue.
>
> *Mine* is the only true story of the incident.

Predicate.   The part of the sentence that makes a statement about the subject. It always includes the sentence verb.

Predicate adjective.   The adjective in the predicate that describes or modifies the subject. It follows a linking verb.

> Charlotte is *friendly.*
>
> This soup smells *good.*
>
> Mr. Thomas appears *ill.*

Predicate noun or nominative.   The noun in the predicate that renames or identifies the subject. It follows a linking verb.

> That woman is a *lawyer.*
>
> Jim was *master* of ceremonies.

Prefix.   A short element (a syllable or syllables) that comes before the main part of the word (the root), adding to or modifying its meaning.

> *sub*marine   *cent*ipede   *contra*dict

Preposition.   A part of speech that shows a relationship between its object (a substantive) and some other word or sentence element.

> She is a friend *of* the family.

Primer style.   The monotonous style of writing that reflects no relative importance of ideas and no emphasis. Primer style is found in writing that does not vary sentence structure through subordination or other rhetorical devices, but uses only simple sentences without variation.

Principal parts (of a verb).   The principal parts of a verb are *first-person singular, present tense; first-person singular, past tense;* and *past participle.* Knowledge of these three principal parts enables one to conjugate any verb.

Pronominal adjective.   An adjective that is the possessive form of a pronoun.

> *your* hat   *their* intentions   *our* home   *my* watch

Pronoun.   A word used in place of a noun; it sometimes refers to a noun or other substantive already mentioned.

Pronoun-antecedent agreement.   The agreement that must exist between a pronoun and its antecedent in person and number.

> Each girl was told to bring *her* lunch with *her* for the outing.

Proper noun.   A noun that names a particular person, place, or thing. It always begins with a capital letter.

    Angela   Senator Smith   Christmas   Atlanta   Idaho

Quotation marks.   Punctuation marks used to enclose direct quotations, titles of short works, smaller units of books, and words from special vocabularies.

Redundancy.   Unnecessary repetition.

    Repeat that *again.*

    She *returned back* to her home.

    The coat that I bought is *blue in color.*

Reflexive pronouns.   Pronouns ending in *-self* or *-selves* and indicating that the subject acts upon itself.

    Jack bruised *himself* on the leg at the playground.

    Millie treated *herself* to a hot fudge sundae.

Relative pronoun.   A pronoun that is used to introduce a dependent adjective clause.

    The information *that* I gave you is correct.

    My uncle, *whom you met last year,* is coming for a visit.

Retained object.   A noun or other substantive remaining as the object when a verb that has both direct and indirect objects is put into the passive voice.

    President Rogers has been given a *vote* of confidence.   (*Vote* is the retained object.)

Root.   The central or main part of a word. A prefix may begin the word, and a suffix may end it, each one modifying the meaning of the root.

    peri*meter*, post*script*, *wis*dom, *false*hood

Run-together sentences.   Sentences without punctuation between independent clauses not joined by a coordinating conjunction.

    Mark ran quickly to the door he opened it and saw the burglar.

Semicolon.   Punctuation mark used to separate independent clauses not joined by a coordinating conjunction, coordinate elements internally punctuated with commas, and independent clauses joined by a coordinating conjunction but heavily punctuated internally.

Sentence.   A group of words combined into a pattern that expresses a complete thought.

Sentence fragment.   A part of a sentence written and punctuated as though it were a whole sentence (a complete thought), although some necessary element has been omitted.

    The baby crying.

    Because I was tired.

    When we arrived at the hotel.

Simple sentence.   A single independent clause that has one subject and one predicate. It may have more than one noun or pronoun as its subject and more than one verb in its predicate.

>   The dog ran across the street.

>   The dog ran across the street and barked at the cat.

>   The dog and the cat fought and made noise.

Subject.   The person, place, or thing being spoken or written about in a sentence.

Subject-verb agreement.   The agreement in person and number that each verb in a sentence must have with its subject. The verb is inflected as to person and number according to those of the clause's subject.

Subjunctive mood.   The mood used in a verb to express a wish or to state a condition contrary to fact. It is also used to express certain formal suggestions or proposals.

>   I wish that I *were* going with you.

>   If I *were* president, no one would go hungry.

>   I move that the nominations *be* closed.

Subordinate clause.   See **Dependent clause.**

Subordination.   In writing or speaking, the reflection that one sentence element is less important or worthy of emphasis than another. Dependent clauses, phrases, and single words may be used instead of full-fledged independent clauses to convey subordinate ideas.

>   Jenny Martin is my cousin, and she is a senior in high school, and she has just been awarded a scholarship to Tulane.   (*no subordination*)

>   My cousin Jenny Martin, who is a senior in high school, has just been awarded a scholarship to Tulane.   (*subordination through use of appositive phrase and dependent adjective clause*)

>   My cousin Jenny Martin, a senior in high school, has just been awarded a scholarship to Tulane.   (*subordination through use of two appositive phrases*)

Subordinating conjunctions.   Conjunctions that introduce dependent clauses, subordinating them in rank to the idea expressed in the independent clause.

Substantive.   A noun, pronoun, or any word or group of words that is used as a noun.

Suffix.   A word part that is added to the end of a word and modifies the meaning of the root.

>   accura*cy*   law*yer*   young*ster*
>   commun*ion*   altru*ism*

Superlative degree.   The inflection of an adjective or an adverb indicating the highest degree of quality, quantity, or manner. It is formed by adding *-est* as a suffix to the simple form of the adjective, or, with adverbs or adjectives of several syllables, by preceding the word with *most*.

kindest	most agreeable	most thoughtfully
poorest	least honorable	most nearly

Tense. The form that a verb takes in order to express the time of an action or a state of being.

Tense sequence. The logic that governs time relationships shown by the verbs in a sentence. If the action in one verb or verbal form occurs before or after the action in the main verb, these differences must be indicated by differences in the tenses.

Terminal marks. The marks of punctuation that signal the end of a sentence. They are the *period,* the *question mark,* and the *exclamation mark.*

Transitional adverb. The adverb, sometimes called conjunctive adverb, that introduces the second of two independent clauses, showing the relationship between the two clauses and frequently modifying the entire sense of the sentence. Sometimes the second adverb comes within the second clause.

Transitive verb. A verb whose action is directed toward a receiver, which may be the object of the verb or (with a transitive verb in the passive voice) its subject.

Bob Horner hit the ball.

A home run was hit by Bob Horner.

Triteness. The use of stale, hackneyed expressions that have lost their original freshness. See also **Cliché.**

Upside-down subordination. The subordination of an important idea to a less important one through careless writing.

When the house caught fire, I was reading the paper.

Vagueness. The too-frequent use of abstract words instead of concrete ones.

The fact that the plan was of a risky nature was known by everyone.

Correction:

Everyone knew that the plan was risky.

Verb. A word used to state or to ask something, expressing action or a state of being. Every sentence must contain a verb.

Verbal. A verb form made from a verb but performing the function of a noun, an adjective, or an adverb. The three verbal forms are the *gerund,* the *participle,* and the *infinitive.*

Verbal phrase. A group of words that contains a verbal and all its modifiers and complements.

Your running too fast has left you out of breath.

Voice.   The form of a verb that indicates whether the subject of the sentence performs the action or is the receiver of the action of the verb. If the subject performs the action, the verb is in the *active voice;* if the subject receives the action, the verb is in the *passive voice.*

> *The chorus sang* "America" at the end of the program. (*Chorus* is the subject; *sang* is the verb in the active voice.)

> "America" *was sung* by the chorus at the end of the program ("America" is the subject; *was sung* is the verb in the passive voice.)

Weak pronoun reference.   Faulty reference by a pronoun to a word that has been merely implied by the context.

> Mother made delicious grape jelly yesterday; I gathered *them* for her.

Wordiness.   Use of more words than are necessary to express an idea clearly and accurately. Excessive predication, redundancy, and certain abstractions are all forms of wordiness, also known as verbosity.

Index

403